# LIVING
## YOUR JOY
## OUT LOUD

# LIVING
## YOUR JOY
## OUT LOUD

CLAIMING AND EXCLAIMING WHO YOU ARE IN CHRIST

JOY BAZEMORE

WESTBOW
PRESS®
A DIVISION OF THOMAS NELSON
& ZONDERVAN

WestBow Press books may be ordered through booksellers or by contacting:

WestBow Press
A Division of Thomas Nelson & Zondervan
1663 Liberty Drive
Bloomington, IN 47403
www.westbowpress.com
1 (866) 928-1240

ISBN: 978-1-4908-9112-5 (sc)
ISBN: 978-1-4908-9113-2 (e)

Print information available on the last page.

WestBow Press rev. date: 12/07/2015

Editorial assistance: Leonard G. Goss, GoodEditors.com

# DEDICATION

For my wonderful husband, David, who loves me unconditionally and
always encourages me to use my God-given gifts, and
whose weirdness perfectly matches my quirkiness;
For my four precious daughters, Grace, Shelley, Hillary, and Heather,
who have taught me much, inspired me often, and given me indescribable joy;
And in memory of my parents, Winston and Margaret Crawley, who taught me to laugh
at myself and demonstrated so beautifully how to live Christ's joy out loud

# SPECIAL THANKS

LOOKING BACK AT the journey the writing of this book has been, I must thank my Thursday morning Bible study group who read the initial really rough draft of the first fifteen chapters. Their love and honest feedback gave me courage to keep writing. And if it weren't for Penny, the finished book would still be hiding in my computer. Thank you for letting God prompt you to light a fire under me.

Thanks also to my dear friend, Karen, one of my staunchest supporters. Every time she learns I'm working on something new, she exclaims, "I want to read it!" Music to an author's ears!

To my publishing team, many thanks for helping me navigate the hills and valleys necessary in making this book the best it can be. Much credit goes to my editors for tightening up my prose while leaving the message intact.

Of course, I want to thank my family for selflessly allowing me to share all the personal anecdotes, even the embarrassing ones.

Finally, my highest praise goes to my Savior, Jesus Christ. Without his sacrifice for my sins, I would have no hope. Without his peace, this world would weigh me down. Without his abounding love, I would have no joy to spread to others. Without Jesus I am nothing. Praise him!

# CONTENTS

# INTRODUCTION

"YOU JUST WANT me to be perfect!" my sixteen-year-old daughter wailed.

Truth be told, I did think her life would be easier if she could be perfect, but that wasn't going to happen anytime soon. And I have felt just as Grace felt many times, especially when reading Proverbs 31 about the wife of noble character. I would say to God, "That woman was perfect, and you want me to be just like her? Well, I can't do it."

It was on one such occasion that God spoke to me and said, "No, Joy, I want you to be like *Jesus*, and I want you to write a book for yourself and for other women about who you are in Christ, and how you can be more like him. For this book I want you to use the letter to the Philippians."

End of discussion.

So I wrote this book. It is not an ordinary study of one of the books of the Bible. It is unique in that I chose the topics by reading and rereading Philippians and looking for words or concepts the apostle Paul used to describe that early group of believers. For example, at the beginning of his letter, Paul addresses the Philippians as saints, so the first chapter is about every believer being a saint. Paul calls them partners, peacemakers, caretakers, and so on, and there are chapters on all the terms Paul uses for his readers.

I begin each chapter with a personal anecdote or other analogy to introduce the topic, and then I break the chapters down into four sections: "The Joyful Truth," "Digesting the Truth," "Living Your Joy Out Loud," and "Joy in Communion with Christ."

*The Joyful Truth* sections are taken from scripture verses that tell us who we are as believers. I explain the Greek word or phrases Paul used in his writing, because many times the nuances of the Greek language are much more meaningful than the English translations. In the first chapter, for example, the joyful truth is that we are saints!

In the *Digesting the Truth* sections, I try explaining in depth what truth from the Scripture means. Here I may use additional Bible passages or quotes from other references to help you understand the concept.

In the sections titled *Living Your Joy Out Loud*, I challenge you to make personal applications to your life and give specific suggestions on how to do so. Finally, in *Joy in Communion with Christ*, I ask you to sing a hymn with me and to pray. I believe the words of the hymns are perfect for summarizing the thoughts in the chapters and for bringing us to a place of personal worship. And no Bible study is any good without prayer, as prayer is the vehicle through which God effects change in our hearts. So please do not skip over this most important step.

Saint Richard of Chicester, an Anglican bishop from the thirteenth century, wrote a prayer that was memorialized in song several years ago: "Oh, Lord, three things I pray—to see Thee more clearly, love Thee more dearly, follow Thee more nearly day by day."[1] I hope this book will help my readers do that. My desire is that you will draw closer to the throne of God and agree with the psalmist, "You make known to me the path of life; you will fill me with joy in your presence, with eternal pleasures at your right hand (Ps. 16:11).

# SAINT

MY MAMA, MARGARET Anna Lawrence Crawley, was born right before Christmas in 1922 to Willie and Nanny Lawrence of Lufkin, Texas. Willie owned a corner grocery store, and consequently, their little family always had food, even during the depression. Nanny was a true southern cook, making biscuits and gravy for practically every meal and baking the best pound cake you ever tasted. One might say my mama grew up "well-fed."

By the time I was born, Mama was only slightly plump, but I remember her saying often, "Everything's better with butter or cream." She was a smart lady, and I wholeheartedly agree with her, though I would probably add, "or cheese, or sour cream, or cream cheese!"

She and I certainly would have seen eye to eye with American chef and food writer James Beard, who declared, "Good bread is the most fundamentally satisfying of all foods; and good bread with fresh butter, the greatest of feasts." And of course, butter comes from cream. I know this firsthand, because once when I was a newlywed I was whipping cream for strawberry shortcake and whipped it a little too long. *Voila!* Butter!

Through the years, the word "cream" has brought to mind the best or richest connotations. An old song proclaimed, "You're the cream in my coffee. . . . I'd be lost without you." And we've all heard, "He's the 'cream of the crop.'" Then there's the one that even children know, "I scream, you scream, we all scream for ice cream!"

## The Joyful Truth

The letter to the Philippians starts with great news: We are cream!

Paul and Timothy, servants of Christ Jesus, to all the saints in Christ Jesus who are at Philippi, with the overseers and deacons: Grace to you and peace from God our Father and the Lord Jesus Christ. I thank my God in all my remembrance of you, always in every prayer of mine for you all making my prayer with joy.

Phil. 4:1-4, ESV

In this very first verse of Philippians, we find the word "saints," translated from the Greek word *hagios*, meaning "holy one, consecrated, acceptable to God."

Maybe you're saying, "I am *no* saint," because you know the Bible says "for all have sinned and fall short of the glory of God" (Rom. 3:23). We are all part of the human race, which is *not* holy and therefore *not* acceptable to God. So how then can we be called *hagios*?

The word *hagios* comes from the same root as *hagiazo*, which means "to sanctify, set apart, *make holy*." The truth that sets us free is that we are not and cannot be holy in or of ourselves. But Jesus Christ, through the sacrifice of his life on the cross to pay for the sin of humanity, has *made* us holy, which is acceptable to God. What a wonderful truth!

## Digesting the Joy

The problem is some truths are harder to believe than others. A good case in point is childbirth. I'll never forget the birth of my first grandchild. My husband, David, and I traveled up to North Carolina to be there for the birth. Ten days after her due date, Shelley finally began having contractions at about 8:00 PM, and we tromped to the hospital at 11:30 PM.

Shelley was definitely in labor, and while my son-in-law, my husband, and I looked on, she learned the unfortunate truth about labor pains. After hours had passed, it was finally time for Shelley to push the baby out. David was asked to leave, but I was allowed to stay. It's a good thing, too, because I was helping her push, every single time, for two hours. I would tell myself that my grunts and grimaces were not productive, but somehow I couldn't quit!

At long last, though no thanks to me, the moment we'd all been waiting for came when Tyler Cason Spears was born. Just moments before, he had been an unknown joy, huddling in his mother's womb. He had been breathing by way of a blood vessel, but through Shelley's groaning force and God's goodness, he made his way into the world and took his first gulping taste of fresh air. What a miracle! When his mewling cries grew into vigorous shouts, my heart left my body and transferred to his.

Likewise, the joyful truth to be digested is that God gave his only Son to die for us. He promises that because of Jesus' sacrifice: "if we confess our sins, he is faithful and just and will forgive us our sins and purify us from all unrighteousness" (1 John 1:9).

Ephesians 2:4-6 tells us that "because of his great love for us, God, who is rich in mercy, made us alive with Christ even when we were dead in transgressions—it is by grace you have been saved. And God raised us up with Christ and seated us with him in the heavenly realms in Christ Jesus."

Through the death and resurrection of Jesus, God has transferred his own heart into our lives. We are reborn. It is sometimes very hard to believe, but nevertheless it is true. As we accept the divine sacrifice and turn from our sin, God allows us to rise to the top as cream does on milk. Then he scoops us off and sets us apart for good works. Just as cream may be poured into hot coffee to make it delicious, we may be poured into a difficult situation to be a blessing. Furthermore, sometimes cream must be whipped in order to serve its purpose as the beautiful, tasty, finishing touch on a dessert. Similarly, we may have to undergo great trials before we can attain the triumph of glorifying God with our lives.

Are you still having trouble believing that you are *hagios*? Look at it this way: Childbirth is somewhat unbelievable, but we have all seen the proof staring back at us from our own mirrors! If you sometimes feel the need for proof of your salvation, look in your spiritual mirror, asking God to point out specific places in your life where he has changed ("rebirthed") you.

Acts 7:58-9:31 records the account of Saul's persecution of the Christians, his conversion experience, and some of the changes that came about in his life. It is interesting to note the changes in Paul's demeanor and purposes after he was converted to Christ. Luke, the writer of Acts, was an eyewitness to Paul's redeemed life. He knew beyond question that Christ had saved Paul because of the transformation he witnessed in the apostle's life. Luke would have said, "Paul is a saint," even though Paul himself said, "Here is a trustworthy saying that deserves full acceptance: Christ Jesus came into the world to save sinners—of whom I am the worst" (1 Tim. 1:15).

Do you have any trouble believing you are a saint? If so, why? Think carefully about what changes came about in your life once you accepted Christ as your Savior. (If you became a Christian at an early age, this question may be more difficult for you. We will address this in a later chapter.)

## Living Your Joy Out Loud

Another interesting New Testament word that comes from the same Greek root as *hagios* is *hagion*, which means "sanctuary." *Sanctuary* can mean several different things, including a sacred place, such as a worship center or temple. In former times, there were places where fugitives from the law were allowed to flee and where they were immune to arrest. These places were called sanctuaries. In our day we might also call a place of refuge or asylum a sanctuary.

As female saints of the Lord, this is where we can have a deep and satisfying ministry. First of all, we welcome the Holy Spirit and allow him to make our lives his sanctuary. Then we look around, for in our homes, in our jobs, in our recreational pastimes, even in our churches, there are many who need sanctuary. They need someone who will listen without judgment, someone who will encourage and bring refreshment to their souls. They cry out for understanding and forgiveness. At some point we all need another person who will let us shout for joy unashamedly or weep the tears of deep sorrow or repentance.

Imagine yourself as a sanctuary. Is there anyone in your life who needs a place of refuge? Your husband may have struggles he cannot share with anyone else. Allow him into your heart, pray for him, and bless him with encouragement. Your children live in a frightening and dangerous age, so be a sanctuary for them. Protect, comfort, and guide them. Your friends and fellow church members (even those with the convincing smiles on their faces) are in the midst of Satan's attacks, so let down your guard and empathize. Pray with them and for them.

One of the best features of a sanctuary is its openness. Our oldest daughter lived in New York City for seven years. What a throng of people in need of sanctuary! Countless churches in that city have responded to the need by leaving the doors of their churches open. At almost any time of day, in any part of the city, a person may walk right into a sanctuary where quiet and peace can be found. In the same way, if we are going to be sanctuaries to others, we will have to be open and available, even if the time is not convenient.

Our greatest privilege as *hagios*, holy and consecrated ones, is to lead people to our Lord, the ideal sanctuary, who said, "Come to me, all you who are weary and burdened, and I will give you rest. Take my yoke upon you and learn from me, for I am gentle and humble in heart, and you will find rest for your souls. For my yoke is easy and my burden is light" (Matt. 11:28-30).

In what specific ways can you bless the people around you with sanctuary?

## Joy in Communion with Christ

Pray, asking God to give you opportunities with people you know. Think about what Christ has done for you so you now have the privilege of being called a saint. Thank him for his love, grace, and righteousness.

Please go to YouTube.com and search "Lord Prepare Me to be a Sanctuary"[2] by michaelatm2603. As you learn the words, sing along with the video, allowing the Holy Spirit to do his work in you.

# PARTNER

OUR THIRD DAUGHTER got married on a gorgeous, glorious summer day. The flowers were astoundingly beautiful, the bride and groom even more so. Smiles abounded, and tears of joy flowed freely. Being mother-of-the-bride was once again a marvelous privilege. With all this perfection, no wonder the almost five hundred pictures turned out fabulously. One of my favorites is a photo of Hillary and Evan as they entered the reception room. No wedding finery, no grins from ear to ear, no flowers. Just a simple picture of their hands, fingers intertwined, a striking symbol of the two joined together now as partners.

Think about how "partnered" hands are used. Did you ever play Red Rover as a child? Two teams would be chosen. One team would stand side by side in a long line on one end of the playground or lawn, and the other team would go to the other end and do the same. They would face each other, team members holding hands tightly. The teams would peruse their opponents to see which player looked the weakest (me, usually).

The captain of the first team would call out loudly, "Red Rover, Red Rover, send Joy right over!" I (or whoever was called) would have to run the length of the playing field and try to break through the clasped hands on the opposing team. If the runner broke through, she would get to "capture" one of that team (usually the strongest or her best friend) to bring over to the other side. If the chain was not broken, the runner would have to join the opponents' team. And so the game would continue until everyone was sick and tired of it.

Another memory from childhood reminds me of a different use for partnered hands. Every once in a while, as a special treat, I got to go horseback riding at a local stable. I recall vividly my initial pitiful efforts at getting into the saddle. First, I would reach up and put my hands on the pommel of the saddle. Then, I would raise my left leg as high as I could, foot aimed towards the stirrup. Next, the horse would move and I'd have to let go of the saddle, swing my body back upright, and hopefully find the ground with my left foot before toppling over. If you've been there, you know exactly what I'm talking about.

After trying this method several times, I learned to accept help. The owners of the stable had been standing around smiling, watching my inept attempts, but when I turned to them with my sad face, one held the horse while another bent down and clasped his hands together, making a "step" for my foot. As I stepped into his hands, he gently raised them, boosting me into the saddle, where I then was able to slip my feet into the stirrups on each side.

At the wedding, the partnered hands were a symbol of unity. In the child's game, the partnered hands were used to fight the enemy, and at the stable, they were used to hold and lift me. All of these examples are meaningful.

## The Joyful Truth

> In all my prayers for all of you, I always pray with joy because of your partnership in the gospel from the first day until now, being confident of this, that he who began a good work in you will carry it on to completion until the day of Christ Jesus.
>
> Phil. 1:4-6

The word in the Bible for *partnership* (in some translations it is *fellowship*) is the Greek word *koinonia*. It means "participation, sharing, contribution." The implication is that we are participants with each other, and with God, in sharing the Good News of Jesus Christ. Every Christian can make a contribution that is eternally important to the kingdom of God.

Let's examine the partnership. First of all, according to verse six, it was God's idea to begin a partnership with us: "He who began a good work in you will carry it on to completion until the day of Christ Jesus" (Phil. 1:6). This means that in our partnership, God gets to be the senior partner. In that role, he establishes the policy of the partnership, and he holds the other partners—you and me—accountable. In other words, God is the overseer of all the operations of the partnership. In addition, as the senior partner, he is the face of the partnership to the world. When people accept my message, they are really accepting the Lord and, conversely, when they reject me they are rejecting the Lord.

The joyful truth is that our senior partner is also the much wiser partner. Unlike so many worldly partnerships, where the one in charge seems inadequate, inept, or ineffective, our senior partner has things under control. According to *The Strongest Strong's Exhaustive Concordance of the Bible*, there are 134 entries in the King James Bible where the word *wisdom* is mentioned. There are an additional 247 entries under the word "wise."

## Digesting the Joy

As I began scanning through the verses listed, the first truth I sensed is that wisdom is all about God. Verse after verse says "the Lord put wisdom . . ." or ". . . the wisdom of God . . ." or ". . . the wisdom that God had put in his heart . . ." or ". . . he will show you the secrets of wisdom." Then I came upon this entry: ". . . for in much wisdom is much grief . . ." *Whoa!* What happened?

The reference was Ecclesiastes 1:18: "For with much wisdom comes much sorrow; the more knowledge, the more grief." *Aha!* I shouted silently. Ecclesiastes is the book that talks about *all* of life being meaningless. I started to skip right to the next thought, but instead I felt compelled to read the verse in context. This is from the paraphrase Bible, *The Message*:

> Call me "the Quester." I've been king over Israel in Jerusalem. I looked most carefully into everything, searched out all that is done on this earth. And let me tell you, there's not much to write home about. God hasn't made it easy for us. I've seen it all and it's nothing but smoke—smoke, and spitting into the wind. Life's a corkscrew that can't be straightened, a minus that won't add up. I said to myself, "I know more and I'm wiser than anyone before me in Jerusalem. I've stockpiled wisdom and knowledge." What I've finally concluded is that so-called wisdom and knowledge are mindless and witless—nothing but spitting into the wind. Much learning earns you much trouble ["with much wisdom comes much sorrow"]. The more you know, the more you hurt.
>
> Eccles. 1:12-18

Imagine Solomon on a therapist's couch. What are his symptoms? When you look beyond hopelessness and meaninglessness, it seems to me Solomon had "I syndrome." The words *I* and *me* are used eleven times in these few verses, while the word *God* is used only once—and that in a negative context.

Solomon was, in effect, saying, "Look at me! I am the teacher; I am the king. I've learned all there is to learn, and it is pointless. Why did God even put us here?" True, Solomon had used wisdom, but it was his own wisdom rather than the wisdom of God.

Human wisdom is centered on self, thinking about self, believing in self, exalting self, relying on self. And yes, that kind of wisdom brings grief. The wisdom of God, on the other hand, begins with his first and foremost commandment: "Love the Lord your God with all your heart and with all your soul and with all your strength" (Deut. 6:5).

In our partnership with God, if he is our first love and we ask for his wisdom, we will get it. We find this promise in the book of James: "If any of you lacks wisdom, you should ask God, who gives generously to all without finding fault, and it will be given to you" (1:5). The wisdom that comes from heaven "is first of all pure; then peace-loving, considerate, submissive, full of mercy and good fruit, impartial and sincere" (James 3:17).

Second Corinthians 9:8 says, "And God is able to bless you abundantly, so that in all things at all times, having all that you need, you will abound in every good work." Philippians 1:6 reads, "Being confident of this, that he who began a good work in you will carry it on to completion until the day of Christ Jesus."

He is doing a good work in us, and as we partner with him, he will do a good work *through* us. If we lean on God's understanding and acknowledge his work, he will direct us: "Trust in the Lord with all your heart and lean not on your own understanding; in all your ways submit to him, and he will make your paths straight" (Prov. 3:5-6).

## Living Your Joy Out Loud

Why have partnerships? Usually, the goal is to produce or enjoy something that couldn't be accomplished by an individual working alone. For instance, law partners often share knowledge, research, secretaries, office space, and so on. Doctors who are in practice together share the workload among patients. Business partners share the debt ensued when opening the business and profits when the business does well. Marriage partners enjoy companionship, a godly physical relationship, children, and more.

God has asked us to be his partners in sharing the gospel, but does he really need our help? Couldn't he accomplish his purposes without us? After all, he created the earth and everything in it merely by speaking.

I love the wonderful truth of these lyrics from "In Me" by Casting Crowns: "How refreshing to know you don't need me. How amazing to find that you want me. So I'll stand on Your truth, and I'll fight with Your strength, until You bring the victory, by the power of Christ in me."[3]

People were *created* to have a relationship with God. When God made every living thing on the earth, in the seas, and in the skies, he declared them "good." Genesis 1:26 tells us God wanted to create something more, something in the divine image, something that would have fellowship with his spirit. So he created a spiritual being dressed in flesh: "Then God said, 'Let us make mankind in our image, in our likeness, so that they may rule over the fish in the sea and the birds in the sky, over the livestock and all the wild animals, and over all the creatures that move along the ground." He even designed a unique place for this special creation.

Genesis 2:8-17 describes the garden where God placed his most extraordinary creation. Later, in the third chapter of Genesis, we read that Adam and Eve heard God walking through the garden. This suggests that God placed them there to enjoy them and so they could enjoy him. Unfortunately, sin came between God and the original human pair, and their magnificent, flawless relationship was destroyed. Nevertheless, God's desire was for reconciliation. The entire Bible is a record of God's reaching out to reconcile with men and women and our completely predictable trouble accepting God as the senior, sovereign partner in the relationship. If we will allow God to have this sovereignty, we will reap joyous dividends. Picture again the clasped hands of the newlyweds. They represent unity (oneness, harmony).

When my four daughters were young, we owned a large conversion van, and I was queen of the road. The five of us spent hours in that van, going to and from all their schools and extracurricular activities. In spite of our rule that each girl could choose only one pursuit outside of school and church, that still meant four other places to go each week. And did I forget to mention music lessons? That was *my* one choice outside of school and church for each of them. So we had to make eight round trips to different places all over town, and the small confines of the van became a breeding ground for arguments and pettiness. Countless times the brakes screeched while I pulled off to the side of the road. I would turn around, give my most daunting look, and ask, "Do we need to sing the song?" All four of them knew the "song" was one I had made up consisting of the following lyrics:

Be kind to one another, be kind to one another,
The Bible says to love our friends, be kind to one another.

Yet, no matter how avidly I preached or how loudly we sang, there wasn't much unity.

The girls are all grown now, and each one knows Christ as her Savior and Lord. Much to my delight, they all love each other and are kind to each other! And I don't think it is just because they finally got the song. I believe it is because they all have a partnership in the gospel, which is a unifying force.

The Red Rover game shows unity as well, but it also demonstrates the weapon of partnership in fighting the enemy. I can still feel the strong emotions I felt as a child when playing the game. *Hold tight! Don't let him through! We have to beat them! It may hurt when they try to break through our hands, but it'll be worth it!*

The gospel has an Enemy. Therefore, you and I, as partners in the gospel, have an enemy as well. He is a strong and wily Enemy. He knows our weaknesses and will capitalize on them. The apostle Peter said, "Be alert and of sober mind. Your enemy the devil prowls around like a roaring lion looking for someone to devour" (1 Pet. 5:8). Our partnership with God is crucial to fighting this adversary, Satan. His schemes against us have no other purpose than to bring shame upon the gospel of Jesus Christ through those of us who say we belong to him. As he did with Eve, he makes us question our beliefs, and he makes us challenge our commitment. He tempts our lusts. If he can get us to falter or fail, our gospel witness is damaged. We must claim our partnership with God and rely on our senior partner's wisdom and strength to fight this relentless foe. We must hold tight and not let Satan through! We must beat him! It may hurt a little along the way, but it will be worth it! Ultimately, we can know joy as we partner with God in stomping on Satan!

A wonderful benefit of this partnership with God is that of lifting up others. Just as the clasped hands of the stable hand formed a step to hoist me into the saddle, our partnership in the gospel can be an encouragement to those we meet every day. I have already touched on this in writing about sanctuary, and I will mention it many other times in this book. Do you know anyone who needs uplifting in the Lord? Who? We can all partner with God in meeting the needs of others.

## Joy in Communion with Christ

As you sing the hymn found below, you will notice that each of the following truths correlates with one of the verses. The truths are, God is my partner in evangelism, God is my partner in worship, and God is my partner in Bible study. Go to hymnal.net and sing with me:

### "COME THOU ALMIGHTY KING"
(Charles Wesley, 1756)

Come Thou, Almighty King,
Help us Thy name to sing, Help us to praise,
Father all glorious, O'er all victorious,
Come and reign over us, Ancient of Days.

Come Thou, Incarnate Word,
Gird on Thy mighty sword, Our prayer attend!
Come, and Thy people bless, and give Thy Word success,
Spirit of holiness, on us descend.

Come, Holy Comforter,
Thy sacred witness bear, in this glad hour!
Thou who almighty art, Now rule in every heart,
And ne'er from us depart, Spirit of pow'r!

Pray and ask God to search you and cleanse any part of you that is not fully reliant on him. Thank him for being the Almighty King, Incarnate Word, and Holy Comforter.

# FRUIT

RECENTLY, WE HAD a large group coming for dinner. The day was cold, so I thought chili would be just the thing. Then I remembered a delicious Mexican-type cornbread recipe a friend had given me and decided to fix that, too. My husband, the quintessential fruit-lover, thought a fruit salad sounded good. I would have served a green salad with the chili and cornbread, but he offered to cut up the fruit, so fruit salad was on the menu.

While eating the meal, my mouth burned from the chili and the jalapenos in the cornbread, and I found the juicy coolness of the fruit salad a wonderful respite. In delectable alternating moments, I would burn my mouth and then toss in the fruity fire extinguisher. I had to admit David's idea was an excellent one.

## The Joyful Truth

Just as the cool sweetness of the fruit contrasted with the spicy saltiness of the chili, God can use us to be delicious, fire-quenching fruit in this fallen world.

Paul describes which fruit would be most effective:

I pray that your love will overflow more and more, and that you will keep on growing in knowledge and understanding. For I want you to understand what really matters, so that you may live pure and blameless lives until the day of Christ's return. May you always be filled with the fruit of your salvation—the righteous character produced in your life by Jesus Christ for this will bring much glory and praise to God.

Philippians 1:9-11, NLT

The word for "fruit" in verse eleven, the *fruit* of your salvation, is the Greek word *karpos*. It translates "fruit, crop, harvest, produce." When Paul prays that our love will overflow more and more, he is praying for the saints to produce a harvest of glory for God.

## Digesting the Joy

Stop a moment and think like a gardener. A harvest doesn't just happen. In order to bring in a crop, several things have to occur. First and most importantly, you have to decide to be a gardener. Then you must decide what to plant and prepare the ground accordingly. Not only that, you must know when to plant the seeds, and you must be sure the seeds have the appropriate amounts of water, light, and fertilizer. In some cases, you must protect the crop from marauders.

In addition, a good gardener knows the three laws of the harvest: First, you reap what you sow. That is, you will harvest whatever crop you planted. There is no getting around this. There is no "getting by." Being sorry you planted corn will not enable you to harvest wheat. In the same way, regretting a spiritual decision will not help you in a dark hour.

For example, no amount of knowledge about celebrities can compare to God's Word hidden in your heart when the going gets rough. Have you ever heard anyone say, "When my husband was diagnosed with cancer, it was a comfort knowing that Oprah is the richest woman in America." And when push comes to shove, it won't do any good to say, "If only I had studied my Bible instead of *House Beautiful* magazine!" It is certainly true that God is merciful, but that does not negate the truth of reaping what we sow.

Second, you will reap more than you sow. What an astonishing and marvelous truth this is. I don't know much about growing vegetables, but think about an ear of corn. Say there are twenty kernels per row and sixteen rows per ear. That is 320 kernels (seeds) on one ear of corn. Imagine if this second law of the harvest were not true, we would have to plant 320 seeds just to yield one ear of corn! But this law is true—we will reap more than we sow. That means a farmer only has to plant a few seeds and yields a big stalk with one to four ears on it. We can thank God for his magnificent design, for in every plant he provides the seed needed for the next planting.

This truth is the same for spiritual harvesting, and my own life is a good example. My goals through the years have been to study God's Word, worship him, and seek his guidance in every decision. Of course, I have been far from perfect, and yet God has multiplied my wisdom and knowledge beyond what I planted. He has helped me recall verses I learned early in childhood or in more dedicated periods of adulthood, and through the Holy Spirit he has allowed me to turn those truths into seeds of counsel for my children and others. And when God causes growth in them, he provides seeds for them to plant in others. What an awesome God we serve!

The third law of the harvest is that you will reap later than you sow. Time must elapse between the planting and the harvesting. There are those who seem to mature as Christians almost immediately, but much more usual is a gradual growth in Christ. Don't forget, though, no growth will take place if seeds are not planted, and furthermore, the Christian life cannot be lived very effectively unless continual nurturing is going on.

The writer of Hebrews rebuked those who had not moved on to maturity in their faith by saying, "though by this time you ought to be teachers, you need someone to teach you the elementary truths of God's word all over again. You need milk, not solid food! Anyone who lives on milk, being still an infant, is not acquainted with the teaching about righteousness" (5:12-13). In chapter eleven of Hebrews the writer lauds Abel, Enoch, Noah, Abraham, and other men and women of Israelite history who had shown great maturity in their faith. I am certain those who grew to spiritual maturity made study, worship, and prayer part of their regimens, and if we are going to attain maturity in our faith, we are going to have to do the same.

Look again at our focal verses for today, and notice the spiritual growth pattern:

I pray that your love will overflow more and more, and that you will keep on growing in knowledge and understanding. For I want you to understand what really matters, so that you may live pure and blameless lives until the day of Christ's return. May you always be filled with the fruit of your salvation—the righteous character produced in your life by Jesus Christ for this will bring much glory and praise to God.

Philippians 1:9-11, NLT

The crop here is righteousness (*dikaiosyne*), which is translated "the act of doing what is in agreement with God's standards, or the state of being in proper relationship with God." If we are saints, then we are already in proper relationship with God. And if we are in proper relationship with God, we will be filled with "the fruit of your salvation—the righteous character produced in your life by Jesus Christ." Our righteousness is complete. "Doing what is in agreement with God's standards" is the part that represents spiritual growth.

How often I have been comforted by the fact that even Paul struggled with doing what is in agreement with God's standards! He wrote, "I know that good itself does not dwell in me, that is, in my sinful nature. For I have the desire to do what is good, but I cannot carry it out. For I do not do the good I want to do, but the evil I do not want to do—this I keep on doing" (Rom.

7:18-19). The apostle attributes the problem to his sinful nature. The truth is every Christian alive has a spiritual nature and a sinful nature warring within us. We want to do good. We want to obey God. We want to please him. But the sinful nature in us wants to take charge, leading us to make our *own* decisions, steer our *own* paths, and fulfill our *own* lusts.

Our sinful natures are the weeds in our gardens, and the only way to kill the weeds is to feed the spiritual seed and pour on the weed-killer. Fruit will be the natural result, as pictured so beautifully in the following psalm:

> Blessed is the one who does not walk in step with the wicked or stand in the way that sinners take or sit in the company of mockers, but whose delight is in the law of the Lord, and who meditates on his law day and night. That person is like a tree planted by streams of water, which yields its fruit in season and whose leaf does not wither—whatever they do prospers. Not so the wicked! They are like chaff that the wind blows away. Therefore the wicked will not stand in the judgment, nor sinners in the assembly of the righteous. For the Lord watches over the way of the righteous, but the way of the wicked leads to destruction.
>
> Psalm 1:1-6, NIV

## Living Your Joy Out Loud

The psalmist mentions "fruit in season" in 1:3. Look back at Philippians 1:9-11 and see what Paul lists as some of the attributes of this crop: "And this is my prayer: that your love may abound more and more in knowledge and depth of insight, so that you may be able to discern what is best and may be pure and blameless for the day of Christ, filled with the fruit of righteousness that comes through Jesus Christ—to the glory and praise of God." The attributes include abounding love, knowledge and depth of insight, discernment, and honesty (integrity).

Abounding love is first mentioned in Exodus 34:6-7 as God reveals his character to Moses: "The Lord, the Lord, the compassionate and gracious God, slow to anger, abounding in love and faithfulness, maintaining love to thousands, and forgiving wickedness, rebellion and sin." God is love. He invented love. His kind of love is not cheap, dry, or shallow. When I think of abounding love in terms of fruit, I think of juicy, sweet watermelon, pineapple, peaches, or oranges.

Through modern technology and art, we have been able to create fake fruit that looks good enough to eat. But if you were to take a bite, you would find Styrofoam, wax, plastic, or other inedible products, not the juicy goodness you expected. People are adept at fake love as well, that which is all talk and no action, or lust rather than real love. Abounding love is not this phony love. According to Exodus 34, it is slow to anger, faithful, forgiving, and compassionate.

Humans, especially those in Western cultures, think of love as a feel-good thing. Yet the description of abounding love found in the verse from Exodus above has only one "feel-good" word: compassion. The other words require *doing* rather than *feeling*. For example, when was the last time you *felt* like being slow to anger? When I think of anger, I think of a roaring fire, out of control, burning up everything in its path. I do not think of a small waft of smoke arising from two sticks patiently rubbed together. Abounding love chooses to pour water over the fire of anger, slowing its growth and thereby its destructive force.

First Corinthians chapter thirteen describes abounding love in even more detail, telling us that it is essential, patient, and kind; it does not envy or boast, is not proud, rude, or self-seeking. Abounding love bears no grudges, does not delight in evil but in the truth, and always protects, trusts, hopes, and perseveres. In short, abounding love is juicy, sweet fruit. By offering abounding love, we can be vessels through which Jesus completely satisfies and edifies our children, husbands, co-workers, friends, or even strangers.

In contrast, when I think of offering knowledge, a crisp apple comes to mind. And just as there are numerous varieties of apples, there are many areas of knowledge. Remember, we are talking about spiritual truth here, not human knowledge about temporal subjects.

Over the years, my children or others have needed the refreshing fruit of my knowledge countless times. I admit, even confess, that I am not the Proverbs 31 woman who spins, buys, imports, rises before dawn, cooks, inspects, plants, shops sales, works far into the night, sews, or upholsters. I have done some of those things at some point in my life, but let's just say the woman in Proverbs 31 is more of a type A personality than me. Even as a type B personality, though, God has given me spiritual knowledge to pass on to others. There have been many times the Lord has furnished me with insight that was helpful to my family. I would say, "There is a spiritual lesson in this," and although my daughters rolled their eyes at the time, as adults they now "arise and call [me] blessed; [my] husband also, and he praises [me]" (Prov. 31:8).

When knowledge is needed, sometimes we will know the answer right away. Yet, not even a saint has expertise in every area, so it is often the apple's job to lead the person to God's Word where all knowledge can be found. In addition, we must not forget that some apples are tart and a little hard to swallow. Once in a while it may be necessary to serve unwelcome truths to those who seek our counsel. For instance, I have had conversations with young women that boil down to something like this:

She: "There just aren't any good guys left."
Me: "There are godly men out there. You're just not looking in the right places." Or,
She: "I'm tired of waiting for a good guy."

Me: "If you marry a bad boy, you'll end up married to a bad boy."
Or,
She: "No one will love me for myself!"
Me: "You're looking for a prince, but are you a princess?"

In 2 Corinthians 2:4, Paul explains the essence of this type of discipline: "I wrote you out of great distress and anguish of heart and with many tears, not to grieve you but to let you know the depth of my love for you." What good is our experience if we don't learn from it and then out of love help others learn as well? The fruit of our knowledge is misused if we tell people only what they want to hear.

Another fruit of righteousness is discerning what is best—in other words, having good spiritual eyesight. Nutritionists agree that the best fruit for eyesight is blueberries. Blueberries are not your everyday fruit basket fruit. Spiritually, however, they need to become a part of our daily diets, and we need to put them in the fruit baskets we offer others. We Christian women have all kinds of *good* things bombarding us, begging for our time, money, support, and emotions. Satan's tactics are many and varied, but they include providing good opportunities, even great ones, in order to distract us from what is best. An ideal example of this problem is found in Luke 10:38-42:

> As Jesus and his disciples were on their way, he came to a village where a woman named Martha opened her home to him. She had a sister called Mary, who sat at the Lord's feet listening to what he said. But Martha was distracted by all the preparations that had to be made. She came to him and asked, "Lord, don't you care that my sister has left me to do the work by myself? Tell her to help me!" "Martha, Martha," the Lord answered, "you are worried and upset about many things, but only one thing is needed. Mary has chosen what is better, and it will not be taken away from her."

Which sister, Mary or Martha, probably had more joy?

I believe Jesus is telling Christian women we need to eat some blueberries! We are all caught up in the world. It is not wrong to entertain guests. In fact, the Bible encourages us to do so. It is not wrong to have a clean house. It is not wrong to prepare for the future. All of those things and more are good, maybe even great, endeavors. But are we spending our lives on all the many things and missing the main thing, the one essential thing? Are we substituting the good for the best? When Jesus said, "You are worried and upset about many things, but only one thing is needed," he was talking about the thing that is better than all others, the only thing that has eternal implications - -

knowing him. Everything else, even human relationships, will pass away.

How do we translate this Scripture into living our joy out loud? When we have learned to choose the only thing over the good things, we are able to help others do the same. Who would deny how much our families, churches, cities, and nation need discernment? Deuteronomy 32:28 says, "They are a nation without sense, there is no discernment in them." Doesn't that sound like America? The extreme importance of sound judgment is expressed in Proverbs 3:21: "My son, do not let wisdom and understanding out of your sight, preserve sound judgment and discretion."

Knowledge is a mind thing, but discernment is a heart thing. Jesus said, "Blessed are the pure in heart, for they will see God" (Matt. 5:8). Then later he said, "But store up for yourselves treasures in heaven, where moths and vermin do not destroy, and where thieves do not break in and steal. For where your treasure is, there your heart will be also. The eye is the lamp of the body. If your eyes are healthy, your whole body will be full of light" (Matt. 6:20-22). Choosing what is best (discernment) is all about the heart. These words of Jesus about heart choices suggest that good eyesight is necessary for the right choices and that even better eyesight will result from those right choices. Furthermore, Jesus seems to be advising intentional and continual action: "store up for yourselves," he says. In other words, keep on looking for and choosing what is best. Keep on having a pure heart.

The final fruit in our fruit baskets is the "pure and blameless" fruit. I call it honesty. When asked what trait I dislike the most, I always answer, "Two-facedness." David, the man after God's own heart, must have felt the same way when he said, "Do not drag me away with the wicked—with those who do evil—those who speak friendly words to their neighbors while planning evil in their hearts" (Ps. 28:3, NLT).

We need to have the fruit of honesty—"what you see is what you get." It is like a banana. If a banana is green on the outside, the inside will be unripe. If the banana peel is brown, the banana itself will be past its prime. When the banana is yellow, it is perfect. We need to be yellow bananas. People need to be able to trust us, or they will not be interested in the love, knowledge, and discernment we try to share.

Picture that fruit salad we had with our chili and cornbread. Everyone ate it on Sunday, but the next day, only my husband would eat it. Why? Because by Monday the bananas in it had gotten brown and gooey. In my opinion, they had ruined the rest of the fruit. Likewise, our other fruit will be ruined if we are anything less than completely honest. That is not to say we should be cruelly so. Ephesians 4:15 (AMP) says, "Let our lives *lovingly* express truth [in all things, speaking truly, dealing truly, living truly]" (my emphasis).

## Joy in Communion with Christ

Being a fruit basket for others is both an honor and a responsibility. While we can enjoy handing out love, knowledge, discernment, and honesty, we must remember that God is the source of these things. I encourage you to sing this song with me. I recommend YouTube.com, *Be Thou My Vision king mojo,* if you want accompaniment to sing to.

"BE THOU MY VISION"
(Traditional Irish hymn)

Be Thou my Vision, O Lord of my heart;
Naught be all else to me, save that Thou art
Thou my best Thought, by day or by night,
Waking or sleeping, Thy presence my light.

Be Thou my Wisdom, and Thou my true Word;
I ever with Thee and Thou with me, Lord;
Thou my great Father, I Thy true son;
Thou in me dwelling, and I with Thee one.

Riches I heed not, nor man's empty praise,
Thou mine Inheritance, now and always:
Thou and Thou only, first in my heart,
High King of Heaven, my Treasure Thou art.

High King of Heaven, my victory won,
May I reach Heaven's joys, O bright Heaven's Sun!
Heart of my own heart, whatever befall,
Still be my Vision, O Ruler of all.

We need to be honest about our sowing habits. What kinds of things do we sow? Do we patiently and earnestly plant those things that will produce a harvest of righteousness? Let us bow down before the Lord and allow him to be the vision, the "landscape designer" of our gardens.

Pray and ask God to give you his love, his knowledge, his heart, and his integrity as you provide refreshing fruit to those around you.

# TARGET

I USED TO be a seventh-grade teacher. I know you are thinking, "Whoa, hormone Hades!" But no. Although the students were mostly typical time-bomb adolescents, I loved teaching them. The thing I detested was all the red tape involved in the education system. Standardized testing has become a huge part of the education process, and students are expected to produce ever-higher scores. Because of the great importance placed on these tests, and therein the growing temptation to cheat, administration personnel and classroom teachers must take every precaution with the test booklets and answer sheets. Teachers are required to count each booklet and answer sheet at the beginning of each day when they are collected from the administration, and they are counted again at the end of each day when the materials are returned to the administration.

One April, on the first day of testing, I collected my homeroom's booklets and answer sheets, counted them in front of the administration, and took them to my classroom. The students took the assigned tests for the day under my very watchful eyes. Then I gathered both booklets and answer sheets to be turned back in. When I got there, I began counting my materials in front of an administrator and found that I was one short on the answer sheets! Everyone in the room could hear my anxious cry. All eyes turned to me, some with accusation, some with empathy for my plight. I was quickly told to go *find* the sheet!

When I got back to the room, I asked the students to be very quiet while I thought about where I could have put the missing answer sheet. I sat down and glanced at my desk and all around the room, trying to recall each step I had taken that morning. I just could not imagine what had happened!

Suddenly, I remembered there was a powerful Someone who could see every nook and cranny of my classroom. I bowed my head and prayed, "God, I know you can see that answer sheet right now. Please tell *me* where it is!" When I looked up, I remembered. Just like that, I remembered that I was helping the students fill in the personal information on the back of their answer sheets when the speech and hearing teacher had come to my room to get one of my homeroom students, a girl who was partially hearing-impaired. She told me the girl would be given the test with the other hearing-impaired students. She then asked the girl to bring her answer sheet but to leave the booklet with me.

I ran down the hallways back to the materials room, and on entering the room, I shouted breathlessly, "I know where it is! I prayed and God told me where it is!" You can imagine the looks I got! Only one woman in the room looked as if she understood. The others' faces reflected a range of reactions from disgust to pity. I felt like I had a bulls-eye on my chest, and there was a firing squad of misunderstanding and intolerance ready to shoot me. But I didn't care. God gave me the solution to the missing answer sheet!

Let me share another anecdote. This happened just a month later. At our middle school, teachers and students are divided into teams. The students are further divided into classes. Each class moves as a group to each teacher on the team, whether science, math, history, English, whatever, throughout the day. The last two years I taught, we had a new teacher on our team, a young woman I will call Linda.

About six weeks into the first of those two years, I was approached by a member of the administration and asked to help Linda, who was having a hard time getting her lesson plans done, getting her grades turned in, and controlling her classes. I had already been helping Linda with class management skills, for practically every day she would come to me and tell me about a "situation" in her class. I had also been showing her the ropes in school policy, attendance, and grade-keeping, just as I had been helped when I was new to the school.

When the administration asked me to "bring her along," I tried my best. But the truth was Linda really didn't like the students, which is a "must" in teaching middle-schoolers. She might have learned how to plan the perfect lesson and how to keep up with all the paperwork required by the school, but she could never gain the upper hand in her classroom without earning the respect of her students. In April of her second year, when teachers' contracts were offered for the next year, Linda did not receive a new contract.

On the last day of school that year, the students were dismissed at noon, and the teachers had that afternoon and the next day to finish posting grades and clean up their homerooms.

After the students had gone, Linda and I were sitting in my room, when she abruptly said, "I think you should know that everyone told me you got me fired."

I was astounded and hurt, and I choked out, "What are you talking about?" She told me that when some of the other teachers found out the school had not renewed her contract, all they said was, "Bazemore." I felt more like a target in that moment than I had in any other day of my teaching career. She had no grounds for believing such a thing, for I tried hard to help Linda as much as I could. I had prayed for her and shown interest in her life even outside of school. I began questioning why other teachers would have intimated such a thing about me, if indeed they had. I am ashamed to say I became very angry and jumped to my feet declaring, "That is a horrible, untrue accusation. I'll just go down to the office and *ask* if I'm the reason! We'll get to the bottom of this."

Linda began a little backpedaling: "You don't have to do that. I just figured you'd want to know what people are saying."

## The Joyful Truth

> It is true that some preach Christ out of envy and rivalry, but others out of goodwill. The latter do so in love, knowing that I am put here for the defense of the gospel. The former preach Christ out of selfish ambition, not sincerely, supposing that they can stir up trouble for me while I am in chains.
>
> Philippians 1:15-17

The word "trouble" in Greek is *thlipsis*, and it means "pressure, affliction, anguish, burden, persecution, oppression, tribulation." Even though the apostle Paul was in prison for preaching the gospel, there were those who envied his reputation as preacher and leader and hoped that in his absence they might take over his status among the young Christians, or cause him more distress (either physically or emotionally, or both). Matthew Henry said it this way:

> They were secretly pleased when he was laid up in prison, that they might have the better opportunity to steal away the people's affections; and they laid themselves out the more in preaching, that they might gain to themselves the reputation they envied him: . . . They thought hereby to grieve his spirit, and make him afraid of losing his interest, uneasy under his confinement, and impatient for release. It is sad that there should be men who profess the gospel, especially who preach it, who are governed by such principles as these.[4]

The sad truth is that if you are a Christian woman and you hold a place of leadership, you will be a target of other Christian women. There may be those who "stab you in the back," thinking they can do your job better than you. Deeds of envy and rivalry characterized by selfishness and insincerity may swarm around you. Most likely, the attacks will come when you are already down. But stay strong! If God has given you a place of leadership, he will also give you the qualifications needed to do the job the way *he* wants it done, along with the grace to handle any naysayers.

The considerably more daunting foe is Satan, and he is *sneaky*. When I "misplaced" the answer sheet, he attacked me first with fear. Then, like a domino effect, came pride (I was *sure* I could have done nothing wrong), forgetfulness (that God was a prayer away), and finally, insecurity about what others thought of my Christianity (although I didn't challenge their looks of disgust or pity).

The truth is I was far more outraged when Linda questioned my motives than when my fellow teachers scoffed at the Lord's ability to tell me where the missing answer sheet was. How worldly I was, tip to toe, on that last day of my relationship with Linda. I was a target, unfairly so, but instead of seizing the opportunity to demonstrate Christ's love to Linda in her time of hurt, I left her sitting there and stomped down to the office to defend myself, perhaps negating any witness I may have been to her in the previous two years.

## Digesting the Joy

When we are being attacked, we must remember it is ultimately Satan who wishes to cause us anguish and longs for our reaction to be a stumbling block to others. We can keep in mind the words of our Lord Jesus Christ: "I have told you these things, so that in Me you may have [perfect] peace and confidence. In the world you have tribulation and trials and distress and frustration; but be of good cheer [take courage; be confident, certain, undaunted]! For I have overcome the world. [I have deprived it of power to harm you and have conquered it for you.] (John 16:33b, AMP).

What does Jesus tell us to be? Cheerful. Courageous. Confident. Certain. Undaunted. All this in the face of tribulation and trials and distress and frustration! It would seem like an unattainable ambition, and it would be if Jesus had not promised to step in, deprive the world of power, and conquer it for us.

If you eat ice cream too fast, you get "brain freeze." If you live in this world, you will experience tribulation. Some hardships just happen because you're alive. Other attacks, similar to Paul's imprisonment and Jesus' execution, come about when we take a stand for our beliefs. Everyone will experience the first type of trouble, but only those who take up Jesus' cross and obediently follow his teaching become targets of the worst kind.

## Living Your Joy Out Loud

I challenge you to set yourselves up as targets, for Christian mothers must take a stand in rearing their children to know and love Christ, and Christian wives must take a stand in honoring their husbands in this man-bashing society.

Television sitcoms have especially tried to teach us the opposite of what the Bible teaches. On any given night, you can feed on a diet of ill-behaved, disrespectful, whiney children who are supposedly funny, and men, particularly husbands and fathers, who are stupid, drunken, or sexually immoral. I have laughed right along with most of you at times, but we need to be careful not to allow the worldly views expressed all around us to deter us from standing up for biblical principles.

And when we stand, we won't be popular. Of course we expect the anti-religious to scorn us. But are we ready to take a stand when other Christian parents allow their children to rule their homes? Will you honor your husband when your friends are criticizing theirs? Are you ready to revere him when you disagree with one of his decisions and everyone is urging you to demand your own way or just do your own thing? Married or unmarried, there are men in your life who have authority over you. Are you willing to give your boss the respect due him when he gets nothing but ridicule from others?

Scripture tells us to discipline our children by teaching them respect for God. In the letter to the Ephesians we are commanded to honor our husbands and obey authority (5:21-6:7). We are standing up for God when we stand up for his teachings, and we can be comforted with the fact that when we are attacked for our beliefs, God stands up for us (see Acts chapter seven).

We must also be ready to explain *why* we believe as we do. This is an area in which the Enemy can easily triumph if we are not prepared. First Peter 3:15 says, "In your hearts revere Christ as Lord. Always be prepared to give an answer to anyone who asks you to give the reason for the hope that you have. But do this with gentleness and respect."

It warms my heart to think of Peter the apostle writing this exhortation. He knew firsthand how it felt to be unprepared when challenged about his faith. Remember what happened? Though he had been the disciple to speak up the loudest and say to Jesus, "You are the Messiah, the Son of the living God" (Matt. 16:16), when it came down to a servant girl asking him if he knew Jesus, he denied it. He wasn't ready to say what he believed. In truth, she didn't ask Peter, "Aren't you with Jesus? Why did you decide to follow him?" What she said was, "You also were with Jesus of Galilee" (Matt. 26:69). Nevertheless, Peter was given a chance to defend his faith in Jesus. A perfect opportunity had presented itself for him to share the gospel, but he disowned the Master. He was unprepared. How fervently, then, must he have written the words, "Always be prepared to give an answer to everyone who asks you to give the reason for the hope that you have. But do this with gentleness and respect" (1 Pet. 3:15).

We should know what Scripture says about the hope that is in us. We can prepare by spending time with Jesus, "the author and finisher of our faith; who for the joy that was set before him endured the cross, despising the shame, and is set down at the right hand of the throne of God" (Heb. 12:2, KJV). Notice that Peter said to give the reason for our hope, but to "do this with gentleness and respect." While we share the Good News with rejoicing, we should be prepared to humbly identify with the one to whom we share.

The last part of the first chapter of Philippians gives us a glimpse into Paul's spirit. Through both implication and direct statement, he reveals how he managed being a target:

> But what does it matter? The important thing is that in every way, whether from false motives or true, Christ is preached. And because of this I rejoice. Yes, and I will continue to rejoice, for I know that through your prayers and the help given by the Spirit of Jesus Christ, what has happened to me will turn out for my deliverance. I eagerly expect and hope that I will in no way be ashamed, but will have sufficient courage so that now as always Christ will be exalted in my body, whether by life or by death. For to me, to live is Christ and to die is gain. If I am to go on living in the body, this will mean fruitful labor for me. Yet what shall I choose? I do not know! I am torn between the two: I desire to depart and be with Christ, which is better by far; but it is more necessary for you that I remain in the body. Convinced of this, I know that I will remain, and I will continue with all of you for your progress and joy in the faith, so that through my being with you again your joy in Christ Jesus will overflow on account of me. Whatever happens, conduct yourselves in a manner worthy of the gospel of Christ. Then, whether I come and see you or only hear about you in my absence, I will know that you stand firm in one spirit, contending as one man for the faith of the gospel without being frightened in any way by those who oppose you. This is a sign to them that they will be destroyed, but that you will be saved—and that by God. For it has been granted to you on behalf of Christ not only to believe on him, but also to suffer for him, since you are going through the same struggle you saw I had, and now hear that I still have.
>
> Philippians 1:18-30

When Paul says, "To live is Christ, and to die is gain," he was saying, "My life is not about prison or persecution. It is about Christ, and he is amazing. It can only get more wonderful!" If we could have this same attitude each day we live, any criticism, ridicule, discrimination, or even bodily persecution we receive would roll like water off our backs.

When Christ was preached, Paul rejoiced. This is another essential key to abundant living. Christendom's most quoted psalm is Psalm 23, which tells us that rejoicing comes from trusting the Shepherd. After listing all the ways the Shepherd cares for us, the psalmist then says, "My cup overflows." Can you sense the joy? The explanation for the joy is thankfulness for everything the Shepherd does. When we are being attacked, let's remember everything the Good Shepherd has done for us and be thankful that if we are suffering we are suffering for him. Our cups will overflow.

Paul gives us assurance and tells us not to be frightened by those who oppose us. He says "this is a sign to them that they will be destroyed, but that you will be saved—and that by God" (Phil. 1:28). The Devil wants to cast us into the "fear fire." God, on the other hand, wants us to remember that our faithful Father is only a prayer away. We can live our joy out loud!

## Joy in Communion with Christ

I encourage you to go to hymnal.net and sing the following hymn with me.

"Stand Up, Stand Up for Jesus"
(George Duffield, Jr., 1858)
Stand up, stand up for Jesus, stand in his strength alone;
The arm of flesh will fail you, ye dare not trust your own.
Put on the gospel armor, each piece put on with prayer;
Where duty calls or danger, be never wanting there.
Stand up, stand up for Jesus, the strife will not be long;
This day the noise of battle, the next the victor's song.
To him who overcometh a crown of life shall be;
He with the King of Glory shall reign eternally.

Gather several small slips of paper (small Post-it notes would be great). On each one list an affliction you are currently suffering. Separate them into two stacks: (1) those that are just part of living in this world and (2) those that are direct hits from Satan.

Look at the first stack and ask that Jesus would remind you to be of good cheer because he is in control. Pray carefully over each one in the other stack, for through the Holy Spirit in you, God wants to empower you to stand firm. Since he wants you to be prepared to give the reason for the hope that you have, pray earnestly.

# WINNER

"SHE IS REALLY something!" the grandfatherly man commented as my daughter, Shelley, flitted around our booth in the corner of the fast-food joint. He was sitting at a table nearby and could easily see her long blonde ringlets bouncing as she crawled onto the seat, hopped down again, skipped just as far as she dared, then turned to grin at me. Her wide smile, almost too big for her face, was enchanting, and her almond-shaped green eyes sparkled with a pixie quality. She jumped and twirled, her athletic little body steady and taut, bringing visions of fluffy pink tutus to the observer's imagination. But it was her voice that captivated completely. She spoke her own little language with a rough-textured, Southern-accented twist. She was indeed "something."

As she grew, this middle daughter of mine continued marching to the beat of her own drum. She never made an intentional decision to be different; she just was. She was a classic tomboy and adored her daddy. They spent much time together riding bikes, shooting basketball, or just playing. Now and then, though, I caught a glimpse of a child standing outside the "girlie" world and wishing she could venture in, but not knowing how.

The summer she was six, Shelley fell in love with competitive swimming. She loved winning those blue ribbons and gold medals! I remember well the summer she was eleven. She swam in the eleven-and-twelve-year-old bracket. So many of her opponents were twelve, but she could hold her own against most of them. However, one twelve-year-old girl on our team, Laura, had beaten Shelley time after time in the breaststroke. When we went to the district swim meet that year, Shelley was determined to beat Laura, and although Shelley's competitive spirit was in high gear, I was not sure it could be done. Eight girls swam the race, but most eyes were on Laura and Shelley, for they swam neck and neck way ahead of the rest of the pack. On the final turn, Laura got a good push off the wall, and my heart sank. Shelley made up the distance pretty quickly, but she kept looking around to see where Laura was, which had the adverse effect of slowing her down. Somehow, though, in the last half of the final lap, Shelley found a new strength and glided past Laura to touch the wall just milliseconds before her opponent. Enjoying the drama, everyone whooped and hollered.

After I hugged her, wet swimsuit and all, I asked her how she had done it. Her answer is a classic: "I saw that she was ahead of me, and I couldn't go any faster, but I did." That determination characterized Shelley's every undertaking.

When she joined the band in seventh grade, she wanted to play the drums. Recalling her two years of dance, I was afraid percussion instruments might not be the best choice for someone with the lack of rhythm she seemed to display. How wrong I turned out to be! She became an exceptional percussionist, right on target rhythmically. In fact, she spent her whole high school career on the snare drum line, an accomplishment few students achieve.

Shelley also excelled in academics, graduating high school with a 4.0 grade average. Granted, she had to study more than our other girls did, but she disciplined herself to accomplish her academic goals. If she made 95 on a test, she wanted to know why she had not made 100. If she struggled to understand something, she would ask countless questions until she did understand.

Shelley particularly enjoyed sports in which she could excel individually. In addition to swimming, she ran track, played tennis, and "kicked" karate. She also played softball, shining as a pitcher and outfielder and enjoying the role of team pep-builder.

Shelley was and is a winner. The huge problem was she only *felt* like a winner when she was winning. It had to be a blue ribbon or a gold medal. It had to be the snare drum line. It had to be a 100. During her college years, when she was no longer swimming or playing softball or running track or playing in the band or making 100s, she no longer felt like she was a winner. Those years and some since have been characterized by extreme angst.

You may be thinking, "What's her problem? I've never been a winner! I never made 100s or placed first in athletics or shined musically. I've never even won a door prize!" And of course, our culture equates winning with beating others at something, or achieving financial success, or fame, and placing all the emphasis on what we accomplish rather than who we are. As Christians, we need to redefine winning so we can redefine who a winner is. We can do so by applying a biblical perspective rather than riding the wave of cultural or contemporary thought. In fact, we are warned about that in Colossians 2:8. "Don't let anyone capture you with empty philosophies and high-sounding nonsense that come from human thinking and from the spiritual powers of this world, rather than from Christ (NLT).

Think about Joseph, the eleventh son of Jacob, a story told in the thirty-seventh chapter of the book of Genesis. Joseph's childhood was probably a happy one. His mother Rachel adored him, for he had been conceived after years of barrenness. His father could finally rejoice in having a son by the woman he loved most. Genesis 37:3a tells us that Jacob "loved Joseph more than any of his other sons, because he had been born to him in his old age; and he made an ornate robe for him." I know what it feels like to want to dote on my grandchildren, for they are the cutest, dearest things in the world. We can only imagine the delight Joseph must have felt in those early sheltered years of innocence as his parents doted on him. Surely he felt he was really something, a real winner.

But as daddy doted on his eleventh son, resentment was brewing among the first ten. The hostile and painful account is found in Genesis 37. Imagine the countryside of Canaan where ten men watch and guard as their sheep eat their fill of the scrubby grass. One of the men glances up to see a familiar figure approaching in the distance. He elbows the brother standing nearby, whispering, "Look who's coming." Like dye diffusing in water, the word spreads, and within moments all ten men have gathered and plotted their despised brother's demise.

When his brothers saw that their father loved him more than any of them, they hated him and could not speak a kind word to him. Joseph had a dream, and when he told it to his brothers, they hated him all the more. He said to them, "Listen to this dream I had: We were binding sheaves of grain out in the field when suddenly my sheaf rose and stood upright, while your sheaves gathered around mine and bowed down to it." His brothers said to him, "Do you intend to reign over us? Will you actually rule us?" And they hated him all the more because of his dream and what he had said. Then he had another dream, and he told it to his brothers. "Listen," he said, "I had another dream, and this time the sun and moon and eleven stars were bowing down to me." When he told his father as well as his brothers, his father rebuked him and said, "What is this dream you had? Will your mother and I and your brothers actually come and bow down to the ground before you?" His brothers were jealous of him, but his father kept the matter in mind. Now his brothers had gone to graze their father's flocks near Shechem, and Israel said to Joseph, "As you know, your brothers are grazing the flocks near Shechem. Come, I am going to send you to them." "Very well," he replied. So he said to him, "Go and see if all is well with your brothers and with the flocks, and bring word back to me." Then he sent him off from the Valley of Hebron. When Joseph arrived at Shechem, a man found him wandering around in the fields and asked him, "What are you looking for?" He replied, "I'm looking for my brothers. Can you tell me where they are grazing their flocks?" "They have moved on from here," the man answered. "I heard them say, 'Let's go to Dothan.'" So Joseph went after his brothers and found them near Dothan. But they saw him in the distance, and before he reached them, they plotted to kill him. "Here comes that dreamer!" they said to each other. "Come now, let's kill him and throw him into one of these cisterns and say that a ferocious animal devoured him. Then we'll see what comes of his dreams."

Genesis 37:4-20

My heart breaks for those ten boys who knew their father loved the eleventh more. I get mad at Jacob, because he surely knew the consequences of a parent showing favoritism. He should have known better, because the same problem had caused a great rift between his brother and himself, when Esau had been preferred by their father and Jacob by their mother. We must question his wisdom in presenting his favorite son with something so obvious as an ornamental robe. We must also question the role of Joseph in the intensity of his brothers' hatred for him.

I like Joseph, and I want to think he was acting out of immaturity or naiveté in telling them about his dreams. He should have kept his dreams to himself. But having read the whole story of the life of Joseph, I might better surmise that Joseph had some personality traits of a natural-born leader, such as self-confidence, outspokenness, and determination. At the age of seventeen, he had not yet learned to temper the negative aspects of those traits with heaping portions of tact.

The fact remains that at this point in his life Joseph was on top of the world. His father was devoted to him, and his dreams held nothing but promise. He was a winner! His circumstances almost immediately soured, however.

Joseph, obediently following his father's order to go make sure his brothers were okay, came upon a decidedly antagonistic group. They immediately ganged up on him and stripped him of his prized possession, the ornamental robe. Then they threw Joseph into an empty well. The Bible does not tell us what Joseph yelled from the pit or how he must have struggled, at least within himself, when his brothers, instead of killing him, sold him into slavery. I cannot imagine that Joseph felt much like a winner at that point.

The biblical account quickly moves on to a more important part of the story. Joseph had to grow as a human being through trials and triumphs, and though he most assuredly felt like a loser at times--hated by his brothers, tricked by Potiphar's wife (Gen. 39), and forgotten by the cupbearer (Gen. 40)—he was forever on his father's mind. "Joseph had his chariot made ready and went to Goshen to meet his father Israel [Jacob]. As soon as Joseph appeared before him, he threw his arms around his father and wept for a long time. Israel said to Joseph, 'Now I am ready to die, since I have seen for myself that you are still alive'" (Gen. 46:29-30).

In the same way, we are on our heavenly Father's mind. Throughout our lives, amidst success or sorrow, God is thinking about us because he treasures us. By the time he was reunited with his family, Joseph had matured in his relationship with God to the point that he could see the truth. Genesis tells us,

> His brothers then came and threw themselves down before him. "We are your slaves," they said. But Joseph said to them, "Don't be afraid. Am I in the place of God? You intended to harm me, but God intended it for good to accomplish what is now being done, the saving of many lives."
>
> Genesis 50: 18-20

## The Joyful Truth

Throughout his struggles Joseph continued to depend on God, and at the end of all his distress, he realized it had been for a holy cause and worth it. When we don't feel like winners, we can bring to mind our heavenly Father's great love for us. We can also bear in mind that our grief is for his glory, just as Paul affirmed:

> I will continue to rejoice, for I know that through your prayers and the help given by the Spirit of Jesus Christ, what has happened to me will turn out for my deliverance. I eagerly expect and hope that I will in no way be ashamed, but will have sufficient courage so that now as always Christ will be exalted in my body, whether by life or by death. For to me, to live is Christ and to die is gain.
>
> Philippians 1:18-21

The Greek word for "deliverance" in this passage is *soteria*. It means "rescue, the state of not being in grave danger and so being safe." We may think the persecution of this world is dangerous, but the persecution of hell is far more so, for it represents everlasting torment. The accolades of this life do not make a winner. Being in Christ is what makes a person a winner. In fact, a Christian has a win-win situation. "For to me," Paul said, "to live is Christ and to die is gain." We already profit when we have Jesus as our Savior; we put in nothing, and Christ becomes our everything.

## Digesting the Joy

Through our Savior and the Holy Spirit, the believer triumphs in countless ways:

> What then are we to say about these things? If God is for us, who is against us? He did not even spare His own Son but offered Him up for us all; how will He not also with Him grant

us everything? Who can bring an accusation against God's elect? God is the One who justifies. Who is the one who condemns? Christ Jesus is the One who died, but even more, has been raised; He also is at the right hand of God and intercedes for us. Who can separate us from the love of Christ? Can affliction or anguish or persecution or famine or nakedness or danger or sword? As it is written: Because of You we are being put to death all day long; we are counted as sheep to be slaughtered. No, in all these things we are more than victorious through Him who loved us. For I am persuaded that not even death or life, angels or rulers, things present or things to come, hostile powers, height or depth, or any other created thing will have the power to separate us from the love of God that is in Christ Jesus our Lord!

Romans 8:39, HCSB

Other verses point to the same truths in illustrating the believer's triumph:

The thief cometh not, but for to steal, and to kill, and to destroy: I am come that they might have life, and that they might have it more abundantly.

John 10:10, KJV

Teach those who are rich in this world not to be proud and not to trust in their money, which is so unreliable. Their trust should be in God, who richly gives us all we need for our enjoyment."

1 Timothy 6:17, NLT.

When I think of all this, I fall to my knees and pray to the Father, the Creator of everything in heaven and on earth. I pray that from his glorious, unlimited resources he will empower you with inner strength through his Spirit. Then Christ will make his home in your hearts as you trust in him. Your roots will grow down into God's love and keep you strong. And may you have the power to understand, as all God's people should, how wide, how long, how high, and how deep his love is. May you experience the love of Christ, though it is too great to understand fully. Then you will be made complete with all the fullness of life and power that comes from God. Now all glory to God, who is able, through his mighty power at work within us, to accomplish infinitely more than we might ask or think.

Ephesians 3:14-20, NLT

## Living Your Joy Out Loud

As children of God, we have the abundance of God at our disposal. Abundant grace and mercy, abundant strength through the Holy Spirit, abundant faith, abundant joy, abundant love, abundant victory! And the list goes on. Yet, death will be even *more* profit as we live with our precious Redeemer and King forever. I guess that means we really are something. We are winners!

## Joy in Communion with Christ

Take a moment and go to YouTube.com, and search *victory in jesus travis cottrell*. Sing along with this upbeat arrangement of a wonderful old gospel hymn.

*As you sing Victory in Jesus*[5], thank God that he is in fact always thinking about us. Why? Because he treasures us. Thank the Father that no one can bring an accusation against God's elect, and no one can separate us from the love of Christ. Thank the Lord for coming to die for us and live within us and for providing abundant life for all Christians.

# WRESTLER

FOR THE LIFE of me, I can't understand the draw of professional wrestling. Even though I know it's not real, I cringe when the participants heave one another to the mat and stomp on each other's chests or heads. I wince when one lifts an opponent in the air, because I know what's coming next. And the worst is the smack talk between the competitors. In sharp contrast to my distaste, my husband's late grandmother loved to watch wrestling on television, and she wouldn't for a moment entertain the idea that it was fake. She believed the hype, the moves, the "injuries," everything. She cheered for her favorites and booed their opponents vehemently.

## The Joyful Truth

The wrestling or struggling I want to discuss is very real. And in this wrestling each one of us is both protagonist and antagonist in our own personal matches.

> If I am to go on living in the body, this will mean fruitful labor for me. Yet what shall I choose? I do not know! I am torn between the two: I desire to depart and be with Christ, which is better by far; but it is more necessary for you that I remain in the body. Convinced of this, I know that I will remain, and I will continue with all of you for your progress and joy in the faith, so that through my being with you again your boasting in Christ Jesus will abound on account of me.
>
> Philippians 1:22-26

Every believer struggles at some point with this question: *If death is more profit, then why do I have to live through this life? It can be so hard!* As long as we are alive in this world, we wrestle. We wrestle with sin, holiness, and happiness. We wrestle with desires for love, home, and children. We wrestle with self-image (body, soul, career, and so on), with time management, and with contentment. To the highest peaks and lowest valleys we journey, and there are times we look forward to heaven with such longing that our hearts wrestle with why we must wait. We "desire to depart and be with Christ, which is better by far" (Phil. 1:23).

When my daughter, Hillary, got married, she and her husband, Evan, went to Mexico on their honeymoon. They had a fabulous time—such fun being together and pure joy knowing they were joined by God and blessed by their families. But two days after their return, they both became very sick. Headache, fever, nausea, and diarrhea assailed them for several days until finally they called their doctor, who prescribed a regimen of antibiotics and other medications.

I went to the pharmacy for them, and when I took the medicines to them I stayed for just a few minutes. During that time I heard my green-faced daughter, who lay sprawled in agony on the couch, say, "Jesus, come take me to heaven right now!" She immediately turned an apologetic face to Evan (sprawled in agony on the floor) and muttered, "I'll miss you," to which he replied weakly, "No, you won't!" He was absolutely right. When we reach heaven, it will be glory forever—more profit!

## Digesting the Joy

So why do we have to stay here, wrestling? Paul eloquently states the dilemma: "What shall I choose? I do not know. I am torn between the two." Paul stayed here in this wrestling match of earthly life, because he had a ministry to fulfill, to "continue with all of you for your progress and joy in the faith, so that through my being with you again your boasting in Christ Jesus will abound on account of me." And that is the same reason we have to stay here.

Included in Jesus' last counsel to his disciples were these words: "You will be my witnesses in Jerusalem, and in all Judea and Samaria, and to the ends of the earth" (Acts 1:8). That is our mission, to be Christ's witnesses. If every Christian was taken to heaven as soon as he or she received Christ, who would be here as the Lord's witnesses? Who would teach the world about a Savior who forgives sins and remembers them no more? I would surely be groping in darkness had it not been for my Christian parents, family members, Sunday school teachers, Christian friends, and pastors who told me of Jesus and lived Jesus in front of me.

Therefore, a better question for us as we resolve to live our joy out loud is, How shall we deal with this wrestling? Before we answer that question, maybe we first need to gain some perspective. We have been speaking figuratively of wrestling, of course, but let's think about actual physical wrestling for a moment. The oldest art depictions of wrestling are found in an

Egyptian tomb, circa 2300 BC. Not surprisingly, throughout history, in both art and written depictions of wrestling, the wrestlers are male, and they are endlessly trying to prove who is stronger, shrewder, or faster.

My husband and I are the proud parents of four girls, but I have visited in homes with boys, and I have also witnessed my husband interacting with his younger brother, nephews, and grandsons. Males, it seems, are born to wrestle! Sometimes they are trying to prove who is best, but often they are merely engaging in the sport of horseplay. Furthermore, I have noticed that in a household filled with boys, the mom is the one screaming, "Be careful! Don't hurt each other! Don't break the furniture!" And to her husband, who is often in the middle of it all, she is pleading, "Don't get them so wound up. I'll never get them to bed!" Yet all her "don'ts" do no good!

What if she said nothing and chose to look on with love, thinking, "Look how much fun they're having. Isn't it wonderful how my husband and my boys enjoy one another? Male bonding is a special gift from God." Is it unrealistic to expect a woman to look at her family's actions from a positive perspective? Absolutely not, and some verses prove it:

An encouraging word cheers a person up.

Prov. 12:25, NLT

Let's agree to use all our energy in getting along with each other. Help others with encouraging words; don't drag them down by finding fault.

Rom. 14:19, MSG

Speak encouraging words to one another. Build up hope so you'll all be together in this, no one left out, no one left behind.

1 Thessalonians 5:11, MSG

Let us consider how to stimulate one another to love and good deeds.

Hebrews 10:24, NASB

## Living Your Joy Out Loud

How would our own daily "wrestlings" be affected if our perspective and attitude changed? Because we often perceive wrestling as a negative, we women probably sound like David did when he asked, "How long, O Lord? Will you forget me forever? How long will you hide your face from me? How long must I wrestle with my thoughts and every day have sorrow in my heart? How long will my enemy triumph over me?" (Ps. 13:1-3).

Grief is a completely normal and acceptable emotion; it is part of life. We grieve the death of a loved one; we grieve when children rebel; we grieve when good friends move away; we grieve the loss of "the way things were." Most of our grumbling, though, has nothing to do with grief. Instead, the culprits are fear, impatience, or perhaps even habit. This was true for David's complaints as well:

> I cried out to God for help; I cried out to God to hear me. . . . I thought about the former days, the years of long ago; I remembered my songs in the night. My heart meditated and my spirit asked: 'Will the Lord reject forever? Will he never show his favor again? Has his unfailing love vanished forever? Has his promise failed for all time? Has God forgotten to be merciful? Has he in anger withheld his compassion?'
>
> Psalm 77:1, 5-9

That certainly sounds like David was wrestling, doesn't it? Later in the same psalm he urges himself to recall the deeds of the Lord, the display of his power through mighty miracles. "Your ways, God, are holy. What god is as great as our God? You are the God who performs miracles; you display your power among the peoples. With your mighty arm you redeemed your people, the descendants of Jacob and Joseph" (Psalm 77:13-15). He thinks of God's greatness and his ability to save. This is a pattern in many of the so-called "groaning Psalms." Through remembrance, wrestling turns to rhapsody.

When did David become a child of God who would become a man after God's own heart? Psalm 139, David reflects on his life, and makes us consider he must have believed he was a child of God even before he was born:

> For you created my inmost being; you knit me together in my mother's womb. I praise you because I am fearfully and wonderfully made; your works are wonderful, I know that full well. My frame was not hidden from you when I was made in the secret place, when I was woven together in the depths of the earth. Your eyes saw my unformed body; all the days ordained for me were written in your book before one of them came to be.
>
> Psalm 139:13-16

To be sure, God gave David the choice to follow him or not, just as he does for us, but God's plan was for David's good and his own delight.

The same can be said for each of us. God's plan for me is for my good and his delight. His plan for you is for your good and his delight. Therefore, those challenges calling on us to struggle are for our good and his delight.

Did David recognize this fact? The simple answer is yes, for no matter where his psalms began, they always ended in praise. David's psalms have ministered to countless believers and caused them to praise God in hundreds of ways. He had to wrestle so we could learn more about our almighty God, whose works are wonderful and whose thoughts are precious.

Paul had to wrestle for the same reason. He could not rush to heaven as he might have wanted, because the believers needed his ministry of lifestyle witnessing, preaching sermons, and writing letters of instruction and encouragement. And where would we be without Paul's writings to guide us in our spiritual growth?

David and Paul wrestled, because it was fruitful for them and for us. Through their struggles we are taught who God is and how we were created to bring delight to him.

We, too, can submit ourselves to the days of trials and questions, to the challenges and the conflicts, remembering that "For his anger endureth but a moment; in his favour is life: weeping may endure for a night, but joy cometh in the morning . . . Thou hast turned for me my mourning into dancing: thou hast put off my sackcloth, and girded me with gladness; to the end that my glory may sing praise to thee, and not be silent. O Lord my God, I will give thanks unto thee for ever" (Ps. 30:5, 11-12, KJV). And perhaps someone is looking on who will come to know the truth through your witness or mine.

My dad lived to the ripe old age of ninety, and although he faced cancer three different times, he was mostly hale and hardy until he was eighty-eight. Then his kidneys started failing, and he began experiencing this wrestling we are talking about. He suffered a loss of his independence, and truthfully, since my mom was already gone, he just wanted to bypass his remaining time and move on to heaven. His mind stayed sharp, however, and during this time he had the opportunity to speak for vespers at his retirement community. The gist of his talk was that the elderly should not feel useless in this time of their lives, because every person is placed on earth to love and be loved as well as to pray for people and be prayed for.

Practicing his own preaching was difficult! He didn't feel like himself, and he started doing something I'd never seen him do before—complain. He was wrestling with wanting his old self back, and wondering if this new self was all he would ever have (it was). Yet he fought to get better. As he showed love to his nurses and doctors by thanking them in spite of his pain, and as he allowed me to see his struggle and pray for him, I was inspired and blessed, and I know God was delighted.

But I wrestled with Dad's temper of mind as well. He was in Richmond, Virginia, and I live in Alabama. I was able to be there some of the time, but not all the time. In addition, the daddy I saw then was not *my* daddy. *My* daddy was invincible. *My* daddy had a quiet strength.

*My* daddy had served God for seventy years and deserved to have it easy, right? I wrestled with those very human feelings and thoughts. When I questioned what good I was doing at his bedside, Daddy said, "You are my cheerleader, Joy." So I tried to put aside my wrestling and encouraged Daddy to look at the positives, knowing God would carry him through.

We must be wrestlers, for we have no other choice. Therefore, let us forge ahead, but as we battle, let us not forget two extremely important truths: we are saints and we are winners!

## Joy in Communion with Christ

Take a few minutes to go to hymnal.net and sing:

"STANDING ON THE PROMISES"
(Russell Kelso Carter, 1886)
Standing on the promises of Christ, my King,
Through eternal ages let his praises ring;
Glory in the highest I will shout and sing,
Standing on the promises of God.

Refrain
Standing, standing,
Standing, standing,
Standing on the promises of God, my Savior,
I'm standing on the promises of God.

Standing on the promises that cannot fail,
When the howling storms of doubt and fear assail,
By the living word of God I shall prevail,
Standing on the promises of God.

Refrain

Standing on the promises of Christ the Lord,
Bound to him eternally by love's strong cord,
Overcoming daily with the Spirit's Sword,
Standing on the promises of God.

Refrain

Standing on the promises I cannot fall,
List'ning every moment to the Spirit's call,
Resting in my Savior as my all in all,
Standing on the promises of God.

Refrain

Don't forget: "For God did not appoint us to suffer wrath but to receive salvation through our Lord Jesus Christ" (1 Thess. 5:9). "Let us consider how we may spur one another on toward love and good deeds" (Heb. 10:24). And, "Sing the praises of the Lord, you his faithful people; praise his holy name. For his anger lasts only a moment, but his favor lasts a lifetime" (Ps. 30:4-5).

Pray and ask God to make you aware of your attitude towards struggling and complaining. Submit yourself totally to the Spirit's control, and accept that God's design is for your good and his delight.

# PEACEMAKER

MY TEMPERAMENT, OR personality type, is the "phlegmatic/sanguine." In other words, I tend to be more introverted, yet I am still people-oriented and sure do like to have fun! One of the less desirable traits we phlegmatics possess is a strong aversion to conflict. When issues arise that could possibly produce confrontation, I would just as soon sweep them under the rug. My loving friend, Sherrie, who is definitely *not* phlegmatic, sometimes has to say to me, "Pick up the rug and deal with it, Joy!"

When I was growing up, if my parents were talking about a matter and their voices seemed to get the slightest bit at odds, my heart would beat faster, and I would whine, "Quit arguing." Their ready reply was, "We're not arguing, we're discussing." Then they would both grin, as if they enjoyed it! But I didn't enjoy it, because I hated conflict. Was I a peacemaker in those instances? I think not. It would be nice if we could create peace by saying, "Everybody please just get along and love each other." But avoiding conflict is not the same thing as seeking peace. The pursuit of peace implies chasing it, tracking it, hunting it down. In other words, peacemakers take action to determine the cause of the conflict and to help reconcile the differences of thought.

Let's examine scripture to help us understand more clearly what Jesus meant when he said, "Blessed are the peacemakers, for they will be called children of God" (Matt. 5:9).

## The Joyful Truth

> If you have any encouragement from being united with Christ, if any comfort from his love, if any common sharing in the Spirit, if any tenderness and compassion, then make my joy complete by being like-minded, having the same love, being one in spirit and of one mind. Do nothing out of selfish ambition or vain conceit. Rather, in humility value others above yourselves, not looking to your own interests but each of you to the interests of the others. In your relationships with one another, have the same mindset as Christ Jesus.
>
> Philippians 2:1-5

When my middle daughter, Shelley, was about ten years old, she gave me a birthday present I didn't particularly appreciate (although I pretended to love it, of course). It was a flat wooden figure of an old-timey washwoman. At the bottom on the base was printed, "If Mama ain't happy, ain't nobody happy!" It was supposed to be funny, but sadly, it was true. My emotions affected the whole household. As much as I tried to teach them otherwise, my children tended to act and respond in the same ways I did.

It's a fact: Women have the power to rule the atmospheres in their surroundings. The Proverbs 31 woman is honored and blessed by her children and husband, because "when she speaks, her words are wise, and she gives instructions with kindness" (Prov. 31:26, NLT). I believe she receives the same treatment she has been giving. She is a peacemaker, causing everyone in her home to become like-minded.

## Digesting the Joy

The Greek word translated "like-minded" is *sympsychos*, which is made up of the prefix "sym," meaning *together*, and "psychos," meaning *mind*. In this particular context, it means "united in *spirit*, harmonious." Paul tells us to be one in spirit and purpose. How do we do that? Have encouragement from being united with Christ; have comfort from his love; have close association with the Spirit; and have some tenderness and compassion.

Remember that Paul wrote his Philippians letter to the *saints* at Philippi. Why, then, did he say, "*If* you have any encouragement from being united with Christ, *if* any comfort from his love, *if* any common sharing in the Spirit, *if* any tenderness and compassion . . ."? Does this mean a person can have a relationship with Jesus Christ and still not be filled with the Spirit at all times? Yes.

Every Christian woman has a sinful nature warring with her new Spirit nature, and sometimes we fail to have the qualities Paul mentions. But when they are not present, we will be unable to promote unity of spirit in our households, workplaces, churches, and so on. If she ain't encouraged by Christ, if she ain't comforted by his love, if she ain't got fellowship with the Spirit, if she ain't tender and compassionate, ain't nobody gonna be that way. And if ain't nobody that way, there ain't no peace in that place!

We do want to make peace, don't we? I have to ask, because some women seem to prefer a little upheaval. They like to "stir the pot" to see what aromas or odors arise. They enjoy a little tug o'war. Maybe they are amused by watching people squirm. Is this good, clean fun? Maybe. But all of us should check our motives, for if in any way we take pleasure in the discomfort of others, we should beware. That was not Jesus' way, for he was a peacemaker.

## Living Your Joy Out Loud

If we want to imitate Jesus in being a peacemaker, we must "Do nothing out of selfish ambition or vain conceit. Rather, in humility value others above yourselves, not looking to your own interests but each of you to the interests of the others" (Phil. 2:3-4). This formula is not difficult: Don't be selfish, be humble, look out for the interests of other people, and have the mind of Christ. In the next chapter, we will look more closely at the attitude of servanthood, but here I want to explore some other aspects of the mind of Christ.

### WHAT WAS JESUS THINKING WHEN HE CHOSE TO BE BAPTIZED?

Have you ever wondered why baptism is such a big deal? Why don't some people want to get baptized? Why are there different traditions regarding baptism? Why do Baptists and some other denominations insist that believers be immersed?

> Then Jesus came from Galilee to the Jordan to be baptized by John. But John tried to deter him, saying, "I need to be baptized by you, and do you come to me?" Jesus replied, "Let it be so now; it is proper for us to do this to fulfill all righteousness." Then John consented. As soon as Jesus was baptized, he went up out of the water. At that moment heaven was opened, and he saw the Spirit of God descending like a dove and alighting on him. And a voice from heaven said, "This is my Son, whom I love; with him I am well pleased."
>
> Matthew 3:13-17

There are three elements to the significance of Jesus' baptism. The first is his conversation with John when he asked John to baptize him. What humility! John was merely Jesus' opening act; Jesus was the real star of the show. John realized this and thought he should in fact be asking Jesus to baptize *him*. But Christ's thinking was entirely contrary to human thought.

Human thought is most often governed by pride—the protection and elevation of almighty self. Jesus' motive, on the other hand, was not self-elevation, but the fulfillment of all righteousness. Think about this: Jesus could have walked into the Jordan River and dunked himself under the water. The symbolism found in the actual baptism would have remained the same. But by subjecting himself to the hands of John the Baptist, he demonstrated his total surrender to the plan of God. To have the mind of Christ, we must be willing to completely humble ourselves before God and others, even those we consider "less important."

The second important element was the baptism itself, which is barely mentioned in the Matthew text. When Jesus came to the Jordan River to be baptized by John, in essence John said, "Well, if you insist, Lord." They got in the water and it was done. But how was it done? How do we know Jesus was actually immersed in the river?

The Greek word used in these verses for "baptize" is *baptizo*, which means "submersion in water." The idea behind baptism is to be overwhelmed by the water, and this takes on greater meaning with immersion, rather than just sprinkling a few drops of water on someone. John called people to repentance and cleansing from their sins, and his baptism was by immersion, an actual full-body washing in the river to symbolize that cleansing.

Jesus' baptism, although the same act of immersion, symbolized something new. It represented the death, burial, and resurrection to come, the forfeiting of himself for the salvation of the whole world. When we are baptized, we are symbolizing our death to self and rebirth in Christ.

What happened after Jesus was baptized and came up out of the water? "At that moment heaven was opened, and he saw the Spirit of God descending like a dove and alighting on him. And a voice from heaven said, 'This is my Son, whom I love; with him I am well pleased'" (Matt. 3:16-17). How beautifully Jesus' baptism correlates with Matthew 5:9, "Blessed are the peacemakers, for they will be called children of God."

Wars, battles, spats and disagreements are all often rooted in selfishness, so if we want to make peace, we have to have the mind of Christ and die to self. Jesus modeled this from the moment his ministry began.

## What was Jesus Thinking when He Performed Miracles?

The book of Matthew emphasizes three facets of Jesus' ministry:

Jesus went throughout Galilee, teaching in their synagogues, proclaiming the good news of the kingdom, and healing every disease and sickness among the people. News about him spread all over Syria, and people brought to him all who were ill with various diseases, those suffering severe pain, the demon-possessed, those having seizures, and the paralyzed; and he healed them. Large crowds from Galilee, the Decapolis, Jerusalem, Judea and the region across the Jordan followed him.

Matthew 4:23-25

Jesus taught in the synagogues, he preached the Good News of the Kingdom, and he healed every kind of disease and demon-possession. News about his dynamic presence spread until large crowds followed him. Jesus taught, preached, and healed, but it was the healing that seemed to attract the most people.

I believe Jesus had compassion on the people, because he understood that humans are somewhat unable to receive spiritual teaching if their bodies or emotions are hurting. He healed all kinds of diseases and hurts. He didn't stop teaching or preaching while he was doing this, for he knew the greatest need was to understand God's plan. But the Lord recognized that the ears of his hearers might be more sensitive to his words if he had first shown them his heart.

Unbelievers frequently call Christians "hypocrites." Is it because our lives aren't perfect? Maybe. But more often I think it is that they sense we have no tenderness or compassion towards them. They want no part of that kind of religion, and I don't blame them. The Gospels record that Jesus was "moved with compassion" towards the masses of hurting people. Will we allow God to move our hearts with compassion towards others? If so, we will be more successful in making peace.

## WHAT WAS JESUS THINKING WHEN HE SAID, "YOU HAVE HEARD IT SAID . . . , BUT I TELL YOU . . . "?

The prophet Isaiah stated, "As the heavens are higher than the earth, so are my ways higher than your ways and my thoughts than your thoughts" (Isa. 55:9). In truth, the mind of Christ is the opposite of our minds. We tend to think and act merely on habit, hearsay, or the whims of culture and our temperaments. In order to be peacemakers and have the mind of Christ, we probably should do the opposite of what comes naturally. The gospel of Matthew recorded Jesus expanding on this concept.

You have heard that it was said to the people long ago, 'You shall not murder, and anyone who murders will be subject to judgment.' But I tell you that anyone who is angry with a brother or sister will be subject to judgment.

Matthew 5:21-22

You have heard that it was said, 'Do not commit adultery.' But I tell you that anyone who looks at a woman lustfully has already committed adultery with her in his heart.

Matthew 5:27-28

It has been said, 'Anyone who divorces his wife must give her a certificate of divorce.' But I tell you that anyone who divorces his wife, except for sexual immorality, makes her the victim of adultery, and anyone who marries a divorced woman commits adultery.

Matthew 5:31-32

Again, you have heard that it was said to the people long ago, 'Do not break your oath, but fulfill to the Lord the vows you have made.' But I tell you, do not swear an oath at all: either by heaven, for it is God's throne.

Matthew 5:33-34

You have heard that it was said, 'Eye for eye, and tooth for tooth.' But I tell you, Do not resist an evil person. If anyone slaps you on the right cheek, turn to them the other cheek also. And if anyone wants to sue you and take your shirt, hand over your coat as well. If anyone forces you to go one mile, go with them two miles.

Matthew 5:38-41

You have heard that it was said, 'Love your neighbor and hate your enemy.' But I tell you, love your enemies and pray for those who persecute you.

Matthew 5:43-44

In effect, these verses in Matthew tell us to discard the old system of thought in favor of having the mind of Christ. As illustrated here, the mind of Christ is slow to anger, pure, generous, and gracious. Jesus knew relationships were more important than rules, motive more important than meticulousness.

What does the peacemaking mind of Christ produce? The apostle Paul said it this way:

Therefore if you have any encouragement from being united with Christ, if any comfort from his love, if any common sharing in the Spirit, if any tenderness and compassion, then make my joy complete by being like-minded, having the same love, being one in spirit and of one mind. Do nothing out of selfish ambition or vain conceit. Rather, in humility value others above yourselves, not looking to your own interests but each of you to the interests of the others. In your relationships with one another, have the same mindset as Christ Jesus."

Philippians 2:1-5

## Joy in Communion with Christ

Do you remember the chorus, "I've Got Peace like a River"? Did you sing it at church camp long ago? I have sung it enthusiastically countless times with no thought towards the connection between the verses. Yet they are related. The flow of peace breaks forth into a fountain of joy that surges into spontaneous worship. If we can be peacemakers, the end result will be glorious worship of our Lord and Savior. Could we desire anything better? Sing now with a new understanding.

### "I've Got Peace Like a River"
(African-American Spiritual)

I've got peace like a river, I've got peace like a river,
I've got peace like a river in my soul.
(Repeat)
I've got joy like a fountain, I've got joy like a fountain,
I've got joy like a fountain in my soul.
(Repeat)
I've got love for my Jesus, I've got love for my Jesus,
I've got love for my Jesus in my soul.
(Repeat)

Pray and meditate specifically upon having the mind of the Prince of Peace.

# SERVANT

THOUGH IT WASN'T really our plan when we got married, my husband and I had four children in less than four years. My sister had a very hard time getting pregnant and had several miscarriages before ever having a child, and I thought my experience would be similar. I wanted to start trying to get pregnant when David and I had been married about a year and a half. I had hoped by the time we were married five years we'd have a baby. David reluctantly agreed. Of course, I got pregnant the first month!

Our beautiful daughter Grace was born nine months later. She was a colicky baby, and sometimes I felt bad for having talked David into parenthood, but at about four months old, she got happy, and then she became so much fun that by the time she was ten months old David was saying, "Let's have another one!"

Once again, I thought it would take some time for me to conceive, but Shelley was born nine months later. Their daddy adored Grace and Shelley, and they adored their daddy as well. Their mama was the one who planned all the details of their care and tended them all day long, but there was no denying it or stopping it: Grace and Shelley were "daddy's girls."

I had heard or read somewhere that baby boys usually love their mamas more than their daddies, so I became determined to try for a boy. David was completely content with his two girls. Of course he was; they thought he hung the moon! I, on the other hand, wanted a child who would adore *me*. Finally, David gave in, so we began trying again.

This time it took two months for me to conceive, and eight and a half months later Hillary and Heather, our twin daughters, were born. (Do you see the irony in that?) At first I felt as if

I was being punished for not being satisfied with the first two, but now I truly know what it means that "in all things God works for the good of those who love him" (Rom. 8:28). What a joy the four of our girls have been! I even got one mama's girl out of the twins. More important, all four of our girls, now grown, are "God's girls."

It is truly a wonder that we didn't stop with just one child, for I distinctly remember when I was in the throes of labor with Grace that I said two things: "I've changed my mind," and "Tell them to just let me die." Well, luckily there is no mind-changing allowed during labor and delivery. I had only two choices: I could either die in fact, which in reality I did not want to do, or I could bear the labor and delivery. Of course, I chose the latter, and within hours our beautiful Grace Katherine was born.

## The Joyful Truth

Sin, too, is something that cannot be undone, and the consequences must be borne. The difference is that there is no happy ending to the burden of sin; it always ends in death. Therein lay God's dilemma. The Father knew we would have to die for our sin, and he could not bear the thought. He wanted to provide another choice, a "happy ending" choice. So Jesus, the Son of God who was God made manifest in human form, gave up his rights and put himself in our place, took the beatings, and died for us to pay the price of our sins.

Scripture assures us that, "In the beginning was the Word, and the Word was with God, and the Word was God. . . The Word became flesh and made his dwelling among us. We have seen his glory, the glory of the one and only Son, who came from the Father, full of grace and truth" (John 1:1, 14).

> In your relationships with one another, have the same mindset as Christ Jesus: Who, being in very nature God, did not consider equality with God something to be used to his own advantage; rather, he made himself nothing by taking the very nature of a servant, being made in human likeness. And being found in appearance as a man, he humbled himself by becoming obedient to death—even death on a cross!
>
> Philippians 2:5-8

The word used for "servant" in this passage is the Greek word *doulos*. It means "servant, slave; a person owned as a possession for various lengths of times; of lower social status than free persons or masters."[6] About *doulos*, *The New Testament Greek Lexicon* says it is a person "devoted to another to the disregard of one's own interest."[7]

Jesus, who is God himself, certainly lived up to that definition. He gave up his status and power to become a man. He gave up his rights and put himself in our place, actually becoming a *doulos*, a slave. He became a person without rights, without name, without honor. A possession. Isaiah describes the ultimate slave state of Jesus.

> He was despised and rejected of men; a man of sorrows, and acquainted with grief: and we hid as it were our faces from him; he was despised, and we esteemed him not. Surely he hath borne *our* griefs, and carried *our* sorrows: yet we did esteem him stricken, smitten of God, and afflicted. But he was wounded for *our* transgressions, he was bruised for *our* iniquities: the chastisement of *our* peace was upon him; and with his stripes *we* are healed. All we like sheep have gone astray; we have turned every one to his own way; and the Lord hath laid on *him* the iniquity of us all.
>
> Isaiah 53:3-6, KJV, emphasis added

During his three years of earthly ministry, Jesus did all sorts of things for people. He provided food and wine, helped the sick, calmed the sea, and even washed feet. But his motive was much deeper than merely meeting a perceived need. He wanted to reveal his Father to the world. Ezekiel 18:23 says, "I, the Lord God, don't like to see wicked people die. I enjoy seeing them turn from their sins and live" (CEV). This is the Father Jesus wanted to portray through every move he made.

## Digesting the Joy

There is an account of a woman caught in adultery found in the gospel of John. Here is how it reads:

> Jesus went to the Mount of Olives. At dawn he appeared again in the temple courts, where all the people gathered around him, and he sat down to teach them. The teachers of the law and the Pharisees brought in a woman caught in adultery. They made her stand before the group and said to Jesus, "Teacher, this woman was caught in the act of adultery. In the Law Moses commanded us to stone such women. Now what do you say?" They were using this question as a trap, in order to have a basis for accusing him.
>
> John 8:1-6

On this particular morning, Jesus went to the temple early to teach. As at other times, the scribes and Pharisees were intent on finding some way to accuse Jesus of one thing or another. They wanted something to stick. Thinking they had found the perfect hook on which to snag him, they brought to Jesus a woman who had been caught in the act of adultery. Adultery was one of the "Big 10" laws of Moses, punishable by death. They supposed Jesus would either have to ignore the law or agree to her execution. If he ignored the law and released her, then they could prosecute him in Jewish courts, saying he was a heretic. Yet if he agreed to her execution, they could accuse him of hypocrisy and insincerity for teaching forgiveness but not showing it. Jesus knew what they were up to and he responded very calmly:

> But Jesus bent down and started to write on the ground with his finger. When they kept on questioning him, he straightened up and said to them, "Let any one of you who is without sin be the first to throw a stone at her." Again he stooped down and wrote on the ground. At this, those who heard began to go away one at a time, the older ones first, until only Jesus was left, with the woman still standing there. Jesus straightened up and asked her, "Woman, where are they? Has no one condemned you?" "No one, sir," she said. "Then neither do I condemn you," Jesus declared. "Go now and leave your life of sin."
>
> John 8:6-11

What was Jesus writing when he stooped down to write in the dirt with his finger? I wish I knew. It may have been his way of "counting to ten" so he would not react with anger. Possibly he was doodling, in effect saying to the scribes and Pharisees that their petty games had become boring to him. Certainly, Bible scholars have made more scholarly guesses, but the fact is that John does not tell us. Evidently we did not need to know. The important thing is that it slowed the pace of the action.

After dragging this poor woman in the way they did, perhaps talking among themselves and even jeering and laughing, they expected a confrontation. This was big! Caught *in the act*! But then Jesus bent down and started writing something. In my imagination, I see the group crowding in and growing quieter, just whispering, "What's he doing? What's he writing?" Then I see the Pharisees growing impatient and asking again, "Well, what will you do with her?"

If anyone in the crowd had not been listening to Jesus before, he listened now. How unexpected Jesus' response must have been! He made no judgment on the woman, but instead cast a bit of doubt on the scribes and Pharisees, and indeed on the whole mass gathered in the temple. Then he stooped down to write again. Was he listing all the sins the multitude might have committed? Again, we do not know. We only know that as he wrote, everyone dispersed, starting with the oldest (those who had sinned the most?).

The woman alone remained with Jesus. Imagine her awe when he asked, not about her sin, but about her accusers. And Jesus' next statement was huge: "I don't condemn you." What? Who was this man? Since at that point only Jesus and the woman were present, how did John, the gospel writer, find out about the end of the story? Perhaps Jesus told the disciples, but my guess is that the woman herself told everyone she knew and that is how the word got around.

We can learn so many lessons from this event, including how Jesus became a servant to this woman. He had given up his right to be equal with God, the Righteous Judge, and had made himself of no reputation, "Who, being in the form of God, thought it not robbery to be equal with God: But made himself of no reputation, and took upon him the form of a servant, and was made in the likeness of men" (Phil. 2:6-7, KJV). He imagined himself in this adulteress' place and had compassion on her. He positioned himself between the sinner and the accusers, though knowing the act would further enrage the scribes and Pharisees. He was saying, "I care more for this lowly woman than I care for myself. I would die in her place."

When Jesus fed the five thousand (Matt. 14:13-21), he was saying, "My Father cares for you. Just as you did not realize you would be here so long today that you would need to pack dinner, you do not know how great the burden of your sin is. I am here to make miraculous provision for you."

When Jesus healed the sick, he was saying, "You have a disease in your soul that is killing you faster than this physical illness. Have faith in me to restore you to spiritual health as well."

When he calmed the sea, Jesus was saying, "There is no longer any need to fear death because I have come to give you life."

When he washed his disciples' feet, not only was Jesus teaching them how to serve, but he was also revealing, "I will humble myself and be your slave. My Father has a plan to use me, and just as I pour the water over your feet to wash them, my blood will be poured out for the cleansing of your sins."

## Living Your Joy Out Loud

At the root of Jesus' every act of service was the revelation of his Father's mercy. In the Old Testament, God's people had been instructed to bring blood sacrifices to atone for their sin. Hebrews 9:22 explains that "the law requires that nearly everything be cleansed with blood, and without the shedding of blood there is no forgiveness." Because people were unable to keep the law, to be "good enough," blood was necessary.

For centuries, God had required the sacrifice of animals to atone for human sins. I cannot fathom the mind of God or understand his timing, but I know he decided to suspend that requirement and give his own Son as a blood sacrifice once and for all. That was God's ultimate plan, to have mercy on the likes of us!

Also in the Old Testament, God instructed the Israelites to build a tabernacle (tent) to be used to worship him. Very specific directions for the tabernacle—for every curtain, pole, bowl and candle stand—were given to Moses, who followed them to the minutest detail. One of the objects God told Moses to build was the Ark of the Covenant, a box which held the tablets on which the Ten Commandments were written. Concerning the lid to this box, God commanded:

> And thou shalt make a mercy seat of pure gold: two cubits and a half shall be the length thereof, and a cubit and a half the breadth thereof. And thou shalt make two cherubims of gold, of beaten work shalt thou make them, in the two ends of the mercy seat. And make one cherub on the one end, and the other cherub on the other end: even of the mercy seat shall ye make the cherubims on the two ends thereof. And the cherubims shall stretch forth their wings on high, covering the mercy seat with their wings, and their faces shall look one to another; toward the mercy seat shall the faces of the cherubims be. And thou shalt put the mercy seat above upon the ark; and in the ark thou shalt put the testimony that I shall give thee. And there I will meet with thee, and I will commune with thee from above the mercy seat, from between the two cherubims which are upon the ark of the testimony, of all things which I will give thee in commandment unto the children of Israel.
>
> Exodus 25:17-22, KJV

I find it thrilling that the word used here for "mercy seat" is *kapporeth*, a Hebrew word meaning "covering." The law was inside the ark, covered by the mercy seat, and God met and communed with man from above the mercy seat. If you picture this in your mind, the law was not between God and man; the covering was between the law and God! That is what mercy is.

When Jesus Christ left his throne in glory to humble himself and take the form of a servant, his blood became the mercy seat between the law and God, so that we could commune with God once more. "For God so loved the world that he gave his one and only Son, that whoever believes in him shall not perish but have eternal life. For God did not send his Son into the world to condemn the world, but to save the world through him" (John 3:16-17).

The lyrics of "Mercy Seat"[8] by Vicki Yohe are exactly right. Take a moment and go to youtube.com and search Mercy Seat – Don Moen, and then listen to the one sung by Ruth Reyna.

If we are going to be servants like Jesus, and if we are going to let Jesus serve through us, we will have to show mercy. We will have to feed the hungry, help the sick, give assistance to the anxious, and deal with the dirty and sinful. Rather than being their accusers, we will need to cover them with love and understanding. Allow me to share an illustration from my young life.

Growing up as a missionary's kid, I understood early on that we were not rich. Still, we always had everything we needed, because my father was a strict believer in having a budget and sticking to it. Knowing that, I am sure it will seem strange to some that we always had a servant. In Asia, where we lived, we were actually considered wealthy, and wealthy people had servants. Our amah (a female servant), Ah-King, was a combination housekeeper, cook, and nanny.

One of Ah-King's duties was to look after me, if everyone else had to be out of the house. She would let me hang around while she squatted to cut vegetables, did the wash, or whatever my mother had asked of her. I remember one day, when I was six, I wandered off to my parents' bedroom while Ah-King worked on supper. Bored and looking for something to pass the time, I drifted into their bathroom and came upon the wonderful sight of my mother's red fingernail polish sitting on the counter! Somehow knowing I shouldn't touch this—but being unable to resist—I proceeded to paint my fingernails while unintentionally daubing bright red patches all over my fingertips and parts of the bathroom counter and sink as well.

Just about the minute I put the brush back in the bottle for the final time, Ah-King came looking for me. Hearing her call my name, I closed the door and locked it quickly, smearing polish on the doorknob. Seconds later, her Chinese-accented voice came through the door. "Miss Joy, you in there?"

I frantically turned the faucet on and began washing my hands. "Yes," I answered. "I'm almost finished. I had to go to the bathroom, and I'm washing my hands." Imagine my little-girl horror when the red stuff wouldn't come off! I scrubbed and scrubbed to no avail, and my dismay quickly turned to dread.

"Miss Joy, what you doing?" Ah-King persisted. "Open door."

Realizing I was a cooked goose, I turned the lock and slowly peaked out, clasping my hands behind my back (which, by the way, is a sure indication that a child has something to hide). Ah-King leveled her slight frame against the large wooden door and pushed into the bathroom.

"Ah-ee-ya!" she cried, seeing the blood-red mess I'd made. "What you been doing in here?"

"I… I was just trying to make my fing-fingernails pretty," I sobbed and stuttered, "but it wo-won't come off. Not e-even when I wash with so-soap!"

When Ah-King looked at my hands, she shook her head and scolded, "Miss Joy, you in trouble. You not suppose to play with your mother's things." Then she took one look at my horrified, tear-stained face and said, "You never do this again?"

I quickly shook my head "No."

So Ah-King opened a drawer and took out a plastic bottle and some cotton pads. She deftly began applying the magic liquid in the bottle to the cotton pads and then to my fingers, the counter, the sink, the cabinet, the floor, and the door. Where red had been, normalcy surfaced. I can still remember the disbelief, relief, and gratitude I felt.

"Are you going to tell on me?" I asked her, bottom lip protruding.

"No, but you be good, you hear?"

Ah-King had the authority of a parent when my parents were away, but she chose to be a servant to me. She put herself in my place, cleaned me up, and then exhorted me to be good. How relieved I was! I couldn't get the "sin" off me, but she knew how to do it, so she had mercy on me. She took responsibility for the dirty cotton pads in the trash can. She acted as if it had never happened. I truly don't remember anything else Ah-King ever did in our home, but I remember her mercy, and how I loved her for it!

## Joy in Communion with Christ

Take a few moments and go to hymnal.net and sing this old hymn.

### "Rescue the Perishing"
(Fanny J. Crosby, 1869)

Rescue the perishing, care for the dying,
Snatch them in pity from sin and the grave.
Weep o'er the erring one, lift up the fallen,
Tell them of Jesus the mighty to save.
Rescue the perishing, care for the dying,
Jesus is merciful, Jesus will save.

Down in the human heart, crushed by the tempter,
Feelings lie buried that grace can restore.
Touched by a loving heart, wakened by kindness,
Chords that are broken will vibrate once more.
Rescue the perishing, care for the dying,
Jesus is merciful, Jesus will save.

I encourage you to pray and meditate on the following:

He was despised and rejected by mankind, a man of suffering, and familiar with pain. Like one from whom people hide their faces he was despised, and we held him in low esteem. Surely he took up our pain and bore our suffering, yet we considered him punished by God, stricken by him, and afflicted. But he was pierced for our transgressions, he was crushed for our iniquities; the punishment that brought us peace was on him, and by his wounds we are healed. We all, like sheep, have gone astray, each of us has turned to our own way; and the Lord has laid on him the iniquity of us all.

Isaiah 53:3-6

"Let any one of you who is without sin be the first to throw a stone at her." Again he stooped down and wrote on the ground. At this, those who heard began to go away one at a time, the older ones first, until only Jesus was left, with the woman still standing there. Jesus straightened up and asked her, "Woman, where are they? Has no one condemned you?" "No one, sir," she said. "Then neither do I condemn you," Jesus declared. "Go now and leave your life of sin."

John 8:7-11

Blessed are the merciful, for they will be shown mercy.

Matthew 5:7

# WORSHIPPER

RECENTLY I RECEIVED an email that was an essay attributed to Jay Leno, but the true author was Craig R. Smith, who is unknown to most people. To me, the important thing about the essay was not its source, but its message. Mr. Smith had read an article that claimed sixty-seven percent of Americans were unhappy with our country. He then began trying to guess what we could be unhappy about. Here are some of the factors he mentioned:

- We have electricity, running water, air conditioning in summer and heat in winter
- We can walk in a grocery store and see more food than many people see in a year
- We have the choice of thousands of restaurants with all types of foods
- If we have a car wreck or a house fire, emergency workers almost immediately show up to help (which means we have cars and houses)
- We have televisions, cell phones, computers, and many other electronic devices
- We have complete religious, social and political freedom[9]

Well, all of those things added together sure seems like reason enough to be unhappy! Unfortunately, many of us are so blessed that we often forget what we have to be grateful for, and we very easily fall into habits of complaining, casting blame, taking things for granted, and becoming greedy for more. We sometimes even forget and take for granted our greatest freedom, which is found in Jesus Christ. After all, "If the Son sets you free, you will be free indeed" (John 8:36); "Now the Lord is the Spirit, and where the Spirit of the Lord is, there is freedom" (2 Cor. 3:17); and "It is for freedom that Christ has set us free. Stand firm, then, and do not let yourselves be burdened again by a yoke of slavery" (Gal. 5:1).

## The Joyful Truth

Philippians 2:8 told us the good news that "being found in appearance as a man, [Christ] humbled himself by becoming obedient to death—even death on a cross!" (brackets added). Jesus left heaven to die for us, but we tend to live out the world's priorities instead of God's. The verses that follow in Paul's letter read this way:

> Therefore God exalted him to the highest place and gave him the name that is above every name, that at the name of Jesus every knee should bow, in heaven and on earth and under the earth, and every tongue acknowledge that Jesus Christ is Lord, to the glory of God the Father.
>
> Philippians 2:9-11

Our redemption is first and foremost for the glory of God the Father. Those who love and obey him are like a sweet aroma. It is true that in Old Testament times the aroma of the sacrifices was pleasing to God, but even then he drew no pleasure from the sacrifices of disobedient people. 1 Samuel 15:22 says, "Does the Lord delight in burnt offerings and sacrifices as much as in obeying the Lord? To obey is better than sacrifice, and to heed is better than the fat of rams." Today we still have the awesome privilege of worshiping the Lord through obedience to his commands.

The word translated "acknowledge" in the verses above is *exomologeo,* which comes from the Greek root *homologeo* and the prefix *ex. Homologeo* means "to confess, acknowledge, agree, admit, declare that something is the truth." The prefix *ex* means "an activity stemming from, out of, or by reason of something." So when I confess "Jesus is Lord," I am not just talking but saying with my actions that he is in control of me. In other words, true confession cannot be lip service, for if the heart hasn't changed, the words are not a confession but only prattle.

## Digesting the Joy

I found it interesting when reading the definitions for both *exomologeo* and *homologeo* that among the long list of synonyms was the word "thank." Evidently, thankfulness is a significant part of acknowledging Jesus as Lord. The following psalm is a brief "worship in a nutshell" where thankfulness is mentioned twice:

Shout for joy to the Lord, all the earth. Worship the Lord with gladness; come before him with joyful songs. Know that the Lord is God. It is he who made us, and we are his; we are his people, the sheep of his pasture. Enter his gates with thanksgiving and his courts with praise; give thanks to him and praise his name. For the Lord is good and his love endures forever; his faithfulness continues through all generations.

Psalm 100:1-8

It sounds like the psalmist understood *homologeo* and *exomologeo*. A person who already has thankfulness in her heart when she enters to worship will find it overflows in her worship.

With my background in preschool work, I am often most touched by the simplest stories, such as the story of worship found in the book of Luke:

Now on his way to Jerusalem, Jesus traveled along the border between Samaria and Galilee. As he was going into a village, ten men who had leprosy met him. They stood at a distance and called out in a loud voice, "Jesus, Master, have pity on us!" When he saw them, he said, "Go, show yourselves to the priests." And as they went, they were cleansed. One of them, when he saw he was healed, came back, praising God in a loud voice. He threw himself at Jesus' feet and thanked him—and he was a Samaritan. Jesus asked, "Were not all ten cleansed? Where are the other nine? Has no one returned to give praise to God except this foreigner?" Then he said to him, "Rise and go; your faith has made you well."

Luke 17:11-19

There are five things to notice about this intriguing story. First, all ten men called Jesus "Master." Second, all ten men were cleansed of their leprosy. Third, only one man threw himself at Jesus' feet in praise and thanksgiving for his healing. Fourth, Jesus was pleased with his gratefulness but disappointed in the lack of gratefulness from the others. And fifth, though all ten men were cleansed of their leprosy, only the one was made "well" (the Greek *sozo*, which means to be in right relationship with God).

Don't you imagine all ten men were exclaiming to each other, "Look! Wow! That Jesus is really something, isn't he?" Yet only one man seemed to comprehend the magnitude of grace bestowed by Jesus the Master. Whereas before, because of their leprosy, all these men had to stand at a distance and raise their voices to speak to people, now they could walk right up to the priests, or anyone else for that matter. They had been outcasts; now they would be members of society once more. They had had to leave their families. Now they could hold their loved ones in their arms again. Yet only one man worshiped at Jesus' feet, and he was a Samaritan, a "foreigner," someone born in a different land. How grieved Jesus must have felt that the only one who loved him enough to worship him rightly was not even one of his own people.

## Living Your Joy Out Loud

Have we been healed of anything? Have our sin-blackened souls been cleansed and made new? Has a burden been lifted? Are we now part of a loving family? How have we, his own people who call him Lord, responded? When I catch my heart becoming cold to my privilege of worship, I turn to such psalms as the following because they are loaded with words that spur me on, especially when I am on my knees:

> I will give thanks to you, Lord, with all my heart; I will tell of all your wonderful deeds. I will be glad and rejoice in you; I will sing the praises of your name, O Most High.
>
> Psalm 9:1-2

> Praise be to the Lord, for he has heard my cry for mercy. The Lord is my strength and my shield; my heart trusts in him, and he helps me. My heart leaps for joy, and with my song I praise him.
>
> Psalm 28:6-7

> Sing the praises of the Lord, you his faithful people; praise his holy name. For his anger lasts only a moment, but his favor lasts a lifetime; weeping may stay for the night, but rejoicing comes in the morning.
>
> Psalm 30:4-5

> I will be glad and rejoice in your love, for you saw my affliction and knew the anguish of my soul. You have not given me into the hands of the enemy but have set my feet in a spacious place.
>
> Psalm 31:7-8

> Your love, Lord, reaches to the heavens, your faithfulness to the skies. Your righteousness is like the highest mountains, your justice like the great deep. You, Lord, preserve both people and animals. How priceless is your unfailing love, O God! People take refuge in the shadow of your wings.
>
> Psalm 36:5-7

> O come, let us worship and bow down; let us kneel before the Lord our maker. For he is our God; and we are the people of his pasture, and the sheep of his hand.
>
> Psalm 95:6-7, KJV

## Joy in Communion with Christ

Join me in singing the following hymn:

"O WORSHIP THE KING"
(Robert Grant, 1833)

O worship the King, all glorious above,
O gratefully sing His power and His love;
Our Shield and Defender, the Ancient of Days,
Pavilioned in splendor, and girded with praise.

O tell of His might, O sing of His grace,
Whose robe is the light, Whose canopy space,
His chariots of wrath the deep thunderclouds form,
And dark is His path on the wings of the storm.

Thy bountiful care, what tongue can recite?
It breathes in the air, it shines in the light;
It streams from the hills, it descends to the plain,
And sweetly distills in the dew and the rain.

Frail children of dust, and feeble as frail,
In Thee do we trust, nor find Thee to fail;
Thy mercies how tender, how firm to the end,
Our Maker, Defender, Redeemer, and Friend.

Now, offer up a heartfelt prayer of thanksgiving to God.

# BODYBUILDER

"WE DON'T WANT *her*. We had to have her last time!"

I can still hear the whine in my classmate's voice. My young life was filled with just such miseries as being chosen last on teams for Red Rover, dodge ball, or kickball, getting hit in the face with the tether ball, and watching in awe and longing as some of the other girls swung across the horizontal ladder monkey bars. When I was fourteen, my own mother beat me at tennis.

As I bemoaned the fact, she counseled, "Don't worry about it. You're just not coordinated."

I later cheered that my high school required only two years of physical education, and my college only two semesters. By the time my grade of C in golf was on my college transcript, I had irrevocably cast myself in the role of klutz. Every physical challenge, no matter how small, seemed to strike the deep chord in my psyche that had for years repeated the mantra, *You are lacking.*

How ironic that I should meet and marry one of the most naturally talented athletes in the South! His psyche's mantra was completely different from mine: *Exercise will make you feel better, so go have some fun--play basketball, football, tennis, golf, volleyball, ride bikes, climb mountains, run, even while mowing the grass!* (I'm not kidding.) Often in our courtship and marriage I have been very thankful for the advice his mother gave me early on, "Don't ever try to keep up with David Bazemore!"

All that said, I could really identify with a silly email I recently received. It read, "I feel like my body has gotten totally out of shape, so I got my doctor's permission to join a fitness club and start exercising. I decided to take an aerobics class for seniors. I bent, twisted, gyrated, jumped up and down, and perspired for an hour. But, by the time I got my leotards on, the class was over." (Ha, ha, ha!)

## The Joyful Truth

Though I wouldn't make it on our church's ladies' softball team, and will not be joining the Tuesday morning tennis group, there really is no excuse for me being out of shape. I can put one foot in front of the other and walk. In fact, I have even managed to jog, lift weights, participate in step aerobics, and do the dance-fitness program Zumba. My current problem is pure laziness, something God is working on.

A Christian woman faces the same kind of choice in her spiritual life.

Therefore, my dear friends, as you have always obeyed—not only in my presence, but now much more in my absence—continue to work out your salvation with fear and trembling, for it is God who works in you to will and to act according to his good purpose.

Philippians 2:12-13

The word *katergazomai* is used for "work out," and it means "to produce, accomplish, or bring about." This is not meant to imply we can accomplish or bring about our own salvation. Paul makes that clear when he says, "For it is *God* who works in you to will and to act according to his good purpose" (emphasis added).

When I was born, I was given my physical body. I didn't do anything to earn it. If I had, I might have wondered why I didn't earn a better model! Nevertheless, I must feed it and give it water. I must exercise it. When I do, the natural consequences will follow: life, growth, health, and energy. God uses what I put in my body and causes the growth. Likewise, when I was born again, God gave me a new spirit. My job is to give it nourishment and a good work out, and when I do that he will cause the growth. If I shirk my responsibility, then I will soon notice a weakness in my spirit that often manifests itself in a greater tendency to submit to temptation.

For this reason Paul writes "continue to work out your salvation with fear and trembling." The Greek used here for "fear" is *phobos*. It means "fear, terror, respect, reverence." Most people will recognize *phobos* as the origin of our English word *phobia*.

I have acrophobia, the fear of heights, which I believe stems from a healthy respect for heights. If a person falls from a tall place, he will almost always die. I had hydrophobia when I was younger. I learned that it probably originated when I was knocked over by a wave at a very young age. After that, I had a healthy respect for what water could do to cut off my breathing!

In the Philippians 2:12 context, the word *fear* should probably be translated "respect or reverence." God does an awesome, mysterious work in the heart of a believer. As we work to build this spiritual body The Creator has given us, we will realize more and more the beauty of the miracle he is performing. On the other hand, if we grow lax in cultivating our relationship with God or in listening to God's voice, the word *fear* might be more appropriate, as laziness in spirit has the potential of getting us into a whole lot of trouble. Paul had heard the church at Philippi was experiencing the trouble of disunity, so he exhorted them to work out their salvation with fear and trembling.

## Digesting the Joy

Philippians 2:12-13 lays out the plan, the process, and the purpose of our spiritual workout. The *plan* is God's Spirit working in us. The disciple John recorded that Jesus said,

> And I will ask the Father, and he will give you another advocate to help you and be with you forever--the Spirit of truth. The world cannot accept him, because it neither sees him nor knows him. But you know him, for he lives with you and will be in you. . . . But very truly I tell you, it is for your good that I am going away. Unless I go away, the Advocate will not come to you; but if I go, I will send him to you. . . . But when he, the Spirit of truth, comes, he will guide you into all the truth. He will not speak on his own; he will speak only what he hears, and he will tell you what is yet to come.
>
> John 14:16-17; 16:7, 13

As God's Spirit works in us, he guides us into all truth. We exercise our spirits by studying God's Word and listening to the promptings of the Holy Spirit. We go where he directs and we do the things he tells us to do. We say the words the Spirit of truth urges us to say. As we intentionally allow the workout of the Holy Spirit, we grow and become more spiritually healthy, and it is in that way we make an impact on others.

Consider the growth of Peter and John, two disciples who had been fishermen before Jesus called them to follow him. Just three years after their call, not long after Jesus had ascended into heaven, they healed a lame man. Through this miracle, Peter was given an opportunity to preach to thousands of people, and the Jewish authorities did not like what they heard, especially the part about Jesus' resurrection from the dead. So they arrested Peter and John and brought them before the Sanhedrin, the high court of the priests, elders, and teachers of the law. They asked by what power Peter and John had healed the lame man.

Then Peter, filled with the Holy Spirit, said to them: "Rulers and elders of the people! If we are being called to account today for an act of kindness shown to a man who was lame and are being asked how he was healed, then know this, you and all the people of Israel: It is by the name of Jesus Christ of Nazareth, whom you crucified but whom God raised from the dead, that this man stands before you healed. Jesus is 'the stone you builders rejected, which has become the cornerstone.' Salvation is found in no one else, for there is no other name under heaven given to mankind by which we must be saved." When they saw the courage of Peter and John and realized that they were unschooled, ordinary men, they were astonished and they took note that these men had been with Jesus.

Acts 4:8-13

Peter's and John's courage must have been something to behold. The authorities of the high court were astonished at the boldness of these unschooled, ordinary men. The reason for the boldness? They were filled with the Holy Spirit.

I have had Spirit-filled moments like that when I knew the words coming from my mouth were not from the southern hick, ordinary woman I am, but from the Holy Spirit living within the bodybuilder Joy. And I can tell you that I felt awe and trembling, especially afterwards! This is the process of God's work. How appropriate that Peter wrote these words later:

By his divine power, God has given us everything we need for living a godly life. We have received all of this by coming to know him, the one who called us to himself by means of his marvelous glory and excellence. And because of his glory and excellence, he has given us great and precious promises. These are the promises that enable you to share his divine nature and escape the world's corruption caused by human desires. In view of all this, make every effort to respond to God's promises. *Supplement your faith with a generous provision of moral excellence, and moral excellence with knowledge, and knowledge with self-control, and self-control with patient endurance, and patient endurance with godliness, and godliness with brotherly affection, and brotherly affection with love for everyone.* The more you grow like this, the more productive and useful you will be in your knowledge of our Lord Jesus Christ.

2 Peter 1:3-8, NLT, emphasis added

"Make every effort to respond to God's promises" can actually be translated, "Keep on making every effort to respond to God's promises." In other words, be a body*builder*. Through the Holy Spirit's power, work out moral excellence, knowledge, self-control, endurance, godliness, brotherly affection, and love. If we keep on making these efforts, if we keep growing like this, we will be useful and productive in God's kingdom. And the purpose for being useful and productive in God kingdom? Paul says it is for God's good pleasure, for when we are useful in his kingdom, he is pleased.

## Living Your Joy Out Loud

Let's say I have worked out my muscles controlling self-control, godliness, and brotherly affection. What does it actually look like when I use them? "Do everything without complaining and arguing, so that no one can criticize you. Live clean, innocent lives as children of God, shining like bright lights in a world full of crooked and perverse people" (Phil. 2:14-15, NLT).

We may have trouble fully comprehending the concept of "working out" our salvation, but there is nothing perplexing about "do everything without complaining and arguing," or "live clean, innocent lives," or "shine like bright stars in a world of crooked and perverse people." God wants us to stand out, doesn't he? He wants us to look different from the crooked and depraved world all around us. How could he expect such a thing? Once again, the answer is that his divine power has given us everything we need for life and godliness.

Each morning we need to put on our workout clothes and work on becoming bodybuilders. No excuses. Because there should be no such thing as a spiritual klutz.

## Joy in Communion with Christ

When you have a chance, go to YouTube.com and search "All I Once Held Dear"[10], *by Robin Mark*. Sing along and meditate on pursuing Christ.

Pray for diligence in building your spiritual body to the glory and pleasure of God.

# CHILD OF GOD

IN TODAY'S PAPER, there is a letter from a distraught man to an advice columnist. He writes that his teenage stepson has been killed, and though many are comforting his wife, no one seems to understand that the young man was a son of his heart, too. When he and his wife married, her son became his. The bond was there. The boy called him "Dad." Yet the man had to face his grief on his own.

Many years ago, a couple in our town adopted a son. For the first three years of his life, they did all the acts of love and care every parent bestows on a child. He was a happy boy and brought them much joy. Then, suddenly, his birth mother decided she wanted him back, and in spite of valid adoption proceedings and official papers, the judge ordered the couple to give up the boy. Their grief was unthinkable.

Sometimes prodigals never return. Sometimes little children have cancer and die. Sometimes parents mistreat their offspring. The parent-child relationship has many twists and turns that are sometimes joyfully "normal" and sometimes extremely heartbreaking. Not so in our relationship with God. We are his children, and he is our never-changing Father, the same-yesterday, today, and forever.

## The Joyful Truth

Do everything without complaining and arguing, so that no one can criticize you. Live clean, innocent lives as children of God, shining like bright lights in a world full of crooked and perverse people.

Philippians 2:14-15, NLT

Doing everything without complaining and arguing, and living clean and innocent lives, are not prerequisites for becoming a child of God. The biblical arithmetic for becoming a child of God is simple: God's grace plus nothing equals salvation. Period. We become God's children the day we trust Jesus as our Savior. The verse above could be rearranged to say, "Children of God, do everything without complaining or arguing so that you may become blameless and pure—that is, without fault—in a crooked and depraved generation."

The word in the original Greek for "child" in this verse is *teknon*, which very simply means "child, son, daughter, offspring, descendant." In other places in the New Testament the word *huios* is used for child, and that word is translated a little differently: "son, child, descendant; a term of endearment."

No doubt scholars have explored the reasons Paul chose to use *teknon* in this setting. Perhaps it was intentional. Perhaps Paul wanted to use the word that specifically included the female gender, because we later learn from this verse, "I plead with Euodia and I plead with Syntyche to be of the same mind in the Lord" (Phil. 4:2), that these two women were having particular trouble getting along with each other.

Regardless of the reason for the choice of word here, it is exciting to note that the same word was used by John in his gospel when he wrote, "Yet to all who did receive him [Jesus, the Word], to those who believed in his name, he gave the right to become children of God—children born not of natural descent, nor of human decision or a husband's will, but born of God" (John 1:12-13, brackets added). Children of God are chosen, planned, privileged children!

## Digesting the Joy

Think about the stages of a person's life. The first stage, premeditation, takes place even before conception. In human families, sometimes this first stage is skipped. That is, rather than being deliberately planned, the pregnancy just happens. This is never the case with God's children, however. The Creator joyfully plans ahead. Our daughter Grace was certainly a planned child, as was Shelley. The twins? Well, I guess you could say *one* of them was planned, though I was hoping for a boy. But which one of our twins was the planned one? The truth is that Hillary and Heather were both part of God's great and glorious plan. So it is with each one of us. Whether our parents planned for us or not, God did, and his ultimate plan was for us to become his own children, part of his wonderful family.

Once a couple knows they are expecting a child, they begin making many decisions. Sadly, for some it is the decision of whether to allow the pregnancy to continue. If in the past you chose abortion for whatever reasons, don't be dismayed. Abortion is on the long, long list of forgivable sins, and Jesus died for those sins. All of them. Every one. No exceptions. His mercy is the covering. Run to the mercy seat where you will find healing for your wounded soul. Allow God's grace to move you forward. (If you need more help with this, Google "Surrendering the Secret by Patricia Layton" to find a support group near you.)

For most couples the nine months before their child is born are months of excited planning, choosing, dreaming, and wondering. Will the child be male or female? What name shall we choose? Who will he look like? What talents will she have? Which room will be hers? How will we pay for college? For that matter, how will we pay for all those diapers? Will we be good parents? Will we both continue working outside the home? Will we choose home schooling? When will he walk, talk, ride a bike?

Have you ever thought about your womb time as God's child, that time before you accepted Christ as your Savior but God knew you were going to be born into his family? What kind of planning, dreaming and choosing did God do? First of all, from the beginning of time, God planned to provide a Savior for us. He knew we would need one. As our Creator, God knew we would have straying, stubborn hearts, and that is why he provided a way of salvation in Jesus, the way and the truth and the life.

Since God knew that people of every generation would question whether Jesus was God's own Son sent to take away the sins of the world, in his infinite wisdom and mysterious omniscience, God told men about the Savior's coming over eight hundred years before Jesus was born! The prophet Isaiah recorded God saying, "Therefore the Lord himself shall give you a sign; behold, a virgin shall conceive, and bear a son, and shall call his name Immanuel" (7:14, KJV). This prophecy was fulfilled and documented in the gospels of Matthew (1:18-25) and Luke (1:26-34).

Matthew records the fulfillment of three other prophecies about our Lord (2:6, 15, 18), and Jesus himself said, "Do not think that I have come to abolish the Law or the Prophets; I have not come to abolish them but to fulfill them" (Matt. 5:17). Furthermore, the gospel of John tells of John the Baptist's assertion that Jesus was the pure Lamb of God portrayed by the prophet Isaiah:

He was oppressed and afflicted, yet he did not open his mouth; he was led like a lamb to the slaughter, and as a sheep before its shearers is silent, so he did not open his mouth. By oppression and judgment he was taken away. Yet who of his generation protested? For he was cut off from the land of the living; for the transgression of my people he was punished. He was assigned a grave with the wicked, and with the rich in his death, though he had done no violence, nor was any deceit in his mouth.

Isaiah 53:7-9

The next day John saw Jesus coming toward him and said, "Look, the Lamb of God, who takes away the sin of the world! This is the one I meant when I said, 'A man who comes after me has surpassed me because he was before me.' I myself did not know him, but the reason I came baptizing with water was that he might be revealed to Israel." Then John gave this testimony: "I saw the Spirit come down from heaven as a dove and remain on him. And I myself did not know him, but the one who sent me to baptize with water told me, 'The man on whom you see the Spirit come down and remain is the one who will baptize with the Holy Spirit.' I have seen and I testify that this is God's Chosen One.

John 1:29-34

Our salvation, then, was a high priority in God's "prenatal" planning.

The second kind of planning God did, before we ever chose to accept Christ as our Savior, was to prepare a place for us in his family. He selected the group of believers with whom you and I would fellowship and he chose the gift or gifts that would be exercised by us among the body of Christ (the church). Paul wrote, "In fact God has placed the parts in the body, every one of them, just as he wanted them to be" (1 Cor. 12:18). Which part are you? Have you discovered your spiritual gift(s)? If not, do some homework on spiritual gifts and find out, because unlike human parents who can only dream about what their child will be, God *knows* your potential because he decides it! His dream for our lives is not an impossible or improbable destination—not if we give him the steering wheel and let him use our gifts for the glory of the Kingdom.

The most exciting part of God's pre-birth plans is that he already knows who we are going to look like! We might not look exactly like him until we are fully-grown Christians, but we will grow to have his mannerisms, his character, his methods, and his style. People will see a child of God and say, "Wow! She is the spitting image of Jesus!"

All of these pre-birth plans lead up to *the* moment--the moment when we are born into God's family. From that moment on, whether we are spiritual infants, children, adolescents, or adults, we have the many lawful rights of a child of God.

## Living Your Joy Out Loud

What rights do we have as children of God? The privilege most written about is prayer. Communication with our heavenly Father, unlike that with humans, is totally fulfilling. For one thing, the Father invites us to talk to him. We sometimes think of prayer as that holy thing that must be about holy things, for Jesus started his model prayer with,

> Our Father, which art in heaven, hallowed be Thy name. Thy kingdom come, Thy will be done on earth as it is in heaven.
>
> Matthew 6:9-10, KJV

Prayer is certainly a holy thing, a holy privilege of conversation with our hallowed heavenly Father. But Jesus also taught that prayer is about asking for our daily bread and seeking deliverance from evil:

> Give us this day our daily bread. And forgive us our debts, as we forgive our debtors. And lead us not into temptation, but deliver us from evil: For thine is the kingdom, and the power, and the glory, forever. Amen.
>
> Matthew 6:11-13, KJV

We are the Father's children, and as such we often just need to call on our daddy to listen, and when we do, he does. In the middle of Psalm 50, in which God is describing the kind of worship he accepts, verse fifteen says, "Call on me in the day of trouble; I will deliver you, and you will honor me."

You who are mothers know you want your children to call on you if they need something. You want them to show they trust you to care about them. The difficulty comes not in whether you want to give them good things but in deciding what will be best for them. God's Word says, "If you, then, though you are evil, know how to give good gifts to your children, how much more will your Father in heaven give good gifts to those who ask him!" (Matt. 7:11). Our Father God insists that his children can ask him anything in Jesus' name. When we trust him to do whatever is best for us, we can feel free to ask, ask, and ask.

Do we always receive the optimum blessing we could from prayer? No, because sometimes we overlook the first principle of communication: Listen more, talk less. James taught this clearly when he said, "My dear brothers and sisters, always be willing to listen and slow to speak" (James 1:19, NCV). One of the good gifts our heavenly Father wants to give is guidance in this frightening world. Yet we can't hear his still, small voice if we are talking all the time.

He wants to give us words of comfort, but we are too busy complaining. He wants to give us joy if we will be still and know that he is God. My paraphrase of Psalm 46:10 is, "Be quiet and God will speak to you." We don't hear our Father talking to us, because we don't give him a chance. If we did, we could bask in the feel of his strong arms and in the sound of his powerful, whispered words meant just for us.

Aside from prayer, another privilege of the child of God is hope. Everyone is drawn to hope. It is that entity in every innocent child that appeals to the hardest heart. We children of God have hope, because our innocence has been given back to us by Jesus Christ's death and resurrection. That isn't to say we sleep on beds of roses. The following verses explain our hope:

> For we know that all creation has been groaning as in the pains of childbirth right up to the present time. And we believers also groan, even though we have the Holy Spirit within us as a foretaste of future glory, for we long for our bodies to be released from sin and suffering. We, too, wait with eager hope for the day when God will give us our full rights as his adopted children, including the new bodies he has promised us. We were given this hope when we were saved.
>
> Romans 8:22-24a, NLT

Hope is the joyful and confident expectation of eternal salvation. The non-believer, one who is not a child of God, may think he or she has hope for the future, but it is an empty hope, for there's no hope in hell. Remember the story of the rich man and Lazarus?

> There was a rich man who was dressed in purple and fine linen and lived in luxury every day. At his gate was laid a beggar named Lazarus, covered with sores and longing to eat what fell from the rich man's table. Even the dogs came and licked his sores. The time came when the beggar died and the angels carried him to Abraham's side. The rich man also died and was buried. In Hades, where he was in torment, he looked up and saw Abraham far away, with Lazarus by his side. So he called to him, "Father Abraham, have pity on me and send Lazarus to dip the tip of his finger in water and cool my tongue, because I am in agony in this fire." But Abraham replied, "Son, remember that in your lifetime you received your good things, while Lazarus received bad things, but now he is comforted here and you are in agony. And besides all this, between us and you a great chasm has been set in place, so that those who want to go from here to you cannot, nor can anyone cross over from there to us." He answered, "Then I beg you, father, send Lazarus to my family, for I have five brothers. Let him warn them, so that they will not also come to this place of torment."
>
> Luke 16:19-27

Once a person has died and gone to hell, there is no hope. For this reason, Peter encouraged his listeners: "Always be prepared to give an answer to everyone who asks you to give the reason for the hope that you have. But do this with gentleness and respect" (1 Pet. 3:15). Paul tells Timothy that the Lord "wants all people to be saved and to come to a knowledge of the truth" (1 Tim. 2:4). In the family of God, the more, the merrier.

## Joy in Communion with Christ

In our hope for eternal salvation lies our hope to meet our Savior. Every time I hear the song "I Bowed on my Knees," I am moved by the images of our hope. I encourage you to go to YouTube.com and search "I Bowed on My Knees" Charles Billingsley. Worship while you listen to this beautiful song. To meet the Son of God face to face—now that will be glory!

Prayer and hope are privileges of the child of God. Let's look at just one more privilege: We get to carry his name. That is, we are *Christians*.

Did you ever do what I did as a preteen and teenager? If I liked a boy a lot, I would practice writing my first name with his last name, such as Joy Peterson or Mrs. Tom Peterson. I would write it all over a notebook or diary. The thrill of taking the name of the man I loved was a wonderful thing to imagine.

On a more serious note, I recall that when our girls were teenagers, as they were getting ready to leave the house I would sometimes say, "Remember whose you are!" They thought I meant, "Don't embarrass your family," but I explained what I really meant: "You belong to Christ. Make him proud!" The privilege of being God's child and bearing the name of Christ carries with it the great responsibility of vigilance so as to bring no reproach to him. We will never be perfect at this, however, and just as I never considered disowning my children when they disappointed or embarrassed me, God will never disown us if we bring criticism to his name. We are his children--planned for, gifted, privileged, and loved.

Take a moment and go to YouTube.com and search "Family of God"[11] by Heber Vega. Sing along.

Take some time to exercise your privilege of prayer. Be still before God. Be quiet. Quit striving. And know that he is all you truly need.

# STAR

CAMPING IS NOT for me. Bugs. Allergies. Humidity. Cold. Hot. Yucky bathrooms. No bathrooms. Snakes. I gave camping a try when I was younger, but I got little sleep and had no fun. The only redeeming moments that came from camping were the ones spent gazing at the star-filled sky. When dusk first darkened into night, one star began a bright burn in the teal blue sky. Then as the next hour passed, the bowl of the night sky turned to navy velvet while the rest of the stars emerged to dance and twinkle on the stage. I sat, staring up, and in those quiet moments I worshiped God. I have never been camping since my youth, but I have watched the sky fill with stars many times. When I do, I feel the same awe and peace I experienced so long ago.

## The Joyful Truth

Considering the beauty and wonder of the stars, how amazing it is to discover that according to Paul in his letter to the Philippians, you and I are stars!

Do everything without grumbling or arguing, so that you may become blameless and pure, "children of God without fault in a warped and crooked generation." Then you will shine among them like stars in the sky as you hold firmly to the word of life. And then I will be able to boast on the day of Christ that I did not run or labor in vain.

Philippians 2:14-16

Here is the account of the creation of the stars from Genesis:

And God said, "Let there be lights in the vault of the sky to separate the day from the night, and let them serve as signs to mark sacred times, and days and years, and let them be lights in the vault of the sky to give light on the earth." And it was so. God made two great lights—the greater light to govern the day and the lesser light to govern the night. He also made the stars. God set them in the vault of the sky to give light on the earth, to govern the day and the night, and to separate light from darkness. And God saw that it was good.

Genesis 1:14-18

The creation of the stars seems almost an afterthought. They aren't the "great lights" that actually give light to the whole earth. They were not made to govern. The sun and moon are the ones that really separate day and night, as well as mark the seasons and days and years. Then why did God include stars? Why the millions of other lights? I believe the answer is "to separate light from darkness." The Hebrew words used for "light" and "darkness" in verse eighteen are not the same words used for "day" and "night" in verse fourteen. Verse fourteen simply means "to separate the day from the night," whereas the connotation of the Hebrew word used for "light" in verse eighteen is that of brightness, clarity, and relief. Its opposite, "darkness," is defined as "blackness, gloom, despair, terror, ignorance." The role of the stars, therefore, is to take part in dispelling the gloom, eradicating despair, doing away with ignorance, and giving clarity and relief to seekers.

The stars accomplish this in three specific ways, the first of which is portrayed beautifully in the book of Psalms:

The heavens declare the glory of God; the skies proclaim the work of his hands. Day after day they pour forth speech; night after night they reveal knowledge. They have no speech, they use no words; no sound is heard from them. Yet their voice goes out into all the earth, their words to the ends of the world. In the heavens God has pitched a tent for the sun.

Psalm 19:1-4

According to these verses, it is fair to say that stars reveal the work of God's hands, and they speak loudly of the glory of the Creator.

## Digesting the Joy

When I went camping as a young woman, it wasn't the nice, warm sun or the bright moon that inspired my worship. It was the hundreds of stars, twinkling silently in their places.

The message the heavens declare is that there is a sovereign, unfathomable God who is the great "I Am," and who deserves our worship and devotion. There is no excuse for ignorance of God, because the proclamation of the stars has done away with it. Unfortunately, the response from humanity has been divided. Some men and women exploit the stars in contriving meaningless horoscopes. They scoff at the truth that the beauty and wonder we observe in the skies is a testimony of God's creative power. They take the gift, but they ridicule the Giver.

Those of us who know the Lord as Creator, Redeemer, and Sustainer, on the other hand, bow in amazement at the magnitude and dimension of our God. We can't comprehend the size of the One who cast the stars in the heavens like so many droplets of water shaken from his fingertips. We can't comprehend the magnitude of the One who walks on planets like stepping stones in a brook and uses the Earth as his footstool. This same God who knows our thoughts is too glorious and wonderful to comprehend. The psalmist was of like mind: "Such knowledge is too wonderful for me, too lofty for me to attain" (Ps. 139:6).

## Living Your Joy Out Loud

How can I be a star whose "starring" role is declaring the glory of God and displaying his craftsmanship? According to Scripture, the answer is the whisper of intentionally blameless behavior. If we are above reproach and pure, we will be stars that shine brightly in the sky as we hold firmly to the word of life (Phil. 2:14-16). After all, the song "This Little Light of Mine" does not proclaim, "I'm going to let it shout," but "I'm going to let it shine." We can say a lot about God by the way we display our bodies, by the purity of our choices, and by the excellence of our motives.

Consistency and dependability in this area are crucial. Think about the stars in the night sky. In the early days of travel, men used the North Star and a constellation called the Southern Cross to navigate in the northern and southern hemispheres, respectively. Thus, although the light of the stars (except the sun) was not bright enough to light the way, the positions of the stars were unchanging and thereby dependable. Men gambled their lives on that certainty. For a more modern example, think about this: Most movie stars, pop stars, and star athletes all have one thing in common (besides wealth), and that is the reliability of their work. True and lasting star status is the result of a predictably excellent or consumer-pleasing performance. When we are faced with temptation to drift or fall in our Christian walk, let's remember that our constancy of excellence is one way we shine out in this depraved world.

I love this old spiritual:

## "I Shall not be Moved"

Jesus is my Savior, I shall not be moved;
In His love and favor, I shall not be moved,
Just like a tree that's planted by the waters,
Lord, I shall not be moved.
In my Christ abiding, I shall not be moved;
In His love I'm hiding, I shall not be moved,
Just like a tree that's planted by the waters,
Lord, I shall not be moved.
If I trust Him ever, I shall not be moved;
He will fail me never, I shall not be moved,
Just like a tree that's planted by the waters,
Lord, I shall not be moved.
On His word I'm feeding, I shall not be moved;
He's the One that's leading, I shall not be moved,
Just like a tree that's planted by the waters,
Lord, I shall not be moved.
Chorus
I shall not be, I shall not be moved;
I shall not be, I shall not be moved;
Just like a tree that's planted by the waters,
Lord, I shall not be moved.

Job said, "Even if he slays me, I shall not be moved."
Daniel said, "Though the lions may maul me, I shall not be moved."
Hannah said, "Though I have no baby, I shall not be moved."
Isaiah said, "When they reject my prophecy, I shall not be moved."
Mary the mother of Jesus said, "I will trust God's promise; I shall not be moved."

But maybe you are thinking, "Wait a minute. There was a star in the Bible that *did* move." And you would be right. Let's consider the significance of the moving star. God was about to do something unique in Bethlehem. He had not done it before, and he has not needed to do it since. He had chosen the time and place carefully.

The people, both major players and supporting actors, had to be informed. For his local missionaries, he chose the shepherds, and he sent angels to tell them of the Messiah's birth. But for some reason we do not yet know, when God selected the missionaries to spread the good news in faraway lands, he chose to use a moving star to lead these men to Jesus. That moving star could be compared to those of us who have a special gifting by God to evangelize, who feel compelled to tell everyone, wherever we go, about Jesus. We are the stars who meet people where they are and lead them to Christ.

**"The star they had seen when it rose went ahead of them until it stopped over the place where the child was."** The second chapter of the gospel of Matthew, verse ten, says that when they saw the star,

- "they were overjoyed" (NIV) .
- "they were filled with joy" (NLT).
- "they were thrilled with ecstatic joy" (AMP).
- "they were overjoyed beyond measure" (HCSB).
- "they rejoiced with exceeding great joy" (KJV).

I have always preferred the King James Version of this verse, because it shows action—they *rejoiced*. I envisage these studious, serious men letting their hair down to dance, sing, and shout because the kingly star they had been following stopped, and at that place they found King Jesus, the Light of the World. How thrilling it is to be a star that leads people to Jesus, for the joy they find in knowing the Savior is unmatchable!

Stars do burn out, but not for a very long time. So a third way in which we, like stars, can separate light from darkness is to persevere in the faith—keep shining. Jude said it far better than I can:

But remember, dear friends, that the apostles of our Master, Jesus Christ, told us this would happen: "In the last days there will be people who don't take these things [the faith and our Lord Jesus Christ] seriously anymore. They'll treat them like a joke, and make a religion of their own whims and lusts." These are the ones who split churches, thinking only of themselves. There's nothing to them, no sign of the Spirit! But you, dear friends, carefully build yourselves up in this most holy faith by praying in the Holy Spirit, staying right at the center of God's love, keeping your arms open and outstretched, ready for the mercy of our Master, Jesus Christ. This is the unending life, the real life! Go easy on those who hesitate in the faith. Go after those who take the wrong way. Be tender with sinners, but not soft on sin. The sin itself stinks to high heaven.

Jude17-23, MSG

Don't be moved. Lead people to Jesus. Keep shining.

## Joy in Communion with Christ

Take a moment and go to YouTube.com, and search *This Little Light of Mine praise in motion music*. Then sing.

"THIS LITTLE LIGHT OF MINE"
(African American spiritual)

This little light of mine, I'm going to let it shine.
This little light of mine, I'm going to let it shine.
This little light of mine, I'm going to let it shine.
Let it shine, let it shine, let it shine.
Hide it under a bushel, NO! I'm going to let it shine!
Hide it under a bushel, NO! I'm going to let it shine.
Hide it under a bushel, NO! I'm going to let it shine.
Let it shine, let it shine, let it shine.
Won't let Satan blow it out, I'm going to let it shine.
Won't let Satan blow it out, I'm going to let it shine.
Won't let Satan blow it out, I'm going to let it shine.
Let it shine, let it shine, let it shine.
Let it shine til Jesus comes, I'm going to let it shine.
Let it shine til Jesus comes, I'm going to let it shine.
Let it shine til Jesus comes, I'm going to let it shine.
Let it shine, let it shine, let it shine!

Pray and ask God to make you immoveable and unchangeable in your depiction of his glory.

# CARETAKER

GARY CHAPMAN, AN expert on marriage and family relationships and author of *The Five Love Languages*, maintains that every person has a love language through which he or she *feels* most loved. The five languages are physical touch, words of affirmation, quality time, gifts, and acts of service. My primary love language is words of affirmation. Mark Twain once said, "I can live for two months on a good compliment."[12] That is me. Verbal appreciation floats my boat.

In his book Chapman describes the five languages fully. He also explains that usually, a person's own love language is the one they "speak" most easily. In other words, since my primary love language is words of affirmation, when I want to show love to someone else I naturally lean toward affirming her with words, whether that is her love language or not. He asserts that all five of the languages speak love to everyone, but he urges us to learn what another person's primary love language is so we can make special efforts to show love in that particular way.

There are ways to communicate words of affirmation that go beyond the simple "nice tie" or "good sermon, pastor" comments. For example, we can offer encouragement by "reinforcing a difficult decision, calling attention to progress made on a current project, or acknowledging a person's unique perspective on an important topic."[13]

In the book of Acts we learn about a man called Barnabas, which means "Son of Encouragement." Whether words of affirmation was his primary love language or not, Barnabas modeled this love language very well. In a courageous and loving gesture, he stood up for Paul when the church at Jerusalem would have ostracized him.

When [Paul] came to Jerusalem, he tried to join the disciples, but they were all afraid of him, not believing that he really was a disciple. But Barnabas took him and brought him to the apostles. He told them how Saul on his journey had seen the Lord and that the Lord had spoken to him, and how in Damascus he had preached fearlessly in the name of Jesus. So Saul stayed with them and moved about freely in Jerusalem, speaking boldly in the name of the Lord.

Acts 9:26-28

Paul himself became quite an encourager, perhaps through his association with Barnabas over a number of years.

## The Joyful Truth

But even if I am being poured out like a drink offering on the sacrifice and service coming from your faith, I am glad and rejoice with all of you. So you too should be glad and rejoice with me. I hope in the Lord Jesus to send Timothy to you soon, that I also may be cheered when I receive news about you. I have no one else like him, who takes a genuine interest in your welfare. For everyone looks out for his own interests, not those of Jesus Christ. But you know that Timothy has proved himself, because as a son with his father he has served with me in the work of the gospel. I hope, therefore, to send him as soon as I see how things go with me. And I am confident in the Lord that I myself will come soon. But I think it is necessary to send back to you Epaphroditus, my brother, fellow worker and fellow soldier, who is also your messenger, whom you sent to take care of my needs. For he longs for all of you and is distressed because you heard he was ill. Indeed he was ill, and almost died. But God had mercy on him, and not on him only but also on me, to spare me sorrow upon sorrow. Therefore I am all the more eager to send him, so that when you see him again you may be glad and I may have less anxiety.

Philippians 2:17-28

This block of Scripture speaks of several ways we can show our love through encouraging others. They tell us we can be glad and rejoice with another person. When Paul wrote to the church at Corinth, he explained in detail the gifts of the Spirit and how they relate to the body of Christ. Each person, gifted in exactly the way God planned and desired, fits into the body and is a vital part of the whole body. We depend on each other for support, for "If one part suffers, every part suffers with it; if one part is honored, every part rejoices with it" (1 Cor. 12:26).

Putting aside envy, pride, or indifference, we should show excitement when others are blessed with good fortune. Children do this so well. Before their lives are touched by ruder tendencies, they automatically rejoice with those who rejoice.

My two-year-old grandson, Bryant, demonstrated this truth recently. He loves to play golf and loves it even more if you will play with him. He is quite good and gets the ball "in the hole" regularly. A few days ago, I was playing with him, and when I got the ball "in the hole," he clapped his hands and shouted, "Yea, Jojo!"

## Digesting the Joy

Applause, smiles, sparkling eyes, words of congratulation, parties, cards, hugs. All of these and more are ways of rejoicing with a person, but the genuine joy you show will be the greatest source of encouragement. The Bible tells us "there is joy in the presence of the angels of God over one sinner who repents" (Luke 15:10, NKJV). When God rejoices, all the angels join in. It is a tremendous picture of heaven and an example for us.

Showing a real interest in others, as when Paul says of Timothy that "I have no one else like him, who will show genuine concern for your welfare" (Phil. 2:20), is another way we can encourage someone.

Are you busy? Me too. Unfortunately, our busyness can be such a detriment to the ministry of encouragement. Sometimes just an encouraging word is all it takes to make someone's day, and it takes but a moment. But there are other times when a person needs a friend to really listen, to advise, to provide a needed item, to pray, maybe even to hover. These kinds of encouragement take time, thought, and sometimes sacrifice.

I have always loved the account of when Jesus had returned to Capernaum and was teaching in a home:

> They gathered in such large numbers that there was no room left, not even outside the door, and he preached the word to them. Some men came, bringing to him a paralyzed man, carried by four of them. Since they could not get him to Jesus because of the crowd, they made an opening in the roof above Jesus by digging through it and then lowered the mat the man was lying on. When Jesus saw their faith, he said to the paralyzed man, "Son, your sins are forgiven."
>
> Mark 2:2-5

The passage doesn't call these men friends, but in the sense that they truly took an interest in this paralyzed man's welfare, and demonstrated their love through action, they were his *dear* friends. They encouraged him through giving their strength, their time, and their determination. He had to have felt blessed. Jesus must have been blessed, too, because he viewed their actions as true faith. Thus, our encouragement has the potential of blessing the recipient, other people who might witness what we say or do, and even Jesus.

Years ago my youth choir at church learned a song called "Pass it On." Part of it goes like this: "It only takes a spark to get a fire going, And soon all those around can warm up in its glowing; That's how it is with God's Love, Once you've experienced it, You spread the love to everyone. You want to pass it on."[14] When we do something for someone else that demonstrates God's love, we are lighting a fire that will spread only God knows how far and wide.

The church at Philippi, hearing of Paul's house arrest in Rome (Acts 28:16, 30-31), collected money to help provide his living expenses while incarcerated. The Philippians entrusted their gift to a beloved brother in Christ, Epaphroditus, and he set off for Rome. Either along the way or after he reached Rome, Epaphroditus contracted a disease that would normally have led to death.

> But I think it is necessary to send back to you Epaphroditus, my brother, co-worker and fellow soldier, who is also your messenger, whom you sent to take care of my needs. For he longs for all of you and is distressed because you heard he was ill. Indeed he was ill, and almost died. But God had mercy on him, and not on him only but also on me, to spare me sorrow upon sorrow. Therefore I am all the more eager to send him, so that when you see him again you may be glad and I may have less anxiety.
>
> Philippians 2:25-28

As Paul writes this letter, he tries to convey his gratefulness for the Philippians, for their gift, and for their courier, Epaphroditus, who risked his life for Paul's benefit. Epaphroditus has finally recovered from his illness, and Paul has decided to send him back to Philippi with this letter so the church there will be encouraged by Paul's words and by seeing Epaphroditus alive and well. As we read these verses, we are inspired to encourage each other the way Paul and his friends encouraged one another.

Paul was encouraged that the Philippians wanted to take part in meeting his physical needs. The ministry we provide in meeting physical needs through church and charity agencies, or individually, can provide life-sustaining goods and services. But we can also supply needed encouragement, because we are helping people through a difficult spot and giving them the will to press on.

In our community, we have a Christian organization that provides counseling and medical help for young women or families with unexpected pregnancies. Through the counseling and medical services and additional assistance given with clothes, diapers, formula, and other baby items, many young women are encouraged to have their babies rather than seeking an abortion. Just as Paul's negative circumstances inspired the Philippians' giving, and their giving inspired him to press on towards the prize, our response to a person's troubles can help put his or her life on a positive track.

## Living Your Joy Out Loud

Unquestionably, the gifts and services we provide others are an encouragement, just as the money was for Paul. But the love behind the gift is often much more encouragement to a person who is down. Even when we cannot afford a large sum, or cannot give a lot of time, or don't feel we know the right words to say, when we act out of love, a person is blessed.

1 Corinthians 13: 1-3 says, "If I speak in the tongues of men or of angels, but do not have love, I am only a resounding gong or a clanging cymbal. If I have the gift of prophecy and can fathom all mysteries and all knowledge, and if I have a faith that can move mountains, but do not have love, I am nothing. If I give all I possess to the poor and give over my body to hardship that I may boast, but do not have love, I gain nothing."

Conversely, if we aren't eloquent and don't have all the "right" answers, but have love, our words are a sweet balm to the hurting. And if we have only a few minutes to visit with an elderly person, and have love, it means the world to her. Thus, when we participate in any ministry where we can share the love of God, we are living out our calling as encouragers.

There is an additional way to encourage someone, and that is to spare the person sorrow, just as God spared Paul "sorrow upon sorrow" by healing Epaphroditus. I believe one of the best ways we can do this is by keeping our promises. Many books concerning the promises of God have been top sellers. Why? Because people need hope and promises stir up hope and belief. Kept promises bring delight, not just to our fellow man but also to our Lord.

"Lord, who may dwell in your sacred tent? Who may live on your holy mountain? The one . . . who despises a vile person but honors those who fear the Lord; who keeps an oath even when it hurts, and does not change their mind . . . Whoever does these things will never be shaken" (Ps. 15:1-5). Broken promises, on the other hand, cause despair. Broken promises are plentiful in our selfish society, but kept promises are rare and reassuring in this uncertain world.

We *must* keep our promises as we consider our Christian witness, because a broken promise raises questions about the integrity of the person who made the promise. And if our integrity is in doubt, our message deserves suspicion also. Even though God always keeps his promises, if his people do not, the world can easily get a negative impression of God. As women of God, we must strive to imitate God in this vital area, being trustworthy rather than manipulative, considering others more important than ourselves. Otherwise, how can we expect our children and our lost neighbors to believe in the joy and hope we profess?

Let me encourage you to meditate on these verses from the book of Matthew:

Then the King will say to those on his right, "Come, you who are blessed by my Father; take your inheritance, the kingdom prepared for you since the creation of the world. For I was hungry and you gave me something to eat, I was thirsty and you gave me something to drink, I was a stranger and you invited me in, I needed clothes and you clothed me, I was sick and you looked after me, I was in prison and you came to visit me." Then the righteous will answer him, "Lord, when did we see you hungry and feed you, or thirsty and give you something to drink? When did we see you a stranger and invite you in, or needing clothes and clothe you? When did we see you sick or in prison and go to visit you?" The King will reply, "Truly I tell you, whatever you did for one of the least of these brothers and sisters of mine, you did for me."

Matthew 25:34-40

## Joy in Communion with Christ

Once again, go to hymnal.net and search *Out in the highways*[15]. Take a few moments to sing this old hymn.

Pray for those who need encouragement from you today, and also for those who need love or acceptance. What promises have you made? Ask the Father to empower you to meet your promises so your integrity and your message of Christ are never in doubt. Ask him to help you minister to the needy with compassion and joy.

# SPONGE

WHEN MY DAUGHTER was seven months pregnant with our first grandchild, I was visiting a young woman who had just had her second baby. Her father, Randy, walked in while I was there and struck up a conversation with me.

"I heard y'all are expecting a grandbaby. Is that right?"

"Yes," I replied, "We're so excited."

"Oh," gushed Randy, "It's better than they say it is!"

I was amused by his response that day, but once my grandson was born, I understood perfectly. Being a grandparent is indescribable, and it is really indescribable being the grandmother of the cutest grandchildren in the world! As my daughter was fond of saying, "Everyone else thinks their child is the cutest, but I'm sorry, they're just wrong. Tyler is the cutest hands down." Indeed, I had to agree. And now that we have other grandchildren, we solve the dilemma by swearing Tyler is the cutest five-year-old boy, while Bryant is the cutest two-year-old boy, and Adelynn is the cutest one-year-old girl in the world!

The thing is, small children are continuously learning and relearning. I recall when Tyler was beginning to walk, he acted like his mother hadn't told him he couldn't play with the rocks in the fireplace or the blinds or the diaper pail. He gravitated to the stairs when he knew good and well they were a "no-no." He loved to treat all toys and handheld objects as if they were balls and should be thrown.

Shelley spent much of her day every day re-teaching the same lessons. Yet he was always learning new things, too. Since they live eight hours away, she has called me every day or two to give me an update on what Tyler has learned or done or said (she is beginning to do the same with Adelynn). Of course, her sister shares Bryant's successes and cuteness with me, too. She even has a blog with pictures and videos chronicling Bryant's progress. Even though I raised four children, I am amazed at how smart these little ones are. They're like sponges!

Why did Shelley have to teach Tyler the same things over and over? Why does *any* parent have to recap the rules or reiterate the reasons? The answer is, for the child's good. The same is true of Christians. What I mean is, new Christians have so much to learn about the life lived in Christ. Yet we older Christians need some of those same lessons taught us again because we all, children and adults alike, are sponges. We soak up, yet we dry out. We learn and we have to relearn. Let's look at what Paul wrote to the Philippians about this.

## The Joyful Truth

> Further, my brothers and sisters, rejoice in the Lord! It is no trouble for me to write the same things to you again, and it is a safeguard for you.
>
> Philippians 3:1

Paul lovingly writes, "It is no trouble for me to write the same things to you again, and it is a safeguard for you." What does he not mind saying multiple times? Simply, "Rejoice in the Lord." In other words, soak up the Lord. Let him fill you.

Our minds are made to be filled. I can't tell you how many times I said of a student, "If he would just use his mind for schoolwork instead of mischief, he could be a straight A student!"

Similarly, God created our spirits to be filled. In the perfect plan of our Father, his Holy Spirit takes residence in our spirits. He moves in and makes himself at home. He inhabits every nook and cranny. And ideally, the Spirit has control over all we do.

In the Bazemore house, we have three kinds of chairs at the breakfast room table--children's chairs, a "queen" chair, and a "king" chair. My husband David, the leader of our home, sits in the "king" chair. That's how I picture my spirit, with the Holy Spirit in control, occupying the King chair. The problem is that I often try to commandeer the King chair. Though I know it's not my place, I sit down there when I am not allowing the Holy Spirit to fill me up and he is not in his chair. Just like the student who uses his mind for mischief, I use my spirit for mischief by taking over the position God created exclusively for the Holy Spirit. How vital it is for me to be a sponge that soaks up the Holy Spirit until I am flooded with rejoicing and he is King!

## Digesting the Joy

Sponges are funny things. I don't have a lot of experience with the real thing, but synthetic sponges mystify me. When you take one out of the packaging, it is soft but not really wet. However, if you leave it sitting out, it will get hard. The edges will be rough, and you could actually scratch a surface with it. It will not do what it was made to do until it is exposed to liquid. But the moment water touches the sponge, it softens up again and can absorb a huge amount. If you squeeze it out, it is again soft, but not really wet. And the cycle continues.

In some ways a Christian is not unlike a sponge. Do you remember that moment when you were "taken out of the wrapper"? You had just received Christ as your personal Savior, and you were brand new. Completely clean. Soft. "Therefore, if anyone is in Christ, the new creation has come: The old has gone, the new is here!" (2 Cor. 5:17). Were you just a child then? A young adult? An adult? It doesn't matter. The old had gone, the new had come. There was a softness in your spirit, a complete openness to the will and ways of the Lord. You began soaking up truth as revealed in Scripture through sermons, Sunday school lessons, Bible studies, and personal devotional times. You became satiated with the blessings of knowing the Lord, and whether you knew it or not, filled with the Living Water, the Holy Spirit.

At the beginning of Jesus' ministry, he had a mountaintop experience much like many of us had when we accepted Christ as our Savior. At his baptism God called him "Beloved Son," and the Holy Spirit descended as a dove upon him. What happened to Jesus immediately after this mountaintop experience? Here is how the gospel of Luke has it:

Now Jesus, full of the Holy Spirit, left the Jordan and was led by the Spirit into the wild. For forty wilderness days and nights he was tested by the Devil. He ate nothing during those days, and when the time was up he was hungry. The Devil, playing on his hunger, gave the first test: "Since you're God's Son, command this stone to turn into a loaf of bread." Jesus answered by quoting Deuteronomy: "It takes more than bread to really live." For the second test he led him up and spread out all the kingdoms of the earth on display at once. Then the Devil said, "They're yours in all their splendor to serve your pleasure. I'm in charge of them all and can turn them over to whomever I wish. Worship me and they're yours, the whole works." Jesus refused, again backing his refusal with Deuteronomy: "Worship the Lord your God and only the Lord your God. Serve him with absolute single-heartedness." For the third test the Devil took him to Jerusalem and put him on top of the Temple. He said, "If you are God's Son, jump. It's written, isn't it, that he has placed you in the care of angels to protect you; they will catch you; you won't so much as stub your toe on a stone?" "Yes," said Jesus, "and it's also written, 'Don't you dare tempt the Lord your God.'" That completed the testing. The Devil retreated temporarily, lying in wait for another opportunity. Jesus returned to Galilee powerful in the Spirit.

Luke 4:1-15, MSG

Satan's craftiness is multi-layered. When he schemes, he plays upon our weaknesses. He lies. He misquotes Scripture. He may leave us alone for a while, but he never gives up. It is as if he has a vise that grasps us and presses and constricts our spirits until we face the danger of being almost totally dry, just like the desert where Jesus was tempted. How was Jesus able to deal with Satan's wiles? He was full of and powerful with the Holy Spirit.

Jesus started out "full of the Spirit" and ended up "powerful in the Spirit." The reason for this is because he was full of the Holy Spirit. The mental image of perpetually being filled with the Spirit reminds me of the ground outside my window. It has been raining for three weeks. Not a constant hard rain, of course, but enough mist and moisture to keep the ground damp. Right now there are puddles everywhere and mud is profuse. But when it stops raining, the ground will immediately begin drying out. The same is true for the Christian. She is either soaking in truth, or she is in the process of drying out. Whereas I am ready for the sun to come out and the ground to dry up, may I never be ready for my heart to wither or die.

## Living Your Joy Out Loud

You may be feeling Satan's vise today. Are you tempted to abandon the struggle? Is your grief too heavy or your disappointment too great? Are you ready to sit on the shelf—where you will dry up completely? That is Satan's plan. Rather than living the abundant life of the working sponge, he wants you to harden your heart and become nothing but rough edges, biting words, and negative demeanor.

Hardness of heart often comes after a disappointment or after succumbing to temptation. Satan convinces us we might as well dry up, because there is no hope. Or sometimes the relentless enemy we face is self. Just like my grandson was determined to go his own way, warnings unheeded, we each have our own minds and wishes. We think we can handle the squeeze from the Devil "just this once," and it won't damage our "sponginess." Or we believe it won't hurt anyone else if we give up soaking in the Spirit.

This bears repeating. God is the great I AM, and he is for you. He lives in you. He wants to empower you. So rejoice in him, and cast yourself at his feet. Rejoice in the Lord. Even when you are feeling somewhat dry "trust in the Lord with all your heart and lean not on your own understanding" (Prov. 3:5). Be led by the Spirit of God. Turn your eyes to *his* goodness. Soak up the memories of what *he* has done. There will always be less than ideal circumstances, because we live in a fallen world. But if we think only of the impossibility of the circumstances rather than the magnificence of our God, we will be dried up sponges with hardened hearts.

Jesus and the disciples lived out a perfect example of this truth:

> By this time it was late in the day, so his disciples came to him. "This is a remote place," they said, "and it's already very late. Send the people away so that they can go to the surrounding countryside and villages and buy themselves something to eat." But he answered, "You give them something to eat." They said to him, "That would take more than half a year's wages! Are we to go and spend that much on bread and give it to them to eat?" "How many loaves do you have?" he asked. "Go and see." When they found out, they said, "Five—and two fish." Then Jesus directed them to have all the people sit down in groups on the green grass. So they sat down in groups of hundreds and fifties. Taking the five loaves and the two fish and looking up to heaven, he gave thanks and broke the loaves. Then he gave them to his disciples to distribute to the people. He also divided the two fish among them all. They all ate and were satisfied, and the disciples picked up twelve basketfuls of broken pieces of bread and fish. The number of the men who had eaten was five thousand. Immediately Jesus made his disciples get into the boat and go on ahead of him to Bethsaida, while he dismissed the crowd. After leaving them, he went up on a mountainside to pray. Later that night, the boat was in the middle of the lake, and he was alone on land. He saw the disciples straining at the oars, because the wind was against them. Shortly before dawn he went out to them, walking on the lake. He was about to pass by them, but when they saw him walking on the lake, they thought he was a ghost. They cried out, because they all saw him and were terrified. Immediately he spoke to them and said, "Take courage! It is I. Don't be afraid." Then he climbed into the boat with them, and the wind died down. They were completely amazed, for they had not understood about the loaves; their hearts were hardened.
>
> Mark 6:35-52

"They were completely amazed, for they had not understood about the loaves." If the disciples had really been soaking up who Jesus was, what would their response have been when Jesus asked them to feed the people?

When Jesus saw the meagerness of the available food, he immediately spoke to God and gave thanks. Was he giving thanks that he had only five loaves and two fishes with which to feed a multitude? Of course not. Jesus was giving thanks for a God who could do miracles, for a Father who cared about each person sitting on the hillside, for the One who desires to feed each of us. He chose to look up and soak in the power of God rather than looking at the limitations of his circumstances.

After the crowd had eaten their fill and gone on their way, Jesus again prayed. I am sure he once again gave thanks for God's provision. But I am also quite certain his prayer included concerns for the swarming masses of people and their lack of spiritual understanding. Though he knew all present had sighed a big "Wow!" when the bread and fish multiplied to feed everyone, he also knew the "Wow" was superficial. Even his disciples' hearts were hardened. They didn't understand about the loaves. Even though they had walked with Him for some time, they didn't "get" Jesus. They still thought of him as a great teacher. Maybe they thought he was just a smarter one of them, only with the ability to do miracles. Some might have believed he was still gathering the support of the masses in readiness to form an army to overthrow the Roman government. Their perception did not take in his divinity. They did not grasp "God with us" and all its implications.

When Mark 6:52 says "their hearts were hardened," the word for "hardened" is *poro'o.* It means "to cover with a thick skin, to harden by covering with a callus." Calluses are not a result of disuse. A callus develops where there was soft skin rubbed over and over by the same shoe, guitar string, garden tool, pen, or whatever. This is the danger most Christians face, especially those of us who were going to church even before we were born. We can go to church, read our Bibles, work on a mission, and still not get Jesus if we don't live in anticipation. We will never get over our spiritual calluses if we don't relinquish our ingrained ideas and expect God to do the unexpected. We need to stop and acknowledge the miracles the Lord performs right before our eyes.

## Joy in Communion with Christ

Soak up the Spirit. Make sure he is the only one who gets to sit in the King chair of your life. Your actions and attitudes will be a testimony to the power of God. Grind down any callus that might have formed in your thought processes about God, and then soak up the truths found in the following psalm:

I will extol the Lord at all times; his praise will always be on my lips. My soul will boast in the Lord; let the afflicted hear and rejoice. Glorify the Lord with me; let us exalt his name together. I sought the Lord, and he answered me; he delivered me from all my fears. Those who look to him are radiant; their faces are never covered with shame. This poor man called, and the Lord heard him; he saved him out of all his troubles. The angel of the Lord encamps around those who fear him, and he delivers them. *Taste and see that the Lord is good; blessed is the man who takes refuge in him.* Fear the Lord, you his saints, for those who fear him lack nothing. The lions may grow weak and hungry, but those who seek the Lord lack no good thing.

Psalm 34:1-10, emphasis added

Extol, praise, boast, rejoice, glorify, and exalt the Lord. Seek him, look to him, call him, and fear him. Taste and see. Soak it up. Squeeze it out. Soak it up. Squeeze it out. Never let yourself get totally dry, weak, or callused, because "those who seek the Lord lack no good thing."

When you have a chance, go to YouTube.com and search "Come, Holy Spirit,"[16] by Bryan Duncan. Listen to Duncan sing this lovely prayer song by Gloria Gaither and Robbie Buchanon.

Use your prayer time today to alleviate any hardness in your spirit. File off calluses or drink up living water. Whatever you need, whatever will bring you to a state of spongy softness.

# GUARD

OUR DAUGHTER ,HEATHER, is a dog-lover from way back. When she was three years old and our dog had puppies, I would often find her with her arm down in their box. She knew she wasn't supposed to pick them up, because Mama Dog might get upset. But she just couldn't keep her hands off them. She would stick her hand down in the box in the hopes one or more of them would rub against it or lick it.

When she was in college and living with her twin sister in a townhouse their dad and I had bought, my brother-in-law offered them two male puppies from his dog's litter. Of course, they couldn't resist. We made the rule that the puppies would have to stay outside, because I am allergic to dogs. But before long, Heather had snuck the dogs inside "because it's just so cold and wet out there." Truthfully, her twin, Hillary, was just as bad.

When the two puppies were about a year old, something happened that we were not prepared for. They began fighting each other. And they weren't playful fights. They were serious, growling, throat-biting fights. Once, Heather tried to get between them and almost got her hand bitten off. We found out this fighting was pretty normal for male dog siblings in their adolescence. They were each trying to claim the territory.

Well, the girls ended up giving one of the dogs away in order to regain a peaceful life. That's pretty much what the apostle Paul is talking about in the third chapter of Philippians. We can't have false teaching warring with the true gospel in our lives or our churches. The ensuing chaos is just too dangerous.

## The Joyful Truth

Watch out for those dogs, those evildoers, those mutilators of the flesh. For it is we who are the circumcision, we who serve God by his Spirit, who boast in Christ Jesus, and who put no confidence in the flesh—though I myself have reasons for such confidence. If someone else thinks they have reasons to put confidence in the flesh, I have more: circumcised on the eighth day, of the people of Israel, of the tribe of Benjamin, a Hebrew of Hebrews; in regard to the law, a Pharisee; as for zeal, persecuting the church; as for righteousness based on the law, faultless.

Philippians 3:2-6

"Watch out for those dogs, those evildoers, those mutilators of the flesh," Paul warns us. The word he uses for the words "watch out" is *blepo*, which means "to see, look at, pay attention, perceive." You've seen the signs posted in public places: *Watch Your Step!* Paul is saying the same thing here. Christians must watch their steps, because Satan, acting through evil people, has set snares everywhere.

When Paul uses the terms "dogs," "evildoers," and "mutilators of the flesh," he is probably talking about the same group of people. On the other hand, he may be referring to them as three different groups: "Watch out for dogs, watch out for evildoers, watch out for those who mutilate the flesh." Bible scholars disagree about whether these descriptions apply to one group or to three different groups, but in my opinion, it doesn't really matter, because the lesson for us is the same either way: We must be on our guard against false teachers. The Christians at Philippi had to watch out for the false teaching that sinners are saved by grace plus good works and circumcision. We, too, must beware of legalism, half-truths, the so-called "prosperity gospel," and other unbiblical doctrines that mutilate the gospel of Jesus Christ.

Jesus specifically taught his disciples to beware of both people and attitudes that could harm their walk of faith. As his disciples, therefore, we should pay close attention any time the Word says, "Be on your guard!" "Above all else," Proverbs tells us, "guard your heart, for everything you do flows from it" (4:23). The heart is the source of all attitudes and actions.

Have you ever found yourself acting on feelings rather than on truth? Me too. This tendency stems from an unguarded heart. Feelings are very real. We could have been hurt by an insult or slight. Or maybe our family is in a financial crisis, and we are feeling afraid. Perhaps we feel angry, because someone has swindled us. All of these feelings--hurt, fear, anger, and others--are real. Acting on these feelings, however, produces harmful results. Listen to David describe his feelings in detail:

Ruthless witnesses come forward; they question me on things I know nothing about.

They repay me evil for good and leave me like one bereaved. Yet when they were ill, I put on sackcloth and humbled myself with fasting. When my prayers returned to me unanswered, I went about mourning as though for my friend or brother. I bowed my head in grief as though weeping for my mother. But when I stumbled, they gathered in glee; assailants gathered against me without my knowledge. They slandered me without ceasing. Like the ungodly they maliciously mocked; they gnashed their teeth at me.

How long, Lord, will you look on? Rescue me from their ravages, my precious life from these lions.

Psalm 35:11-17

I offer you my heart, Lord God, and I trust you. Don't make me ashamed or let enemies defeat me. Don't disappoint any of your worshipers, but disappoint all deceitful liars. Show me your paths and teach me to follow; guide me by your truth and instruct me. You keep me safe, and I always trust you.

Psalm 25:1-5, CEV

David was determined to act on the truth set out by God, not on his feelings of defeat, loneliness, worry, or sadness. He offered his heart to God, asking him to protect it. In Psalm 141:4 David again asks God to guard his heart against evil and the men who do evil. He says, "Do not let my heart be drawn to what is evil so that I take part in wicked deeds along with those who are evildoers; do not let me eat their delicacies" (NIV). "Don't let me want to do evil or waste my time doing wrong with wicked people. Don't let me even taste the good things they offer" (CEV). "Post a guard at my mouth, God, set a watch at the door of my lips. Don't let me so much as dream of evil or thoughtlessly fall into bad company. And these people who only do wrong—don't let them lure me with their sweet talk!" (MSG). "Don't let me drift toward evil or take part in acts of wickedness. Don't let me share in the delicacies of those who do wrong" (NLT). The lure of evil is strong, and we need supernatural help to avoid its snares and remain righteous.

Notice that the doing of evil is preceded by a change of heart, a slipping of thoughts. It is no coincidence that Satan is depicted in the Bible as a serpent, for he tempts our thoughts and desires to slither and slide into God-forbidden, dangerous territory.

## Digesting the Joy

The subject of guarding the desires of our hearts was addressed by Jesus many times. On one occasion, he said, "Watch out! Be on your guard against all kinds of greed; life does not consist in an abundance of possessions" (Luke 12:15).

I like the King James Version of this verse, because it uses a different word for greed—"covetousness." "Take heed, and beware of covetousness: for a man's life consisteth not in the abundance of the things which he possesseth."

In the Ten Commandments, God pointed out that coveting could apply to many things: "You shall not covet your neighbor's house. You shall not covet your neighbor's wife, or his male or female servant, his ox or donkey, or anything that belongs to your neighbor" (Exod. 20:17). In other words, we need to be careful that the desires in our lives reflect the desires of God's heart rather than the desires of this world. Why? Because this world is not all there is. In fact, this life is just a slight breeze compared to the hurricane of eternity, so things that matter in eternity should be our focus now.

Let me return briefly to the warning Paul gave the Philippians: "Watch out for those dogs, those evildoers, those mutilators of the flesh" (3:2). In his letters to the young churches, one of Paul's main themes is to "guard what you have been taught." For example:

I urge you, brothers and sisters, to watch out for those who cause divisions and put obstacles in your way that are contrary to the teaching you have learned. Keep away from them. For such people are not serving our Lord Christ, but their own appetites. By smooth talk and flattery they deceive the minds of naïve people. Everyone has heard about your obedience, so I am full of joy over you; but I want you to be wise about what is good, and innocent about what is evil.

Romans 16:17-19.

Even from your own number men will arise and distort the truth in order to draw away disciples after them. So be on your guard!

Acts 20:30-31a

Then [when we all reach unity in the faith and in the knowledge of the Son of God] we will no longer be infants, tossed back and forth by every wind of teaching and by the cunning and craftiness of men in their deceitful scheming.

Eph. 4:13-14, my paraphrase

While Paul became a missionary to the Gentiles, Peter was accepted by the early church as the chief preacher to the Jewish population. From Peter as well we find this exhortation concerning the guarding of our hearts. He said, "In your hearts revere Christ as Lord. Always be prepared to give an answer to everyone who asks you to give the reason for the hope that you have. But do this with gentleness and respect" (1 Pet. 3:15). This implies guarding what we have been taught. Peter wrote again in his second letter:

There are some things in those [epistles of Paul] that are difficult to understand, which the ignorant and unstable twist and misconstrue to their own utter destruction, just as [they distort and misinterpret] the rest of the Scriptures. Let me warn you therefore, beloved, that knowing these things beforehand you should be on your guard, lest you be carried away by the error of lawless and wicked [persons and] fall from your own [present] firm condition [your own steadfastness of mind]. But grow in grace (undeserved favor, spiritual strength) and recognition and knowledge and understanding of our Lord and Savior Jesus Christ (the Messiah). To Him [be] glory (honor, majesty, and splendor) both now and to the day of eternity.

2 Peter 3:16-18, AMP

Peter wanted his readers to beware of those who would mislead them, noting that the best way to beware is to *really* get to know Jesus.

One way I get to know Jesus is by studying what he did and said. The gospels of Matthew, Mark, and Luke all include what Jesus said about the signs of the end times. His first admonition to his followers was, "Watch out that you are not deceived. For many will come in my name, claiming, 'I am he,' and 'The time is near.' Do not follow them" (Luke 21:8). If we follow Peter's advice and *really* get to know Jesus, then we will not be fooled by impostors.

Jesus also declared, "You must be on your guard!.. If anyone says to you, 'Look, here is the Messiah!' or, 'Look, there he is!' do not believe it.' . . . Be on guard! Be alert! You do not know when that time will come. . . What I say to you, I say to everyone: 'Watch!'" (Mark 13:9, 21, 33, 37).

## Living Your Joy Out Loud

Jesus was instructing the disciples to live in such a way that their "talk" and "walk" would match up. This is so crucial to living our joy out loud, and one of the most critical pieces of advice Scripture gives us is about guarding our mouths, lips, and tongues. "The hearts of the wise make their mouths prudent, and their lips promote instruction," reads Proverbs 16:23.

Take some time and meditate on the message of these verses:

You brood of vipers, how can you who are evil say anything good? For the mouth speaks what the heart is full of."

Matthew 12:34

Those who guard their lips preserve their lives, but those who speak rashly will come to ruin.

Proverbs 13:3

But now you must also rid yourselves of all such things as these: anger, rage, malice, slander, and filthy language from your lips. Do not lie to each other, since you have taken off your old self with its practices.

Colossians 3:8-9

Do not let any unwholesome talk come out of your mouths, but only what is helpful for building others up according to their needs, that it may benefit those who listen.

Ephesians 4:29

It has been said that living the Christian life is not hard, but it is impossible. There is no doubt that we cannot make ourselves righteous; the Holy Spirit who resides within us has that assignment. And yet we are to make every effort to grow in our faith, feeding it and watering it. We are supposed to be guards, taking heed lest we fall and cause someone else to do the same. But thankfully, "because of your partnership in the gospel from the first day until now" (Phil. 1:5), we are partners with God in the spread of the gospel. Our partner is Yahweh, the great I AM.

On the first day of the third month after the Israelites left Egypt--on the very day--they came to the Desert of Sinai. After they set out from Rephidim, they entered the Desert of Sinai, and Israel camped there in the desert in front of the mountain. Then Moses went up to God, and the Lord called to him from the mountain and said, "This is what you are to say to the house of Jacob and what you are to tell the people of Israel: 'You yourselves have seen what I did to Egypt, and how I carried you on eagles' wings and brought you to myself. Now if you obey me fully and keep my covenant, then out of all nations you will be my treasured possession. Although the whole earth is mine, you will be for me a kingdom of priests and a holy nation.' These are the words you are to speak to the Israelites.

Exodus 19:1-6

After these words of reassurance, God enumerated to Moses the statutes he wanted his people to follow. He explained how he wanted them to treat each other and told them about the land he would give them. Finally, in verse twenty of chapter twenty-three in Exodus, God says, "See, I am sending an angel ahead of you to guard you along the way and to bring you to the place I have prepared. Pay attention to him and listen to what he says. Do not rebel against him; he will not forgive your rebellion, since my Name is in him."

Similarly, He has sent us the Holy Spirit to bring us safely to the place he has prepared for us: "Guard the good deposit that was entrusted to you—guard it with the help of the Holy Spirit who lives in us" (2 Tim. 1:14).

I told you about the dogs our daughters had and how eventually one had to be given away. Well, the other dog, Sampson, moved with Heather to Birmingham when she went there to get her master's degree. It was scary for us to let her go, but it helped knowing Sam would protect her with his very life. Now, what if Heather had put Sam out in the back yard at night and then carelessly left her front door unlocked? Without Sam's warning growl, a burglar or other intruder could have come in, and if he reached Heather's bedroom, he would have found her vulnerable. How pointless having a watchdog would have been at that point! Her protector, right there on the other side of the back wall, yet Heather in grave danger.

Our protector and guide lives with us. He will help us guard the good deposit Christ has made, but we must not put him in the back yard. We must keep him close where he can do his work of guidance and protection. We must pay attention to him and listen to what he says.

## Joy in Communion with Christ

Take a few minutes to go to hymnal.net and search "I Know Whom I Have Believed" and sing. The refrain is taken from the King James Version of 2 Timothy 1:12.

### "I KNOW WHOM I HAVE BELIEVED"
(Daniel W. Whittle, 1883)

I know not why God's wondrous grace
To me He has made known,
Nor why, unworthy, Christ in love
Redeemed me for His own.

Refrain
But I know whom I have believed
And am persuaded that He is able
To keep that which I've committed
Unto Him against that day

I know not how the Spirit moves,
Convincing us of sin,
Revealing Jesus through the Word,
Creating faith in Him.

Refrain

I know not when my Lord may come,
At night or noonday fair,
Or if I'll walk the vale with Him
Or meet Him in the air.

Refrain

Which Scripture in this chapter impacted you the most? Write a prayer concerning the lesson you learned from that Bible text.

# THE CIRCUMCISION

OUR FOUR DAUGHTERS attended public school, so over the years we came in contact with close to 160 different teachers. Some of them were all business, but others were more laid-back. Some of our daughters' teachers were exquisitely creative, while a few were just plain dull. Most importantly, some seemed able to easily transfer knowledge from their own minds and hearts into the minds and lives of their students. But not all, by any means. Many were forgettable, like their subject matters.

What made the difference between those fabulous, memorable educators and the others? Not gender, for both women and men made up each group. Not age. Mrs. Worth was a very young teacher when she taught our twins. She had a rapport with the students and a knack with helping them understand novels, essays, short stories, and poetry. Though never harsh, she was a natural disciplinarian. The kids would say she was one of the unforgettable ones.

Neither was grade level a determining factor for excellent teaching. Mr. Searcy, one of only two teachers that all four girls experienced, taught eighth grade Earth Science. He was strict and difficult. But he was excellent. All four girls, though not fans of science, enjoyed learning in his class. Conversely, our daughter Shelley had a teacher in the eighth grade who knew her subject well, but when Shelley, whose strategy for making A's was to ask as many questions as it took in order to understand, asked a question in this particular class, the teacher would spout knowledge but never really answer the question. Now, granted, we mainly heard our daughter's side of the story, but since I was teaching in the same school at the time, I knew many of the teachers, and though I found this woman to be good at class management and very smart, highly educated, organized, and so on, I heard from quite a few parents that their children just couldn't grasp this teacher's subject matter.

So what made the difference between those successful and well-liked teachers and the others? I believe the answer is giftedness. Some people attend elite schools of education where they are taught the philosophy, methods, and mechanics of education. They make outstanding grades in their college classes and subsequently are hired by good school systems. They are able to make lesson plans and follow them through. Some even become good teachers. But a few, like Mrs. Worth and Mr. Searcy and others, are *gifted* teachers. They don't have to become good. They just are.

## The Joyful Truth

Here is a wonderful truth: Out of God's love and mercy, he has given us the gift of sainthood and the gift of *the* circumcision. It is a *giftedness* we should explore.

> Watch out for those dogs, those evildoers, those mutilators of the flesh. For it is we who are the circumcision, we who serve God by his Spirit, who boast in Christ Jesus, and who put no confidence in the flesh—though I myself have reasons for such confidence. If someone else thinks they have reasons to put confidence in the flesh, I have more: circumcised on the eighth day, of the people of Israel, of the tribe of Benjamin, a Hebrew of Hebrews; in regard to the law, a Pharisee; as for zeal, persecuting the church; as for righteousness based on the law, faultless.
>
> Philippians 3:2-6

Many verses in the Bible help us explore the nature of the word *gift*. Some depict the practice of using a gift as either a bribe or as payment for something expected. For example, "And be sure to say, 'Your servant Jacob is coming behind us.' For he thought, 'I will pacify him with these gifts I am sending on ahead; later, when I see him, perhaps he will receive me'" (Gen. 32:20). Or, "Make the price for the bride and the gift I am to bring as great as you like, and I'll pay whatever you ask me. Only give me the young woman as my wife" (Gen. 34:12).

1 Samuel 9:6-8 says, "But the servant replied, 'Look, in this town there is a man of God; he is highly respected, and everything he says comes true. Let's go there now. Perhaps he will tell us what way to take.' Saul said to his servant, 'If we go, what can we give the man? The food in our sacks is gone. We have no gift to take to the man of God. What do we have?' The servant answered him again. 'Look,' he said, 'I have a quarter of a shekel of silver. I will give it to the man of God so that he will tell us what way to take.'"

Two more examples would be Proverbs 19:6, "Many curry favor with a ruler, and everyone is the friend of one who gives gifts," and Daniel 2:6, "But if you tell me the dream and explain it, you will receive from me gifts and rewards and great honor. So tell me the dream and interpret it for me."

Additionally, there are countless places in Scripture that describe gifts given in response to blessings or as a sign of loyalty. For example, Deuteronomy 16:16-17 says, "Three times a year all your men must appear before the Lord your God at the place he will choose: at the Feast of Unleavened Bread, the Feast of Weeks and the Feast of Tabernacles. No man should appear before the Lord empty-handed: Each of you must bring a gift in proportion to the way the Lord your God has blessed you."

The gift we have been given in *the* circumcision is another kind of gift entirely. God has gifted us, not because of something we have done, and with no expectation of reciprocation, but merely because of his love and mercy. Paul was born a Jew of high ranking, followed the Jewish customs to the letter, went to the best schools, learned all the law, and became a noted religious leader. He did every Jewish thing the right way. He was circumcised and circumspect. As far as righteousness based on the law was concerned, Paul was faultless. Nevertheless, he didn't become "*the* circumcision" until he knew Jesus as Savior and Lord.

Exactly who is the circumcision? "For it is we who are the circumcision, we who serve God by his Spirit, who boast in Christ Jesus, and who put no confidence in the flesh" (Phil. 3:3).

Put no confidence in the flesh. I have struggled with this, even though I am not a type A personality. For years I felt unworthy of the grace of Jesus unless I was working or worrying myself weary in the causes of the kingdom of heaven. What I was doing was putting confidence in the flesh—in my ability to sacrificially live for God. Except for not having been circumcised on the eighth day, I could have been Paul. If anyone else thinks she has reasons to put confidence in the flesh, I had more: born into a Christian family, I was the child of missionaries to the Philippines, the granddaughter, on my father's side, of a preacher and his wife who was a Christian speaker, and on my mother's side, of a deacon in the Baptist Church and his wife who was a first grade Sunday school teacher for forty years; in regard to the law, I went to church every time the doors were open, every revival service, even during college, and married an equally "holy" Baptist boy from a Christian home; as for zeal, I continued serving in several capacities in the church while raising a family; as for legalistic righteousness, I wondered why everyone was not as dedicated a Christian as I.

Talk about putting confidence in the flesh! I praise God for not giving up on me and for not letting me drown in that mess of superior intentions and legalism. Instead, the Lord reached down, shook me up a bit, and helped me realize the giftedness of *the* circumcision.

## Digesting the Joy

Why do many Christians have such trouble with the free gift of grace? Why is it so hard to accept? Maybe it's because we are such doers. Maybe it's because some of us want to play such an active role in the coming Kingdom. Our beloved former minister of music, who went home to sing with the Lord in 2001, once said, "I think when we get to heaven, God is going to say, 'I didn't mean for it to be so hard.'"

Paul would have agreed. In his first letter to the church at Corinth, he made the point that some people were married and some unmarried, some were Jews and some Gentiles, and some believers were slaves and some were free when God called them to become followers of Jesus. He said, "All of you, slave and free both, were once held hostage in a sinful society. Then a huge sum was paid out for your ransom. So please don't, out of old habit, slip back into being or doing what everyone else tells you. Friends, stay where you were called to be. God is there. Hold the high ground with him at your side . . . I want you to live as free of complications as possible" (1 Cor. 7:23-24, 32, MSG).

Is your To-Do list long and guilt-ridden? Is the quality of your marriage, the security of your job, or the fulfillment found in your hobbies based solely on your achievement of certain goals? Consider the words of Jesus:

> Come to me, all you who are weary and burdened, and I will give you rest. Take my yoke upon you and learn from me, for I am gentle and humble in heart, and you will find rest for your souls. For my yoke is easy and my burden is light
>
> Matthew 11:28-30

The gift of the circumcision is rest. Jesus did not say, "Stop burdening yourself! Cease! Rest already, will you?" No, he said, "Come, and I will give you the gift of rest" (my paraphrase). The Greek word used for "rest" is *anapausis*, which is derived from two root words: *ana* and *pauo*. *Ana* means "each, in turn, every man," while *pauo* means "to stop, cease, finish, or refrain." In effect, Jesus said, "Come yoke yourself with me and you will stop your heavy laboring forevermore."

Even though Jesus said this to a crowd of people, the *ana* part of *anapausis* was Jesus making it personal, just in case anyone listening thought Jesus was preaching to someone else in the crowd! The *ana* says, "I will cause *each of you* to cease . . . ." He will cause *you* to lay down your burdens of sin and legalism, and he will cause *me* to lay down mine. And with our burdens removed, we will find rest for our souls and learn to live freely and lightly.

I love *The Message* paraphrase of these verses: "Come to me. Get away with me and you'll recover your life. I'll show you how to take a real rest. Walk with me and work with me—watch how I do it. Learn the unforced rhythms of grace. I won't lay anything heavy or ill-fitting on you. Keep company with me and you'll learn to live freely and lightly" (Matt. 11:28-30).

What a gift the Savior has given us!

## Living Your Joy Out Loud

God modeled resting, and his kind of rest very obviously declares, "The work is done. Time to quit."

> For God so loved the world, that he gave his only begotten Son, that whosoever believeth in him shall not perish, but have everlasting life.
>
> John 3:16, KJV

> For it is by grace you have been saved, through faith--and this not from yourselves, it is the gift of God--not by works, so that no one can boast.
>
> Ephesians 2:8-9

> For just as through the disobedience of the one man the many were made sinners, so also through the obedience of the one man the many will be made righteous.
>
> Romans 5:19

Jesus Christ died for our sins, was buried, rose from the grave, and after conquering death he now sits enthroned in heaven and waits for the perfect, Father-planned moment to return to earth to retrieve us. Through his glorious work, we have become the Circumcision, and we can rest. Cease. Let go. Once we let go and let him gift us in this way, then we can freely, wholeheartedly worship by the Spirit of God and glory in Christ Jesus.

## Joy in Communion with Christ

Take a few minutes to go to YouTube.com and search "I Will Sing of My Redeemer – You Set Me Free" Heber Vega. The original hymn was written by Philip P. Bliss in 1876. The medley you will hear was written by Travis Cottrell, who sings it here. Listen, sing along, and then pray.

# DEBTOR

THE ECONOMY WAS the main issue to emerge in the presidential elections of 2008 and 2012. People of all economic levels voted for the candidate they thought would rescue their pocketbooks. Foreign policy, national security, and health and education difficulties took the back seat to people's financial woes. Those experiencing financial hardship appeared to come in two main groups.

For some, the woes were caused by the national financial downturn. People had lost their jobs, and the domino effect of unemployment, less spending, smaller demand, and unemployment became a cycle that had millions of people in debt. The people suffering the second sort of financial difficulty were suffering in large part because they had not said a financial "whoa!" Their spending had gone out of control, with their greed and self-delusion having gotten them in debt up to their eyeballs.

Whether through faulty choices or the state of the economy, the average American had almost $11,000 in credit card debt, which is, I think it is fair to say, a lot of debt. The American people wanted a fast economic solution that wouldn't hurt too much, and they trusted any candidate who promised to help them.

Unfortunately, the American government has the same problem as the American people. They have spent far beyond what they take in. President after president and congress after congress have been irresponsible, in part because they have wanted to maintain the illusion of the American Dream. Doing the difficult thing, such as cutting back on programs, enacting reforms, or thinking about the consequences for our descendants has been, well . . . too difficult.

We are in a mess. Even those of us who have conducted our financial lives with care and who have no present debt have lost huge chunks of our retirement funds, which makes us more susceptible to debt in the future. Debt is a scary thing, so it is hard to imagine anyone finding joy in being a debtor. Yet the apostle Paul considered everything as loss for the sake of Christ, and he encouraged the Philippians to do the same.

## The Joyful Truth

> But whatever were gains to me I now consider loss for the sake of Christ. What is more, I consider everything a loss because of the surpassing worth of knowing Christ Jesus my Lord, for whose sake I have lost all things. I consider them garbage, that I may gain Christ and be found in him, not having a righteousness of my own that comes from the law, but that which is through faith in Christ—the righteousness that comes from God on the basis of faith.
>
> Philippians 3:7-9

The King James Version of Philippians 3:8 says, "I count all things but loss for the excellency of the knowledge of Christ Jesus my Lord: for whom I have suffered the loss of all things, and do count them but dung, that I may win Christ." The Greek word used for "suffer loss" is *zemioo*, a passive verb. Why is it important to point this out?

Every sentence has a subject which is the main focus of the sentence, usually a person, place, or thing. In addition, every sentence has a verb, that part of the sentence showing some action. For example, in the sentence "Mrs. Bazemore taught the class," *Mrs. Bazemore* is the subject, and *taught* is the verb. Mrs. Bazemore is doing the teaching, so *taught* is an *active* verb. But if we change the sentence around and say, "The class was taught by Mrs. Bazemore," *class* is the subject, and *was taught* is the verb. But did the class do the teaching? No, Mrs. Bazemore taught. So *was taught* is a *passive* verb.

Now let's apply this lesson to our Scripture. Paul said, "I have suffered the loss for Jesus and to know Jesus." *I (Paul)* is the subject, and *have suffered* the loss is the verb. On the face of things it seems like Paul is the one suffering the loss. But because Paul uses the Greek verb *zemioo*, which is passive, he is saying that he is *not* the one suffering loss. Then who else could have suffered loss? Jesus, of course. He lost all things for Paul. He left his throne and his status. He became poor and unknown. Above all, he lost his purity when he took on the sins of the whole human race. He lost all things for Paul, and he lost all things for you and me.

I didn't become a debtor by choosing to lose all things, but Christ chose to lose all things, and I thereby became indebted to him. The verb is passive, because Jesus did the action.

While indebtedness is a sobering state, accepting the reality of our indebtedness to Christ can be a joyful experience.

## Digesting the Joy

At the end of every seven years you must cancel debts. This is how it is to be done: Every creditor shall cancel any loan they have made to a fellow Israelite. They shall not require payment from anyone among their own people, because the Lord's time for canceling debts has been proclaimed. You may require payment from a foreigner, but you must cancel any debt your fellow Israelite owes you. However, there need be no poor people among you, for in the land the Lord your God is giving you to possess as your inheritance, he will richly bless you, if only you fully obey the Lord your God and are careful to follow all these commands I am giving you today. For the Lord your God will bless you as he has promised, and you will lend to many nations but will borrow from none. You will rule over many nations but none will rule over you. If anyone is poor among your fellow Israelites in any of the towns of the land the Lord your God is giving you, do not be hardhearted or tightfisted toward them. Rather, be openhanded and freely lend them whatever they need. Be careful not to harbor this wicked thought: "The seventh year, the year for canceling debts, is near," so that you do not show ill will toward the needy among your fellow Israelites and give them nothing. They may then appeal to the Lord against you, and you will be found guilty of sin. Give generously to them and do so without a grudging heart; then because of this the Lord your God will bless you in all your work and in everything you put your hand to. There will always be poor people in the land. Therefore I command you to be openhanded toward your fellow Israelites who are poor and needy in your land.

Deuteronomy 15:1-11

God knew beforehand that people would fall into debt. His foreknowledge is something we can understand. If we know about a meeting coming up, what do we do? We prepare for it. If we know that when our child arrives home from school he is going to have a bad grade on a report, we begin planning what we will say to our child. Foreknowledge permits forethought and planning.

According to the above verses, what was God's plan? God knew his people would be in debt, and he had a plan for settling it. According to verses four through six, the reason for people's or nation's debts is that they do not fully obey the commands of the Lord: "There need be no poor people among you, for in the land the Lord your God is giving you to possess as your inheritance, he will richly bless you, if only you fully obey the Lord your God and are careful to follow all these commands I am giving you today. For the Lord your God will bless you as he has promised, and you will lend to many nations but will borrow from none. You will rule over many nations but none will rule over you."

God's heart towards debtors is seen in verses seven and eight: "If anyone is poor among your fellow Israelites in any of the towns of the land the Lord your God is giving you, do not be hardhearted or tightfisted toward them. Rather, be openhanded and freely lend them whatever they need." And he warns us in the ninth verse to "be careful not to harbor this wicked thought: 'The seventh year, the year for canceling debts, is near,' so that you do not show ill will toward the needy among your fellow Israelites and give them nothing. They may then appeal to the Lord against you, and you will be found guilty of sin."

Another joyful truth is that God is softhearted, generous, and ungrudging towards the poor and needy (debtors), and the one who cancels his brother's debt will be blessed by God: "Give generously to them and do so without a grudging heart; then because of this the Lord your God will bless you in all your work and in everything you put your hand to."

In the New Testament we also find the subject of debt and the cancellation of it. Early on, as Jesus was giving his disciples a model of prayer, he taught them to say, "Forgive us our debts, as we also have forgiven our debtors" (Matt. 6:12). The Lord knew beforehand that his followers would *be* debtors and *have* debtors, both monetarily and relationally speaking.

What was his plan concerning debt? It was for us to show others the grace that God has shown us: "For if you forgive other people when they sin against you, your heavenly Father will also forgive you. But if you do not forgive others their sins, your Father will not forgive your sins" (Matt. 6:14). Evidently, this truth was difficult to digest, for at least two additional situations arose later in which Jesus felt compelled to reteach this truth. He did so by using parables, such as the one in the gospel of Matthew:

Therefore, the kingdom of heaven is like a king who wanted to settle accounts with his servants. As he began the settlement, a man who owed him ten thousand bags of gold was brought to him. Since he was not able to pay, the master ordered that he and his wife and his children and all that he had be sold to repay the debt. At this the servant fell on his knees before him. "Be patient with me," he begged, "and I will pay back everything." The servant's master took pity on him, canceled the debt and let him go. But when that servant went out, he found one of his fellow servants who owed him a hundred silver coins. He grabbed him and began to choke him. "Pay back what you owe me!" he demanded. His fellow servant fell to his knees and begged him, "Be patient with me, and I will pay it back." But he refused. Instead, he went off and had the man thrown into prison until he could pay the debt. When the other servants saw what had happened, they were outraged and went and told their master everything that had happened. Then the master called the servant in. "You wicked servant," he said, "I canceled all that debt of yours because you begged me to. Shouldn't you have had mercy on your fellow servant just as I had on you?" In anger his master handed him over to the jailers to be tortured, until he should pay back all he owed. This is how my heavenly Father will treat each of you unless you forgive your brother or sister from your heart.

Matthew18:23-35

Another parable is found in Luke's gospel:

When one of the Pharisees invited Jesus to have dinner with him, he went to the Pharisee's house and reclined at the table. A woman in that town who lived a sinful life learned that Jesus was eating at the Pharisee's house, so she came there with an alabaster jar of perfume. As she stood behind him at his feet weeping, she began to wet his feet with her tears. Then she wiped them with her hair, kissed them and poured perfume on them. When the Pharisee who had invited him saw this, he said to himself, "If this man were a prophet, he would know who is touching him and what kind of woman she is—that she is a sinner." Jesus answered him, "Simon, I have something to tell you." "Tell me, teacher," he said. "Two people owed money to a certain moneylender. One owed him five hundred denarii, and the other fifty. Neither of them had the money to pay him back, so he forgave the debts of both. Now which of them will love him more?" Simon replied, "I suppose the one who had the bigger debt forgiven." "You have judged correctly," Jesus said.

Luke 7:36-43

Jesus knew what Simon the Pharisee was thinking, and he knows what we are thinking. These parables from Matthew and Luke teach that debt is debt, and the size of the debt doesn't matter to God. In addition, God expects us to model his behavior by forgiving our debtors.

## Living Your Joy Out Loud

As I said earlier, I didn't become a debtor by choosing to lose all things the way Jesus Christ chose to lose all things. Because he did, I thereby became indebted to him. Let me apply the biblical truths about debt to my relationship with Christ.

### GOD KNEW I WOULD BE INDEBTED TO CHRIST, AND HE PREPARED A PLAN FOR SETTLING THAT DEBT!

The plan to send Jesus as our Savior was on the Father's "To-Do" list all along. John 1:1-2 says, "In the beginning was the Word, and the Word was with God, and the Word was God. He was with God in the beginning." A way to paraphrase this would be, "The Word was first, the Word present to God, God present to the Word. The Word was God, in readiness for God from day one" (MSG). In readiness for what? "Through him all things were made; without him nothing was made that has been made. In him was life, and that life was the light of all mankind" (John 1:3-4).

Jesus was ready to create. Every creation on earth, even the earth itself, was created by Jesus, the Word. More importantly, "Nothing was made without the Word. Everything that was created received its life from him, and his life gave light to everyone. The light keeps shining in the dark, and darkness has never put it out" (John 1:3-5, CEV).

God's plan for debt is to take us from darkness (indebtedness) to light (freedom). Jesus is the One who keeps on shining in the dark, willing to give light to all his creation. What a joyous truth that God had a plan to cancel our debt!

## God is Softhearted, Generous, and Ungrudging towards Debtors

Have you seen the commercials for companies that allegedly help you get out of debt? The people seem so kind. How badly they feel for you! How they want to help you! What a sigh of relief they breathe when you choose to call them! Here is a reality check: The kind people are actors. The company has paid them to look and act concerned. The company has paid the network to place the commercial on the air. They have to get their money from somewhere, and that somewhere will be you.

In contrast, God wants to clear our debt, and his kindness is not an act. It's the real thing, because he loves us unconditionally, immeasurably, unfathomably. There is barely a chapter in the entire Bible that doesn't contain some message of God's compassion and faithfulness, even to sinners, and especially to repentant sinners. God's Word is truly a love letter.

## The One who Cancels his Brother's Debt will be Blessed by God

God pronounced a blessing on Jesus the day he began public ministry. When Jesus came up out of the water after his baptism, a dove (the Holy Spirit) descended from heaven, and God said, "This is my Son, whom I love; with him I am well pleased" (Matt. 3:17). Jesus, in his human state, had not yet suffered anything but the normal pains of being alive on this earth. Nevertheless, the Father knew. He had full knowledge of the plan of redemption, and he knew Jesus would do what was necessary. God saw the future, in which his Son would die to pay the sin-debt of every person, and he was well pleased.

In the same way, God will bless us as we forgive one another. If you have ever experienced the joy of this blessing, then you have sensed the voice of God saying, "Well done, my child."

### Debt is Debt. The Size of the Debt doesn't Matter to God

If I owe $22,351 to credit card companies, I am in debt. If I owe $223.51 to a local business, I am in debt. If I owe my friend $22.35, I am still in debt. I cannot claim freedom from debt until all financial obligations are paid. The same is true spiritually.

Until I choose to let Jesus cancel my debt, no matter how big and bad or how small and insignificant the sin may seem, I am in debt. And even if the amount or wickedness of my sin could be gauged, how would I know how bad was too bad or how good was good enough? God, in his sovereignty and mercy, decided to provide a way for *all* sin to be cancelled, *all* debt to be paid. Take it or leave it, but if you want joy, take it.

### God Expects us to Model His Behavior by Forgiving our Debtors

Our forgiveness of others' wrongs against us is one of the paramount ways in which we share our testimonies. In an imitation of Christ's death, it paints the perfect picture out of actions, not words. Francis of Assisi, an early thirteenth century monk, said, "Preach the gospel at all times, and when necessary use words." Along that same line, he said, "It is no use walking anywhere to preach unless our walking is our preaching."

## Joy in Communion with Christ

Please go to hymnal.net and search "Alas and did my Savior bleed." Sing along.

### "At the Cross"
(Isaac Watts, 1707)

Alas! and did my Savior bleed, and did my Sovereign die?
Would he devote that sacred head for sinners such as I?

Refrain
At the cross, at the cross, where I first saw the light,
and the burden of my heart rolled away;
it was there by faith I received my sight, and now I am happy all the day.

Was it for crimes that I have done, he groaned upon the tree?
Amazing pity! Grace unknown! And love beyond degree!

Refrain

Well might the sun in darkness hide, and shut its glories in,
when Christ the mighty Maker died for man, the creature's sin.

Refrain

Thus might I hide my blushing face while Calvary's cross appears;
dissolve my heart in thankfulness, and melt mine eyes to tears.

Refrain

But drops of tears can ne'er repay the debt of love I owe.
Here, Lord, I give myself away; 'tis all that I can do.

Refrain

# STUDENT

WERE YOU A good student? "Yes, *summa cum laude!*" some of you are affirming. "No, I winged it," others are mumbling. For many, "Well, I tried, but…" just about wraps it up.

I can tell you as a former teacher that good grades are not always an accurate gauge of a good student. Many of you probably learned material as I did—just long enough to test well on it. Or perhaps you didn't have to study much, because good grades came naturally. Neither of those scenarios necessarily brings the term "good student" to mind.

My thesaurus gives "scholar" and researcher" as synonyms for "student," thus implying that if a person is a student at all, then he or she is a "good student." My *Family Word Finder* seems to really grasp the concept, for it includes "observer, examiner, spectator, reviewer, watcher, interpreter, analyst, commentator, and reader" as synonyms for "student." It defines "studious" as "devoted to study, earnest, diligent, painstaking, purposeful, laborious, determined, intent." Furthermore, it gives a lesson on word origin: "Study" and "student" come from the Latin *studere*, which means to apply oneself, to be diligent.[17]

Maybe the way to ask the question is like this: Were you a student? Did you apply yourself? Were you diligent in examining, reviewing, interpreting, and commenting on your course subjects? Were you devoted, earnest, determined and purposeful? Were you intent and focused in your objective? Perhaps now only a few of you can say, "Yes!" As for me, I'm afraid I have to respond, "Only sometimes."

As we wade thoughtfully in the waters of this chapter, allow me to challenge us to become students like Paul, who determinedly desired to know his subject matter.

## The Joyful Truth

What is more, I consider everything a loss because of the surpassing worth of knowing Christ Jesus my Lord, for whose sake I have lost all things. I consider them garbage, that I may gain Christ and be found in him, not having a righteousness of my own that comes from the law, but that which is through faith in Christ—the righteousness that comes from God on the basis of faith. I want to know Christ—yes, to know the power of his resurrection and participation in his sufferings, becoming like him in his death, and so, somehow, attaining to the resurrection from the dead. Not that I have already obtained all this, or have already arrived at my goal, but I press on to take hold of that for which Christ Jesus took hold of me. Brothers and sisters, I do not consider myself yet to have taken hold of it. But one thing I do: Forgetting what is behind and straining toward what is ahead, I press on toward the goal to win the prize for which God has called me heavenward in Christ Jesus. All of us, then, who are mature should take such a view of things. And if on some point you think differently, that too God will make clear to you. Only let us live up to what we have already attained. Join together in following my example, brothers and sisters, and just as you have us as a model, keep your eyes on those who live as we do. For, as I have often told you before and now tell you again even with tears, many live as enemies of the cross of Christ. Their destiny is destruction, their god is their stomach, and their glory is in their shame. Their mind is set on earthly things.

Philippians 3:8-19

We can learn so much from this block of Scripture. If we start at the end, we immediately discover the source of any problems we might experience. If our minds are on earthly things, we cannot possibly know Christ and become like him. When our stomachs, that is, our worldly cravings, are our god, then Jesus cannot be our Lord. If we glory in shameful acts and pursuits, then our destiny is destruction, not eternal life. Paul was shaking his head over just such poor examples and begged the Philippians not to follow them but to take note of those who, like him, were living diligently and purposefully for Christ.

In twenty-first century America, "many live as enemies of the cross of Christ" (Phil. 3:18). Some are very obvious, and usually we can stay far away from them. But others are a great deal subtler in their wickedness, and it is more difficult keeping our distance from them.

We often slowly adapt our lives to fit the worldly model, erroneously thinking that the "small" sins are just misdemeanors, really inconsequential when compared to the felonies like murder or adultery. Let's not fool ourselves. This subtle impiety is no less indicative of self-reliance, self-absorption, or self-promotion than the obvious evil we so like to disparage. God's Word teaches us that anything lifting self to a place of worship is directly in opposition to the cross of Jesus Christ, for his cross represents a total surrender of self. Let us make every effort to follow Christ with the purpose of knowing his heart and becoming like him.

I am reminded of the man who was pastor of my church back during my teenage years. A couple of years ago I spent time with Dr. Copeland and his wife of sixty-some years, and I learned that they had courted completely through letters. Four hundred and thirty-five letters! With the stresses of physical desire and where to go on a date out of the picture, they came to understand one another's hearts. By the time they married, they truly *knew* each other, and their compatibility was evident to me even as a teenager. Their humor, their love of learning and music, their attention to living healthfully and their mutual forthrightness in speech confirmed their unity in spirit.

While talking with them, I felt my heart saying, "That's how I want to know Christ! I want to learn of him with none of the physical demands of this world warring with what is really important. I want to know him so well that he and I have an evident unity of spirit. I want to love what he loves and find deep satisfaction in just being with him." Can you relate to these desires? The joyful truth is that all of them can be fulfilled!

## Digesting the Joy

You have probably heard "The Serenity Prayer" by Reinhold Niebuhr. "God grant me the serenity to accept the things I cannot change, courage to change the things I can, and wisdom to know the difference." Have you heard this variation? "God grant me the serenity to accept the people I cannot change, the courage to change the one I can, and the wisdom to know it's me" (author unknown).

Ouch! The first step towards knowing Christ in an all-encompassing way is to see our need and then develop a "want to" mind-set of rejoicing in the Lord. Paul had lofty goals in mind as he endeavored to know Christ. He wanted to gain Christ, "and be found in him, not having a righteousness of my own that comes from the law, but that which is through faith in Christ—the righteousness that comes from God on the basis of faith. I want to know Christ—yes, to know the power of his resurrection and participation in his sufferings, becoming like him in his death, and so, somehow, attaining to the resurrection from the dead" (Phil. 3:9-11). .

Maybe we identify totally with Paul, but maybe we are just beginning our journey with Christ and those goals sound like a foreign language to us. Or maybe we understand the words but are wondering where a person would begin putting goals like that into motion. Let's take note of two other people in the Bible, Zacchaeus and the rich young man, who illustrated a desire to know Christ, but whose lives were more like the average person's than Paul's seemed to be:

> Jesus entered Jericho and was passing through. A man was there by the name of Zacchaeus; he was a chief tax collector and was wealthy. He wanted to see who Jesus was, but because he was short he could not see over the crowd. So he ran ahead and climbed a sycamore-fig tree to see him, since Jesus was coming that way. When Jesus reached the spot, he looked up and said to him, "Zacchaeus, come down immediately. I must stay at your house today." So he came down at once and welcomed him gladly. All the people saw this and began to mutter, "He has gone to be the guest of a sinner." But Zacchaeus stood up and said to the Lord, "Look, Lord! Here and now I give half of my possessions to the poor, and if I have cheated anybody out of anything, I will pay back four times the amount." Jesus said to him, "Today salvation has come to this house, because this man, too, is a son of Abraham. For the Son of Man came to seek and to save the lost."
>
> Luke 19:1-10

Paul wanted to gain Christ and have the righteousness that comes from God. Zacchaeus likewise wanted to gain righteousness by making recompense for any damage he had caused. When he made this commitment Jesus told him salvation was his.

The rich young man appears in a scene found in Matthew 19, where Jesus and his disciples are perhaps relaxing under a tree, or maybe resting along the shore. They left Galilee so Jesus could get some rest, but the multitudes followed, because they were so hungry for Jesus' teaching and desperate for his healing. He had become a celebrity. Even his mere touch was coveted, so many parents brought their children to be embraced and blessed by the Lord. Then, a man approached with a wrenching question:

> "Teacher, what good thing must I do to get eternal life?" "Why do you ask me about what is good?" Jesus replied. "There is only One who is good. If you want to enter life, obey the commandments." "Which ones?" the man inquired. Jesus replied, "'Do not murder, do not commit adultery, do not steal, do not give false testimony, honor your father and mother,' and 'love your neighbor as yourself.'" "All these I have kept," the young man said. "What do I still lack?" Jesus answered, "If you want to be perfect, go, sell your possessions and give to the poor, and you will have treasure in heaven. Then come, follow me." When the young man heard this, he went away sad, because he had great wealth.
>
> Matthew 19:16-22

The rich man was also interested in gaining the righteousness of God. Like Zacchaeus, he was a son of Abraham, and like Paul, he was concerned to obey all the commandments so he could obtain eternal life. But his great wealth prevented him from gaining the kingdom of Christ, because he was unwilling to choose the treasure of heaven over his earthly treasure.

## Living Your Joy Out Loud

What can we take away from the simple stories of Zacchaeus and the rich young man?

### A Student of Jesus Looks for Him

Before anything else can happen, we first have to recognize a lack in our lives. I recently found a bug in my bathroom that looked like an ant with wings. I was afraid it might be a termite, but I didn't really know what termites look like. So I got on my computer and searched for pictures. After that, I was pretty sure it was an ant. But I still didn't know what to do about it, if anything. I recognized that I needed help beyond my own expertise, so I called my exterminator to look at it and advise me.

If we want to learn things we have to go to school; school rarely comes to us. Effort has to be made. Many people do not know Jesus intimately, because either they do not recognize a lack in their lives, or they are too lazy to pursue a relationship with him. It's just easier to run with the crowd, go with the flow, seek earthly fulfillment.

Zacchaeus and the wealthy young man lived in a day when many in their communities were looking for the Messiah. But they put feet to their curiosity in order to meet Jesus personally. If they had waited just a short time, it would have been too late.

Time is short. Compared to eternity, each of our lives is like a grain of sand in the bottom of the Pacific Ocean. But where a person spends eternity depends on one choice made during this fleeting existence: Will we seek him? If not, what is holding us back?

### A Student of Jesus Relinquishes his Pride in Order to See Jesus

"Dare to be different." I don't recall where I first heard this admonition—maybe from my mother. Pride tells us to be like everyone else. Self-preservation tells us not to rock the boat. Self-righteousness tells us we can accomplish everything on our own. Satan tells us that seeing Jesus is not that important. But a student of Jesus does not listen to pride, does not work for preservation or gratification of self, and definitely does not pay attention to anything the Enemy has to say.

We need to get out there, climb a tree like Zacchaeus, press through the crowds, dare to be different! Meeting, following, and knowing Jesus is our highest calling.

## A STUDENT OF JESUS IS RIDICULED BY THOSE WHO DON'T UNDERSTAND

If you want to know the truth, ridicule from non-Christians *really* bugs me. Sometimes I feel like they are so brainless. After all, the truth is so obvious, isn't it? Silly me. Our Lord Jesus experienced derision, so why shouldn't I? He was misunderstood, misinterpreted, and mistreated. But he was not miserable, because he accepted the inevitable consequences of living a holy life in an unholy world. We who will be his students must endure the same.

## A STUDENT OF JESUS GIVES UP ALL TO MAKE JESUS HIS EVERYTHING

The saddest Christian anyone will ever see is she who will not give up the rubbish of this world to gain Christ. She will be like the rich young man who went to see Jesus:

He went away sad, for he had many possessions (NLT).
He went away sad, for he had great wealth (NIV).
He went away grieving; for he was one who owned much property (NASB).
Crest-fallen, he walked away. He was holding on tight to a lot of things, and he couldn't bear to let go (MSG).

Let's instead make Philippians 3:12 our prayer: "Not that I have already obtained all this, or have already arrived at my goal, but I press on to take hold of that for which Christ Jesus took hold of me."

## A STUDENT OF JESUS OBEYS HIM

When Jesus said, "Zacchaeus, come down immediately. I must stay at your house today," Zacchaeus came down, and that move was the beginning of a great relationship. His obedience opened up the door to his house, and much more significantly, opened the door to his heart.

## A STUDENT OF JESUS IS CHANGED

Luke gives us front row seats to witness the immediate, miraculous change in Zacchaeus's heart. He traded in what was once his great infatuation, money, for the greatest love a human can know: the love of our Savior for us.

Our pursuit of Jesus may be like that of Zacchaeus and Paul. Or it may be more like the rich young man. According to Paul, the end desire of our pursuit should be "to take hold of that for which Christ Jesus took hold of me" (Phil. 3:12).

Like a one-hour television drama, Zacchaeus' sin problem seems to have been solved in one single episode. But close scrutiny of the rest of the New Testament contradicts this possibility. Even Jesus' closest friends, though seemingly passionate in loyalty to him, tripped up on occasion.

For instance, Peter definitely had his stops and starts. Paul admitted to the same: "Although I want to do good, evil is right there with me. For in my inner being I delight in God's law; but I see another law at work in me, waging war against the law of my mind and making me a prisoner of the law of sin at work within me. What a wretched man I am! Who will rescue me from this body that is subject to death? Thanks be to God, who delivers me through Jesus Christ our Lord! (Rom. 7:21-25).

Undeniably, a student is not a student without failures and ensuing growth. The task is not to fake perfection, but to "press on."

Press on to know Jesus Christ our Lord. Climb a tree and get out on a limb.

## Joy in Communion with Christ

I encourage you to go to hymnal.net and search "More about Jesus." Sing:

### "MORE ABOUT JESUS"
(Eliza E. Hewitt, 1887)

More about Jesus would I know,
More of His grace to others show;
More of His saving fullness see,
More of His love Who died for me.

Refrain
More, more about Jesus.
More, more about Jesus,
More of His saving fullness see,
More of His love Who died for me

More about Jesus let me learn,
More of His holy will discern;
Spirit of God, my teacher be,
Showing the things of Christ to me.

Refrain

More about Jesus; in His Word,
Holding communion with my Lord;
Hearing His voice in every line,
Making each faithful saying mine.

Refrain

I encourage you now to take some time to pray.

# CLEAN SLATE

WHEN I WAS a teacher, I used to love walking into my classroom on the first day of school each fall. The carpet had been shampooed; the bookshelves had been dusted; the desks were lined up like soldiers; and, best of all, the dry-erase boards were blindingly clean and white, ready for a new year. Something about the shiny, smudge-free surfaces called to me to cover them with learning opportunities! It was a thrill filling them with examples and assignments, and it was equally delightful to slide the eraser over them each afternoon in preparation for the next day's challenges.

There were times when I left an announcement or reminder of a test written in a small box on the top left corner of the board. When the day was over, I'd erase everything but that. The rest of the board was dazzling white, except for *that*. In the morning, when I would glance at the beautiful, clean board, there it was. I couldn't bask in the clean slate, because it wasn't entirely clean! I'm really not an obsessive compulsive, but those who teach school know what I'm talking about. Others may identify, because they find extreme pleasure in keeping an immaculate house or office. They just can't go to bed or leave on vacation until every toy, dish, paper, or rubber band is put away and every surface shimmers or sparkles. They like a clean slate.

The distressing truth is that while we may be compulsive about maintaining cleanliness around us, we often neglect the dirt in our souls and hearts. We tote our sin around like a backpack, either refusing to put it down and let it go, or becoming so accustomed to the extra weight that we don't notice it.

## The Joyful Truth

Forgetting or neglecting our sin is not the sort of "forgetting" Paul is talking about in Philippians:

Not that I have already obtained all this, or have already arrived at my goal, but I press on to take hold of that for which Christ Jesus took hold of me. Brothers and sisters, I do not consider myself yet to have taken hold of it. But one thing I do: Forgetting what is behind and straining toward what is ahead, I press on toward the goal to win the prize for which God has called me heavenward in Christ Jesus. All of us, then, who are mature should take such a view of things. And if on some point you think differently, that too God will make clear to you. Only let us live up to what we have already attained.

Philippians 3:12-16

The term in Greek for "forgetting" in this passage is *epilanthanomai*, and it simply means not remembering or recalling. "Forgetting what is behind" means don't overanalyze, don't cast blame; just forget.

Paul is quite radical in his statement about forgetting what is behind us. He admitted he hadn't yet attained the goal he had been trying for years to reach. But he persevered. He was not going to allow his life to be about his failures, and he pled with the Philippians to follow his example. A good paraphrase of verse fifteen is "So let's keep focused on that goal, those of us who want everything God has for us" (MSG).

Paul didn't mention repentance, but we cannot leave the past behind and press towards Jesus without having our sins cleansed. The Holy Spirit who lives within us won't allow it.

Here is a truth worth remembering: If you haven't confessed your sin and left it behind, then no matter how diligently you try to press on to the prize, you will be like a truck trying to get out of a muddy rut--the harder you try, the deeper you sink. Imagine the dry-erase board. If I had not erased it daily, then mess and confusion would have ensued, and the students could never have figured out their assignments. They wouldn't have been successful on tests, and they probably would have given up.

In thinking about Paul's pressing on, I am reminded of my daughter, Heather. She was a sunshiny child, smiling and laughing so much that we almost nicknamed her "Happy," though "Curtain-Climber" would also have suited. She was so enthralled with life that she climbed on everything from the moment she could crawl. She never seemed to learn from her mishaps, and she always seemed to forget the consequences!

When she was only eleven months old and barely walking, she climbed the monkey bars at our local park and, before my husband could go after her, she fell from a seven-foot-high platform.

Unhurt and unstoppable, at two years of age she climbed on top of the refrigerator and ate half a bottle of iron-fortified children's vitamins. The consequences of ipecac and vomiting eighteen times didn't deter her. She fell face first on the floor and broke her nose when she was three, after climbing on a chair to watch me fix pizza. By the time she was four, Heather was climbing up and jumping off the high dive at our community swimming pool. Once, when she was there with a friend's family, she slipped and fell from the high dive platform onto the pavement. Thankfully, a boy at the bottom of the ladder broke her fall and she merely cracked her skull! Heather's forgetting of these accidents was due, I think, partly to immaturity and partly to her adventurous personality.

When Paul tells us to be mature, he doesn't mean we should become fuddy-duddies. In fact, I sense in him the same fervor I sensed in Heather: the need to strain, to press on, to go for the prize! "All of us, then, who are mature . . . let us live up to what we have already attained." In explaining to the Corinthians his diverse actions among the Gentiles and the Jews, Paul said, "To the weak I became weak, to win the weak. I have become all things to all men so that by all possible means I might save some. I do all this for the sake of the gospel that I may share in its blessings. Do you not know that in a race all the runners run, but only one gets the prize? Run in such a way as to get the prize" (1 Cor. 9:22b - 24). He was telling the brothers and sisters in Corinth not to dwell on what had happened in the past, but to keep focused on the main thing, the winning of the prize.

## Digesting the Joy

Peek into the lives of three women who exemplified this concept of staying in the game to win the prize. Let's first look at Miriam in the book of Exodus:

Then Pharaoh gave this order to all his people: "Every Hebrew boy that is born you must throw into the Nile, but let every girl live." Now a man of the tribe of Levi married a Levite woman, and she became pregnant and gave birth to a son. When she saw that he was a fine child, she hid him for three months. But when she could hide him no longer, she got a papyrus basket for him and coated it with tar and pitch. Then she placed the child in it and put it among the reeds along the bank of the Nile. His sister stood at a distance to see what would happen to him. Then Pharaoh's daughter went down to the Nile to bathe, and her attendants were walking along the riverbank. She saw the basket among the reeds and sent her female slave to get it.

She opened it and saw the baby. He was crying, and she felt sorry for him. "This is one of the Hebrew babies," she said. Then his sister asked Pharaoh's daughter, "Shall I go and get one of the Hebrew women to nurse the baby for you?" "Yes, go," she answered. So the girl went and got the baby's mother. Pharaoh's daughter said to her, "Take this baby and nurse him for me, and I will pay you." So the woman took the baby and nursed him. When the child grew older, she took him to Pharaoh's daughter and he became her son. She named him Moses, saying, "I drew him out of the water."

Exodus 1:22-2:10

Miriam stood at a distance to see what would happen to her baby brother, Moses. When Pharaoh's daughter took him out of the Nile, Miriam offered to find a Hebrew woman to nurse the baby. Pharaoh's daughter agreed, and for several years, Miriam's mother continued to nurse young Moses. Then, when the child grew older, she took him to Pharaoh's daughter and he became her son. To win the prize of life for Moses, Miriam and her mother had to forget the order of Pharaoh and press on.

Next, let's look at Ruth:

Boaz took Ruth and she became his wife. When he made love to her, the Lord enabled her to conceive, and she gave birth to a son. The women said to Naomi: "Praise be to the Lord, who this day has not left you without a guardian-redeemer. May he become famous throughout Israel! He will renew your life and sustain you in your old age. For your daughter-in-law, who loves you and who is better to you than seven sons, has given him birth." Then Naomi took the child in her arms and cared for him. The women living there said, "Naomi has a son!" And they named him Obed. He was the father of Jesse, the father of David.

Ruth 4:13-17

Ruth married an Israelite from Bethlehem who had come to her country to live. When he, his father, and his brother died, her mother-in-law, Naomi, decided to return to Bethlehem in Judah. She told Ruth to go back to her own family, but Ruth would not listen. She was determined to go with Naomi. Much later, Ruth married a man from Judah named Boaz, and they had a son. Ruth was another who had to forget what was behind and press on to find her place in God's plan to give birth to Obed the grandfather of King David.

Finally, let's take a look at Mary Magdalene:

Jesus traveled about from one town and village to another, proclaiming the good news of the kingdom of God. The Twelve were with him, and also some women who had been cured of evil spirits and diseases: Mary (called Magdalene) from whom seven demons had come out . . . .

Luke 8:1-3

Then the disciples went back to where they were staying. Now Mary stood outside the tomb crying. As she wept, she bent over to look into the tomb and saw two angels in white, seated where Jesus' body had been, one at the head and the other at the foot. They asked her, "Woman, why are you crying?" "They have taken my Lord away," she said, "and I don't know where they have put him." At this, she turned around and saw Jesus standing there, but she did not realize that it was Jesus. He asked her, "Woman, why are you crying? Who is it you are looking for?" Thinking he was the gardener, she said, "Sir, if you have carried him away, tell me where you have put him, and I will get him." Jesus said to her, "Mary." She turned toward him and cried out in Aramaic, "Rabboni!" (which means "Teacher"). Jesus said, "Do not hold on to me, for I have not yet ascended to the Father. Go instead to my brothers and tell them, 'I am ascending to my Father and your Father, to my God and your God.'" Mary Magdalene went to the disciples with the news: "I have seen the Lord!" And she told them that he had said these things to her.

John 20:10-18

Mary Magdalene also had to forget what was in her past, a past that included demon possession, in order to be a part of Jesus' inner circle of followers. She was tenacious in her faith and held on to deliver the Good News to the disciples.

## Living Your Joy Out Loud

Miriam, Ruth, and Mary Magdalene had no idea what the "big plan" was before they took their first steps. But they all persevered in the faith to win the prize. We have full knowledge of the ministry God had for Moses, Miriam's brother, and King David, the great-grandson of Ruth. And we know the news of the resurrection of Christ brought to the early church by Mary Magdalene. These women had only the God-given desire to run for the prize, and they ran their race with perseverance.

We should not let anything stop us. There *is* a big plan, and the Master Designer has it all under control. But first we must forget what is behind by taking our sin, hurt, insecurity, the mistakes our parents made, or any other past trouble slowing us down, and "Forgetting what is behind and straining toward what is ahead . . . press on toward the goal to win the prize for which God has called me heavenward in Christ Jesus. All of us, then, who are mature should take such a view of things" (Phil. 3:13-15).

Make this day the day you put things behind you that do not help you press on toward the goal for which God has called you. Don't let the things of the past be a nuisance. Don't snag your pants on it. Don't let it disturb your peace, disrupt your pace, or dampen your plan. Start with a clean slate, and press on, for the prize is worth it.

## Joy in Communion with Christ

Take a short break and go to YouTube.com, and search "Higher Ground a Hymn a Week." Join in the worship and singing.

### "HIGHER GROUND" (OR "I'M PRESSING ON THE UPWARD WAY")
(Johnson Oatman, Jr., exact date unknown)

I'm pressing on the upward way,
New heights I'm gaining every day;
Still praying as I'm onward bound,
"Lord, plant my feet on higher ground."

Refrain
Lord, lift me up and let me stand,
By faith on heaven's tableland,
A higher place than I have found,
Lord, plant my feet on higher ground.

My heart has no desire to stay
Where doubts arise and fears dismay;
Though some may dwell where those abound,
My prayer, my aim, is higher ground.

Refrain

I want to live above the world,
Though Satan's darts at me are hurled;
For faith has caught the joyful sound,
The song of saints on higher ground.

Refrain

I want to scale the utmost height
And catch a gleam of glory bright;
But still I'll pray till heav'n I've found,
"Lord, plant my feet on higher ground."

Refrain

Weighing a life lived under the law against a life lived through Jesus, Paul wrote, "That old law had glory, but it really loses its glory when it is compared to the much greater glory of this new way. If that law which disappeared came with glory, then this new way which continues forever has much greater glory." (2 Cor. 3:10-11, New Century Version).

Meditate on how these verses encourage a Christian to make a clean slate (forget and press on). Then pray.

# CITIZEN OF HEAVEN

BELOW ARE FIFTY of the one hundred questions on the test given to those who want to become naturalized citizens of the United States of America. This version of the test took effect on October 1, 2008. How many can you answer correctly? (No peeking at the answers until afterwards.)

1. What is the supreme law of the land?
2. The idea of self-government is in the first three words of the Constitution. What are these words?
3. What do we call the first ten amendments to the Constitution?
4. What is *one* right or freedom from the First Amendment?
5. What is freedom of religion?
6. What is the economic system in the United States?
7. Name *one* branch or part of the government.
8. What stops one branch of government from becoming too powerful?
9. Who is in charge of the executive branch?
10. Who makes federal laws?
11. How many U.S. Senators are there?
12. We elect a U.S. Senator for how many years?
13. The House of Representatives has how many voting members?
14. Who does a U.S. Senator represent?

15. Why do some states have more Representatives than other states?

16. What is the name of the Vice President of the United States now?

17. If both the President and the Vice President can no longer serve, who becomes President?

18. What does the President's Cabinet do?

19. What are two Cabinet-level positions?

20. What is the highest court in the United States?

21. How many justices are on the Supreme Court?

22. Who is the Chief Justice of the United States?

23. Under our Constitution, some powers belong to the federal government. What is *one* power of the federal government?

24. Under our Constitution, some powers belong to the states. What is *one* power of the states?

25. Who is the Governor of your state?

26. What is the political party of the President now?

27. What is the name of the Speaker of the House of Representatives now?

28. There are four amendments to the Constitution about who can vote. Describe *one* of them.

29. What is *one* responsibility that is only for United States citizens?

30. What are *two* rights of everyone living in the United States?

31. What is *one* promise you make when you become a United States citizen?

32. What is one reason colonists came to America?

33. Why did the colonists fight the British?

34. There were 13 original states. Name *three*.

35. Name *one* war fought by the United States in the 1800s.

36. What did the Emancipation Proclamation do?

37. What did Susan B. Anthony do?

38. Name one war fought by the United States in the 1900s.

39. Who was President during the Great Depression and World War II?

40. Who did the United States fight in World War II?

41. During the Cold War, what was the main concern of the United States?

42. What movement tried to end racial discrimination?

43. What major event happened on September 11, 2001 in the United States?

44. Name one of the two longest rivers in the United States.

45. What ocean is on the East Coast of the United States?

46. Name *one* state that borders Canada.
47. Name *one* state that borders Mexico.
48. Why does the flag have 13 stripes?
49. What is the name of the national anthem?
50. Name *two* national U.S. holidays.

You may now look at the answers at the end of this chapter. I got 92% correct when I took the quiz, not an outstanding score for someone who was born, raised, and educated in the United States, and who used to teach seventh-grade civics. How did you do?

I am glad our government tries to familiarize prospective citizens with the workings of our nation, and I hope studying this material and taking the test makes them more appreciative of living in the greatest country in the world. But I wonder if we who don't have to take the test are as grateful as we should be.

God blessed America when she began as a nation espousing belief in God and making laws that reflected a biblical worldview. God still blesses America, even when we as a country have slid into an amoral society. I don't know why God has continued to bless us as we have turned our backs on him, but I do know that ingratitude is something he abhors.

From the earliest history of the Israelite nation, God gave warnings to the Jewish people about the dangers of prosperity:

> The Lord your God will soon bring you into the land he swore to give you when he made a vow to your ancestors Abraham, Isaac, and Jacob. It is a land with large, prosperous cities that you did not build. The houses will be richly stocked with goods you did not produce. You will draw water from cisterns you did not dig, and you will eat from vineyards and olive trees you did not plant. When you have eaten your fill in this land, be careful not to forget the Lord, who rescued you from slavery in the land of Egypt. You must fear the Lord your God and serve him.
>
> Deuteronomy 6:10-13, NLT

> But that is the time to be careful! Beware that in your plenty you do not forget the Lord your God and disobey his commands, regulations, and decrees that I am giving you today. For when you have become full and prosperous and have built fine homes to live in, and when your flocks and herds have become very large and your silver and gold have multiplied along with everything else, be careful! Do not become proud at that time and forget the Lord your God, who rescued you from slavery in the land of Egypt.
>
> Deuteronomy 8:11-14, NLT

God gave them a land flowing with milk and honey. Not only was it the best soil in the region, but the ground had already been broken, planted, watered, and harvested. Cities had been built. Roads were developed. Flocks of sheep and herds of cattle were grazing in abundance.

Like a pre-shrunk cotton tee-shirt, this land was ready for the wearing, and the Israelites didn't have to worry about whether it would "fit them" later. God promised success. Yet he knew his people. He had experienced their impatience, their stubbornness, their idolatry, their whining, and their fear. So he gave them a warning: "You must fear the Lord your God and serve him. . . . Beware that in your plenty you do not forget the Lord your God and disobey his commands, regulations, and decrees." In order to insure their remembrance, God gave the law of the tithe:

> A tithe of everything from the land, whether grain from the soil or fruit from the trees, belongs to the Lord; it is holy to the LORD. . . . Every tithe of the herd and flock—every tenth animal that passes under the shepherd's rod—will be holy to the Lord. No one may pick out the good from the bad or make any substitution. If anyone does make a substitution, both the animal and its substitute become holy and cannot be redeemed.
>
> Leviticus 27:30, 32-33

If we were paid in cash and had to count our earnings as we received them, would it be easier to lay aside every tenth dollar for the Lord? If so, would it prompt us to be grateful for the other nine, or would we grimace at every penny taken out, as we do with taxes?

When I was a child, I had a friend whose dad had a large wooden paddle upon which was written, *"Attitude Adjuster."* My friend had a healthy respect for that paddle, and a healthier respect for her dad. She did not grow up hating her father or beating her children. She grew up loving and appreciating her father, because he loved her enough to help her change her attitude and make some good choices. If we have an unhealthy attitude about giving, we can let the Holy Spirit adjust that attitude.

## The Joyful Truth

> Join together in following my example, brothers and sisters, and just as you have us as a model, keep your eyes on those who live as we do. For, as I have often told you before and now tell you again even with tears, many live as enemies of the cross of Christ. Their destiny is destruction, their god is their stomach, and their glory is in their shame. Their mind is set on earthly things. But our citizenship is in heaven. And we eagerly await a Savior from there, the Lord

Jesus Christ, who, by the power that enables him to bring everything under his control, will transform our lowly bodies so that they will be like his glorious body.

Philippians 3:17-21

The Greek word used for "citizenship" in the twentieth verse is *politeuma*, derived from the root word *polis*, which means "city." With the addition of just one letter you get the word *politeumai*, which means "to fulfill one's duty, or to conduct oneself, or to lead one's life." Thus, built right into the Greek word for citizenship is the idea of *doing* something.

President John F. Kennedy had the same idea. He died when I was in the fifth grade, so I don't remember much about him or his presidency, except for his assassination and the seemingly unending television coverage of all that ensued. But I do remember that during those hours of accolades and analysis, more than once I heard his recorded Massachusetts-accented voice saying, "Ask not what your country can do for you; ask what you can do for your country" (from his inauguration speech, 1961). For me, that plea was his legacy. If Americans ever truly heeded that urging, in the years since then we have made a U-turn.

When the 2010 census was going on, I saw a commercial several times that implored people to fill out their census forms and mail them in so they could get all the federal funding they deserved. Yes, our mantra now seems to be, "Ask not what you can do for your country; ask what it can do for you."

When the country of Haiti experienced its catastrophic 7.0 magnitude earthquake in 2010, hundreds of thousands were without shelter, tens of thousands died or were injured, thousands were starving and many, many looked for loved ones who were buried alive under the rubble. The people of America and the world were deeply touched by the plight of these poorest people in the Western hemisphere, and millions of dollars were donated to hundreds of relief organizations. My own immediate reaction was, "I must go help!"

Most of us are good at responding to desperate circumstances, especially those that take place somewhere far removed from our everyday lives. But are we as touched by the needs in our own communities and churches? Are we as prompt and generous in our gifts of money and service? Are we good citizens of heaven?

Many people want to receive the eternal blessings that come with being citizens of heaven, but they don't want to give anything. They don't mind going to worship services, that is, if the music suits them and they get their ears tickled with the sermon. But how many of us seem to have the attitude that we are owed something by the Church?

The Church should provide our children's spiritual upbringing. The Church should supply new, state-of-the-art facilities. The Church should offer opportunities for fellowship. The

Church should meet our needs when we are sick or impoverished. And how is the Church supposed to do all this? Well, that is the Church's responsibility! Do we not see the connection between the Church and ourselves? Does this foundational misunderstanding stem from a lack of true relationship with Jesus Christ?

## Digesting the Joy

Entitlement is an age-old attitude. Even our Lord's disciples thought they were entitled to more than the others: "An argument started among the disciples as to which of them would be the greatest" (Luke 9:46). The gospel of Mark records another instance where some of the disciples had the wrong idea about heavenly citizenship, and Jesus had to correct them:

> Whoever wants to become great among you must be your servant, and whoever wants to be first must be slave of all. For even the Son of Man did not come to be served, but to serve, and to give his life as a ransom for many.
>
> Mark 10:43-45

The attitude that we deserve something because we have chosen to follow Jesus is not correct and not biblical. We have already been given so much more than we deserve. In Luke 14:33, Jesus said, "Those of you who do not give up everything you have cannot be my disciples." He made it clear that instead of demanding even more, we citizens of heaven should expect to give up what is dearest to us for the sake of the Kingdom.

We love to think of Jesus as the tender shepherd, leading his frolicking little lambs along a sunlit, clear-cut pathway. It is much more difficult to picture Jesus as the bruised and beaten Lamb of God carrying his cross down the Via Dolorosa, calling us to deny ourselves and take up our crosses to follow him. Yet that is precisely what he asks of us.

In Luke's account of Jesus' ministry, this serious word about the cost of being a disciple is followed by Jesus' parables of the lost sheep, the lost coin, and the prodigal son. With tax collectors, "sinners," Pharisees, and teachers of the law all gathered around, Jesus strikingly, through the use of repetition, conveyed the worth of each repentant sinner to our holy God.

## Living Your Joy Out Loud

After Jesus talked to his followers about the high cost of discipleship, he then taught them about the correct attitude towards money.

There was a rich man who was dressed in purple and fine linen and lived in luxury every day. At his gate was laid a beggar named Lazarus, covered with sores and longing to eat what fell from the rich man's table. Even the dogs came and licked his sores. The time came when the beggar died and the angels carried him to Abraham's side. The rich man also died and was buried. In Hades, where he was in torment, he looked up and saw Abraham far away, with Lazarus by his side. So he called to him, "Father Abraham, have pity on me and send Lazarus to dip the tip of his finger in water and cool my tongue, because I am in agony in this fire." But Abraham replied, "Son, remember that in your lifetime you received your good things, while Lazarus received bad things, but now he is comforted here and you are in agony. And besides all this, between us and you a great chasm has been set in place, so that those who want to go from here to you cannot, nor can anyone cross over from there to us." He answered, "Then I beg you, father, send Lazarus to my family, for I have five brothers. Let him warn them, so that they will not also come to this place of torment." Abraham replied, "They have Moses and the Prophets; let them listen to them." No, father Abraham," he said, "but if someone from the dead goes to them, they will repent." He said to him, "If they do not listen to Moses and the Prophets, they will not be convinced even if someone rises from the dead."

Luke 16:19-31

Jesus' thought process should affect our idea of heavenly citizenship, because he moved from denying oneself to the high value of each soul to the correct use of monetary blessings. We are members of the body of Christ, citizens of heaven, and I believe we hold a citizen's responsibility to *do* something for the Kingdom. The Lord's Prayer (Luke 11:2-4), a prayer many of us say at least once a week, contains the line, "Thy kingdom come, thy will be done, on earth as it is in heaven." In order for God's will to be done on earth as it is in heaven, it must begin with me and with you.

We must ask not what our churches (our salvation, our beliefs) can do for us. We must ask what we can do for the sake of Jesus.

## Joy in Communion with Christ

Here is an old chorus to sing along with, which is attributed to S. Sundar Singh:

### "I HAVE DECIDED TO FOLLOW JESUS"

I have decided to follow Jesus;
I have decided to follow Jesus;
I have decided to follow Jesus;
No turning back, no turning back.
Though I may wonder, I still will follow;
Though I may wonder, I still will follow;

Though I may wonder, I still will follow;
No turning back, no turning back.
The world behind me, the cross before me;
The world behind me, the cross before me;
The world behind me, the cross before me;
No turning back, no turning back.
Though none go with me, still I will follow;
Though none go with me, still I will follow;
Though none go with me, still I will follow;
No turning back, no turning back.
Will you decide now to follow Jesus?
Will you decide now to follow Jesus?
Will you decide now to follow Jesus?
No turning back, no turning back.

Answers to quiz (the ones subject to change because of year or the place one lives are left blank):

1. The Constitution
2. "We, the people"
3. The Bill of Rights
4. Speech, religion, assembly, press, petition
5. You can practice or not practice any religion
6. Capitalism (market economy)
7. Executive (president), legislative (Congress), judicial (the courts)
8. Separation of powers, checks and balances
9. The President
10. Congress
11. 100
12. 6
13. 435
14. All the people of the state
15. Because some states have more people
16.
17. The Speaker of the House

18. Advises the President
19. Secretary of: agriculture, commerce, defense, education, energy, health and human services, homeland security, housing and urban development, interior, state, transportation, treasury, veterans' affairs, labor, and Attorney General
20. The Supreme Court
21. Nine
22.
23. Print money, declare war, create and army, make treaties
24. Provide education, provide protection (police), provide safety (fire departments), give driver's license, approve zoning and land use
25.
26.
27.
28. Serve on a jury; vote
29. Apply for a federal job, vote, run for office, carry a U.S. passport
30. Freedom of expression, freedom of speech, freedom of assembly, freedom to petition the government, freedom of worship, the right to bear arms
31. Give up loyalty to other countries; defend the Constitution and laws of the United States; obey the laws of the United States; serve in the military, if needed
32. Freedom, political liberty, religious freedom, economic opportunity; escape persecution
33. Because they didn't have self-government; because of taxation without representation
34. New Hampshire, Massachusetts, Rhode Island, Connecticut, New York, New Jersey, Pennsylvania, Delaware, Maryland, Virginia, North Carolina, South Carolina, Georgia
35. War of 1812, Mexican-American War, Civil War, Spanish-American War
36. Freed the slaves
37. Fought for women's rights, fought for civil rights
38. World War I, World War II, Korean War, Vietnam War, Persian Gulf War
39. Franklin Roosevelt
40. Japan, Germany and Italy
41. Communism
42. Civil rights movement
43. Terrorists attacked the United States
44. Missouri, Mississippi
45. Atlantic

46. Maine, New Hampshire, Vermont, New York, Pennsylvania, Ohio, Michigan, Minnesota, North Dakota, Montana, Idaho, Washington, Alaska

47. California, Arizona, New Mexico, Texas

48. Because there were 13 original colonies

49. "The Star-Spangled Banner"

50. New Year's; Martin Luther King, Jr. Day; President's Day; Memorial Day; Independence Day; Labor Day; Columbus Day, Veterans' Day; Thanksgiving; Christmas

# CROWN

JESUS BECAME MY personal Savior in 1961. Though only seven years old, I truly and tremblingly gave myself to him and asked him to live in my heart forever. In the years since, I have sometimes regretted making my profession of faith so early, before committing some really bad sins that could have "beefed up" my testimony! I'm just kidding (sort of). I would hear someone's amazing testimony and think, *How bad could I have been at seven-years-old that Jesus would need to come in and completely change my life?*

The truth is that every person, no matter his or her age, is just as "bad" as the next, because each person is born with a sin nature. The Lord said "every inclination of the human heart is evil from childhood" (Gen. 8:21). Romans 3:23 tells us that "all have sinned and fall short of the glory of God."

This is true even of infants and toddlers, and if you have ever been around them you have seen that sin nature in its early stages. The moment a child realizes there are choices in life, he begins asserting his preferences. He fusses at not being able to do what he wants when he wants. Or she gravitates towards the "no-no's." The "Toddler's Creed" humorously illustrates another of the ugly truths in the human sin nature:

## THE TODDLER'S CREED

If I want it, it's mine.
If I give it to you and change my mind later, it's mine.

If I can take it away from you, it's mine.

If I had it a little while ago, it's mine.

If it's mine, it will never belong to anybody else, no matter what.

If we are building something together, all the pieces are mine.

If it looks just like mine, it is mine.[18]

This sounds a bit like covetousness, doesn't it? When Jesus became my personal Savior, I needed a personal Savior as much as anyone ever needed one. My heart was ruled by selfishness, egotism, and covetousness. I wanted all the "pretties" I saw: That girl's boxy red purse with the brass buckle; that friend's shiny black shoes; that boy's really sweet mama; that candy store's malted milk balls; that acquaintance's nifty bicycle horn; that neighbor's gleaming swing set with a super slippery slide attached; that teacher's colored chalk; that library's date stamper; that. . . I think you get the picture. If mere desire could have made them mine, they would've been *mine*.

That desire was never felt more profoundly than when I first laid eyes on a tiara. I believe the first occasion I saw one was a GA (Girls' Auxiliary) coronation service at Derbyshire Baptist Church in Richmond, Virginia. In those days, many Southern Baptist girls took part in GA, an organization whose purpose was to teach and promote missions work around the world. In view of earning badges and other symbols of accomplishment, each girl in GA would work on memorizing Scripture, participate in mission action, and create artistic expressions and symbols of the Christian life. Step-by-step and year-by-year a girl worked to become a maiden, a lady-in-waiting, a princess, a queen, a queen with a scepter, and a queen regent. All the hard work culminated in a coronation service at the end of each school year.

Well, before I was even old enough to be a GA, my older sister, Anne, had graduated through the prerequisite steps and was ready to be crowned Queen at the coronation service. She and two other girls, dressed in long white dresses, hair styled into updos, stood on the platform, and one by one their mothers placed tiaras on their heads, signifying they had reached the rank of queen.

Immediately, a burning desire came over me that was so great I can hardly describe it even now. I wanted to be up there in flowing white dress. But more than that, I wanted that tiara! Its glitz out-sparkled anything I had ever owned, and the shape of it was divine, so triangularly did it point toward heaven. I knew for certain that if I had a tiara, my life would never be the same.

Perhaps you have coveted a tiara at some point in your life. What is it about a tiara that warrants our passion? What touches that female chord within us and makes us quiver with excitement at the thought of wearing one? I cannot believe that it is merely the shininess, for as exhilarating as baubles and patent leather are, they do not equal the thrill of owning and wearing a tiara. After all, one may own many pairs of patent leather shoes and many a varied bauble in her lifetime, but how many women ever actually possess tiaras of their very own? Marilyn Monroe said it best in her 1953 movie, *Gentlemen Prefer Blondes:* "I always say a kiss on the hand might feel very good, but a diamond tiara lasts forever."

## The Joyful Truth

We are tiaras of sorts. We are beautiful, longed for, and treasured. Read the first verse of Philippians chapter four: "Therefore, my brothers and sisters, you whom I love and long for, my joy and crown, stand firm in the Lord in this way, dear friends!" The New Living Translation puts that verse this way: "Therefore, my dear brothers and sisters, stay true to the Lord. I love you and long to see you, dear friends, for you are my joy and the crown I receive for my work." Paul called the Philippian believers his crown, the reward for his work.

Jesus is a name I have heard all my life. My parents were missionaries serving among Chinese-speaking people in the Philippines. Their commitment to telling others about Jesus' saving grace was part of my earliest memory. My mother passed away in 2001 at the age of seventy-nine, but my father lived to be ninety years old, still occasionally teaching Sunday school and leading vespers at his retirement center up until eight months before he died. As recently as two years before his death, he went as a visiting professor of missions to the Taiwan Baptist Theological Seminary in Taipei. He loved to tell the story of Jesus and his love.

I remember preschool Sunday school and Sunbeams very well. Church was a happy and loving place to be. Mrs. Maxine Bersch, my Sunday school teacher when I was in kindergarten, was a wonderful storyteller and had a warm, comfy lap. I could tell she loved the Bible! Mrs. Bersch was the first person I remember besides my parents to help me understand that I was a sinner and in need of a Savior.

Soon I began reading for myself and understanding a little more of who I was and who Jesus was. At that point, the person who had the most influence on me was my older sister. I guess you could say Anne had a burden for my salvation. She spoke to me about it constantly, saying, "Don't you know you're a sinner? Do you want to go to heaven? If you do, you need to ask Jesus to save you from your sins!" "If you died, you wouldn't get to go to heaven like Mama, Daddy, Winston, and me." The more she talked to me, the more burdened I felt about my sin. Of course I wanted to go to heaven, and of course, I didn't want to be separated from my loving family.

The time had come for me to answer a very important question. *Would I ask Jesus into my heart and trust him to save me?* On a Sunday night in the fall of 1961, I answered *Yes.* I walked down the aisle of the school cafeteria where our church was meeting and told our pastor that I wanted Jesus in my life. Later that week, he visited me in our home, and soon after that I was baptized. I was scared to death of water, but I obeyed Jesus' desire for me to follow him in baptism on a cold December Sunday afternoon.

Who will receive a crown for their work of telling me about Jesus? Does God award partial crowns, or does he give multiple crowns representing the same person's soul? I don't know. But I do know that my salvation brought great joy to many people. Think about this: Whose crown are you? Are there any believers who are your "joy and crown"?

## Digesting the Joy

Do you remember the Burger King crown—the fake gold-coated cardstock with just as phony emeralds, sapphires, and rubies liberally painted on? I used to take my girls to Burger King, not because their kids' meals were superior or their toys more fun. We went for the free crowns. Each of the four girls could get one and wear it at the same time as her sisters wore theirs, yet somehow they all felt extremely special. And when a crown got lost or worn out or left out in the rain, we could go get another for the price of an order of fries.

Real crowns are not so generously dispensed. Every time I have seen one it was locked up behind thick glass. What are the distinguishing qualities of a real crown?

### A Crown is Valuable

Why is a crown valuable? Unlike the Burger King crown, real crowns are scarce. Not everyone owns one. Part of the value comes in the rarity, and they are rare because of the precious materials used to make them. But they are also rare and valuable because of who they represent.

### A Crown Represents Royalty and Sovereignty

Christians are valuable, rare representations of the royal King, Jesus Christ. When Paul called the Philippian Christians his "crown," he was not patting himself on the back. Actually, he was giving the Philippians themselves a precious compliment. He was saying, much as Peter did in his first letter, "You are God's chosen and special people. You are a group of royal priests and a holy nation. God has brought you out of darkness into his marvelous light. Now you must tell all the wonderful things that he has done" (1 Pet. 2:9, CEV).

## A Crown is Stored in a Secure Place

Because of its value, a crown is stored in a secure place. The crown jewels of England include scepters, swords, bracelets, a bejeweled orb, a chalice, a golden bird, a spoon, and hundreds of other, smaller items. But the four crowns are the icing on the cake.

The Imperial Crown of State is a gorgeous white gold crown. On the front are a ruby and a diamond, each the size of a ping pong ball. The rest of the gold is encrusted with a total of 2,783 diamonds, seventeen sapphires, 277 pearls, eleven emeralds, and five rubies, all shown in their best light by the purple velvet lining.

St. Edward's Crown is yellow gold with wine-colored lining and contains a mixture of 444 precious stones. The third crown, a white gold crown made for Queen Elizabeth, the Queen Mother, displays the legendary Koh-i-noor, a 105.6 carat diamond. The Imperial Crown of India is another yellow gold crown set with more than 6,000 diamonds with rubies, sapphires and emeralds.[19]

I have seen these crowns in person, and I must say they are impressive! I didn't see them as closely as I would have liked, however, because they are sealed in a lighted glass vault in the Jewel House at the Tower of London, protected by the Coldstream Guards, a regiment of the British army. We could only look, and we were made to move along rather quickly. In fact, we were behind a barrier about four feet from the case, probably so as not to get fingerprints all over the glass. Still, the jewels, especially the crowns, were amazing to behold.

Every reader of this book is an extremely valuable crown that is stored in a secure place. Ephesians 1:13-14 and 4:30 identify the indestructible "glass" behind which we are sealed: "And you also were included in Christ when you heard the message of truth, the gospel of your salvation. When you believed, you were marked in him with a seal, the promised Holy Spirit, who is a deposit guaranteeing our inheritance until the redemption of those who are God's possession—to the praise of his glory. . . . And do not grieve the Holy Spirit of God, with whom you were sealed for the day of redemption."

Unlike the crowns of earthly kingdoms, which are periodically taken out of their secure places, we will remain sealed (secure) until the day of redemption.

## Living Your Joy Out Loud

The unfathomable miracle of the seal of the Holy Spirit upon us, however, is that we can remain sealed and secure while not being locked up. What I am saying is that the one noteworthy way in which we are very different from a crown of an earthly kingdom is that God wants to use us in this world *every day*. He doesn't want to place us in the ivory towers of evangelical churchdom where other people just visit and wish they could be royalty. He wants to use us to bring others into the royal priesthood. In fact, Scripture makes it very clear that the Holy Spirit does more than just seal us until the day of our redemption (all italics are my emphasis):

Whenever you are arrested and brought to trial, do not worry beforehand about what to say. Just say whatever is given you at the time, for *it is not you speaking, but the Holy Spirit.*

Mark 13:11

At that time Jesus, *full of joy through the Holy Spirit*, said, "I praise you, Father, Lord of heaven and earth, because you have hidden these things from the wise and learned, and revealed them to little children. Yes, Father, for this is what you were pleased to do."

Luke 10:21

But when he, the Spirit of truth, comes, *he will guide you into all the truth.* He will not speak on his own; he will speak only what he hears, and he will tell you what is yet to come.

John 16:13

But you will receive *power* when the Holy Spirit comes on you; and you will be my witnesses in Jerusalem, and in all Judea and Samaria, and to the ends of the earth.

Acts 1:8

Then the church throughout Judea, Galilee and Samaria enjoyed a time of peace and was strengthened. Living in the fear of the Lord and *encouraged by the Holy Spirit,* it increased in numbers.

Acts 9:31

May the God of hope fill you with all joy and peace as you trust in him, so that you may overflow with *hope by the power of the Holy Spirit.*

Romans 15:13

Do you not know that your *bodies are temples of the Holy Spirit*, who is in you, whom you have received from God? You are not your own.

1 Corinthians 6:19

We are stunning, sparkly creations, fashioned by royalty for royalty, and like that tiara I coveted, we can unashamedly and unequivocally point towards heaven. We can point that way not because we have been packed up and sealed for delivery there, but because we are full of joy, love, power, and hope from the Holy Spirit.

## Joy in Communion with Christ

I encourage you to go to cyberhymnal.org and sing "Seal Us, O Holy Spirit"[20]:

"SEAL US, O HOLY SPIRIT"
(Isaac H. Meredith, 1900)

Seal us, O Holy Spirit,
Grant us Thine impress, we pray;
We would be more like the Savior,
Stamped with His image today.

Refrain
Seal us, O Holy Spirit,
Help us Thy likeness to show;
Then from our life unto others
Streams of rich blessings shall flow.

Seal us, O Holy Spirit,
Make us Thine own from this hour;
Let us be useful, dear Master,
Seal us with witnessing power.

Refrain

Seal us, seal us,
Seal us just now, we pray;
Seal us, O Holy Spirit,
Seal us for service today.

Now take some time to pray.

# PILLAR

A WEASEL WORD is a word used to "weasel out" of saying what you actually want to say. Let me give you some examples.

While researching this topic, I ran across an old blog in which a woman remarked that she thought she had actually been brought up to use euphemisms for "No" instead of saying, "No." For example, she would say, "I don't think it will work out," or "Perhaps another time," which both meant "No," but sounded less abrupt. Weasel words.

Modern day parents are particularly guilty of using weasel words like "We'll see," when they really mean "No." Several years ago, when I worked at my church, I heard a nine-year-old boy ask his father if a friend could come over to swim that afternoon. His father answered, "We'll see," and walked on down the hallway. So I asked Brandon what he thought his father meant by "We'll see." Brandon immediately replied, "Not on your life!" I practically laughed my head off.

Have we Christian women resorted to using weasel words concerning our devotion to the Lord? Do we use them so we do not seem abrupt, fanatic, intolerant, stern, or old-fashioned? What part of "Love the Lord your God with all your heart and with all your soul and with all your mind and with all your strength" (Mark 12:30) sounds like a suggestion or euphemism? What has happened to our loyalty and steadfastness? When did we become defensive about our faith?

## The Joyful Truth

Paul loved the people he had won to the Lord. They were his joy and crown. His relationship with them was much like a wise, loving father's relationship with his children, so he repeatedly encouraged them to stick with their faith. Here at the beginning of Philippian's chapter four, the apostle writes, "Therefore, my brothers and sisters, you whom I love and long for, my joy and crown, stand firm in the Lord in this way, dear friends!" (Phil. 4:1).

In the koine (common) Greek language of the New Testament, "stand firm" is the word *steko*, which can be translated "be steadfast," and is derived from two other words, *histemi* (take a stand; establish; continue) and *tolmeroteron* (more boldly).

Paul used the word *steko* many times in his writing: "Be on your guard; stand firm in the faith; be courageous; be strong" (1 Cor. 16:13); "It is for freedom that Christ has set us free. Stand firm, then, and do not let yourselves be burdened again by a yoke of slavery" (Gal. 5:1); "Whatever happens, conduct yourselves in a manner worthy of the gospel of Christ. Then, whether I come and see you or only hear about you in my absence, I will know that you stand firm in the one Spirit, striving together as one for the faith of the gospel" (Phil. 1:27); and, "So then, brothers and sisters, stand firm and hold fast to the teachings we passed on to you, whether by word of mouth or by letter" (2 Thess. 2:15).

The Greek word *steko* sounds a bit like the English word *stick*. The meaning is certainly appropriate. According to thesaurus.com, *stick* can have several connotations. As a verb, it can mean to adhere, endure, become embedded, remain, or it can mean to prod, stab, or pierce. As a noun, a stick is a staff, a stake, or a branch. This is a fitting image because it is as if Paul is saying, "You must take yourself, full of faith, and stand tall like a staff. Choose your position, and stab yourself into that spot. Then become embedded there. Remain. Adhere. Endure."

## Digesting the Joy

Take a look at how six different translations of the Bible render *steko*, to stand firm or to be steadfast, in Philippians 4:1. What particular words do they use to remind us of the concept of standing fast?

My dear, dear friends! I love you so much. I do want the very best for you. You make me feel such joy, fill me with such pride. Don't waver. Stay on track, steady in God (MSG).

Therefore, my dear brothers and sisters, stay true to the Lord. I love you and long to see you, dear friends, for you are my joy and the crown I receive for my work (NLT).

Dear friends, I love you and long to see you. Please keep on being faithful to the Lord. You are my pride and joy (CEV).

Therefore, my beloved and longed-for brethren, my joy and crown, so stand fast in the Lord, beloved (NKJV).

My dear brothers and sisters, I love you and want to see you. You bring me joy and make me proud of you, so stand strong in the Lord as I have told you (NCV).

Therefore, my brethren most dear-worthy and most desired, my joy and my crown, so stand ye in the Lord, most dear brethren (WYCLIFFE).

Paul was not beginning a new thought in this verse. He was completing a thought started in Philippians 3:20-21: "Our citizenship is in heaven. And we eagerly await a Savior from there, the Lord Jesus Christ, who, by the power that enables him to bring everything under his control, will transform our lowly bodies so that they will be like his glorious body." And *then* he says, "Therefore, my brothers and sisters, you whom I love and long for, my joy and crown, stand firm in the Lord in this way, dear friends!"

Therefore, don't waver; stay on track; stay steady; stay true; keep on being faithful; stand fast; stand strong; stand in the Lord. Love the Lord your God with all our heart and with all your soul and with all your mind and with all your strength.

Paul absolutely understood that *sticking to* the faith would take both confidence in and remembrance of the One who had saved them, who had sustained them thus far, and who was coming for them one day.

## Living Your Joy Out Loud

I am reminded of three men who had planted their feet firmly in God's Word. Their names were Shadrach, Meshach, and Abednego, and their story is in the third chapter of the book of Daniel. Having heard the Scriptures since childhood, they knew by heart this text in Exodus:

I am the Lord thy God, which have brought thee out of the land of Egypt, out of the house of bondage. Thou shalt have no other gods before me. Thou shalt not make unto thee any graven image, or any likeness of any thing that is in heaven above, or that is in the earth beneath, or that is in the water under the earth. Thou shalt not bow down thyself to them, nor serve them: for I the Lord thy God am a jealous God.

Exodus 20:2-5, KJV

These men stood firm in their convictions. They were far from home in the land of Babylon, among pagans who bowed down to idols and who worshipped the image of gold King Nebuchadnezzar had set up. But God had blessed them in that land. King Nebuchadnezzar had been pleased with them and advanced their positions in his kingdom.

Shadrach, Meshach, and Abednego never used weasel words concerning their devotion to the Lord. They were the very definition of standing firm in the faith, being courageous, and being strong. And even if it meant their lives, they refused to bow down to the golden idol. Nebuchadnezzar was furious with them, and he ordered the furnace heated seven times hotter than usual and commanded some of the strongest soldiers in his army to tie up Shadrach, Meshach, and Abednego and throw them into the blazing furnace. The fire, however, did not harm the men. In fact, not a single hair on their heads was singed, their robes were not scorched, and there was no smell of fire on them.

Shadrach, Meshach, and Abednego stuck to the faith of our fathers with confidence in and remembrance of the One who had saved them.

The religion of Islam is based upon five pillars. Muslims believe that if they do these five things throughout their lives, they will go to heaven. The Five Pillars of Islam are:

1.  Confession ("There is no god but Allah, and Mohammed is his prophet.").
2.  Praying five times a day, facing Mecca.
3.  Giving alms (2.5% of their income) to the poor.
4.  Fasting from sunup to sundown during the holy month of Ramadan.
5.  Making a pilgrimage to Mecca at least once in one's lifetime (this pilgrimage is called the Hajj).

Christianity has only one pillar, and that is Jesus Christ. When we accept Jesus as our Savior and Lord and invite him into our lives, we become pillars as well, and just like Jesus, we can withstand the trials by fire in this life.

## Joy in Communion with Christ

Take some time to pray, thanking God for our pillar, Jesus Christ. Ask him to help you stand firm, stay on track, stay true to him. Then go to YouTube.com and search Lincoln Brewster's "Love the Lord."[21] Listen to this song, and as you begin to catch on to the tune, sing along.

# YOKEFELLOW

IN THE MIDST of a heated quarrel a husband blasted at his wife, "You know, I was a fool when I married you." Smirking, she replied, "Yes, dear, I know, but I was in love and didn't notice."

Many a foolish man and infatuation-blinded woman have yoked themselves together in marriage and come to question or even regret the decision later. But the foolish and blind are not the only ones with ups and downs in marriage.

My husband and I discussed and decided early in our courtship that we would not use the "D" word—divorce. Now that doesn't mean I haven't at times thought the grass might be greener in another yard, and I'm sure my almost perfect, certainly more-perfect-than-I husband has wondered the same thing. We can even identify with the old joke, "Divorce? Never! Murder? That's another matter!"

## The Joyful Truth

In 2 Corinthians 6:14, the apostle Paul uses an interesting metaphor: "Do not be yoked together with unbelievers. For what do righteousness and wickedness have in common? Or what fellowship can light have with darkness?" Can you get a picture in your mind of a husband and wife "yoked together"?

I can imagine it quite easily, because growing up as a missionaries' kid, I had the privilege of traveling in Southeast Asia and observed firsthand the teams of water buffalo yoked together. And if you ask me, that yoke looked like a heavy, loathsome burden on two tired, resigned beasts. With this sort of oppression illustrated right before my very eyes, it is a wonder I wanted to get married at all. And it's no wonder Matthew 11:28-30 confused me for a while. Jesus, addressing the crowds, said, "Come to me, all you who are weary and burdened, and I will give you rest. Take my yoke upon you and learn from me, for I am gentle and humble in heart, and you will find rest for your souls. For my yoke is easy and my burden is light."

*Come to me, all you who are weary and burdened? Are you picturing the yoked water buffalo? Take my yoke upon you? I thought we were going to rest! For my yoke is easy and my burden is light? What is it made out of? Styrofoam?*

Jesus' compassion for the masses of people under the oppression of the Pharisaic law compelled him to invite them to a different kind of life. It was not an unyoked, undisciplined life. The difference was in the yokefellow. Jesus was saying, "Rather than yoking yourself with the Law, which leaves all the work to you, yoke yourself with Me, and I will carry the weight. The only thing is, you will have to go in the direction I go, or you will feel the pull of the yoke on your neck once more" (my paraphrase). Now that I understand this passage of Scripture, it is one of my favorites!

"Do not be yoked together with unbelievers," Paul teaches us. "For what do righteousness and wickedness have in common? Or what fellowship can light have with darkness?" Though many Christians tend to apply its directive almost exclusively to marriage, that was not Paul's intention. In fact, the sixth chapter of Second Corinthians is a plea to the Christ-followers of Corinth to stay under Jesus' light yoke.

Think about this: If you have allowed Jesus to put his yoke on you and are walking along with him, one of two things must happen if you want to become yoked with anyone else. Either that person *must* come under Jesus' yoke with you, or you have to step out from under Jesus' yoke to get under the other person's and go his or her way. I am not saying that being unyoked from Jesus means losing one's salvation; I don't believe that at all. What I am talking about is achieving success for God's glory.

In this aspect of life, we can't partner with Jesus and with someone else who isn't partnered with Jesus. One paraphrase expresses this quite well: "Please don't squander one bit of this marvelous life God has given us. . . Don't become partners with those who reject God. How can you make a partnership out of right and wrong? That's not partnership; that's war. Is light best friends with darkness? Does Christ go strolling with the Devil? Do trust and mistrust hold hands? Who would think of setting up pagan idols in God's holy Temple? But that is exactly what we are, each of us a temple in whom God lives" (2 Cor. 6:1, 14-16, MSG).

We have all seen teams of horses attached to wagons. The idea is that two or four animals will produce twice as much power or four times as much power to pull the wagon. This power is an awesome thing when all the animals go in the same direction. Let's suppose all four horses were attached to the coach, but each horse was allowed to choose his own direction to pull. The wagon would overturn at the least and could be broken into pieces, ruining the cargo. The purpose for which the horses were employed—to pull the wagon in a safe and timely manner in a single direction—would be defeated.

As Christians, yoking ourselves together with people who are of the same mind and heart is vital—in our marriages, in our businesses, and in our churches. The purpose for the union is the glorification of Jesus Christ, and if one member of the team has another plan, then the whole purpose can be spoiled.

> I plead with Euodia and I plead with Syntyche to be of the same mind in the Lord. Yes, and I ask you, my true companion, help these women since they have contended at my side in the cause of the gospel, along with Clement and the rest of my co-workers, whose names are in the book of life.
>
> Philippians 4:2-3

The Greek word translated "true companion" ("yokefellow" in the KJV and ASV) is actually not a noun but an adjective, *syzgos or synzygos,* meaning "yoked together; united by the bond of marriage, relationship, office, labor, study, business, or the like." The prefix *sy- or syn-* means "together" or "same" (synthesis, synchronized, synagogue, syndicate). Some scholars believe this was an actual person's name: Syzygus. And that would make sense, since Paul seems to be speaking to specific people in this paragraph. But the plea could have been made to anyone who had remained true to the cause of the gospel.

Basically, what Paul is saying is, "You are a fellow who is yoked with me. We are working together, at the same time, in the same direction, for the same purpose, and for the same Master. Help these women who have been yoked with us to get back under the yoke." The cause is the gospel, the greatest cause ever to be undertaken.

## Digesting the Joy

There is an irony in the names of the women who were having a disagreement. The name "Syntyche" is built from the prefix *syn*, meaning "together," and *tynchano*, meaning "to take part in" or "to be extraordinary." The name Euodia is a Greek word which means "good-scentedness, fragrance, or sweet-smelling."

My name is Joy, and at times people have said to me, "You have the perfect name" or "You really live up to your name!" At other times, I've felt great conviction for making a mockery of my name.

These two women in Philippi to whom Paul was writing were shaming their names. They who had formerly been under the yoke of Jesus had stepped out from under it and gone their own ways. Unfortunately, the whole church was being affected by their conflict. I have said this before, and I'll say it again: One woman's emotions can easily direct the whole household's emotions. And obviously, two women's disagreement could just as easily infect the whole church, and thereby its effectiveness in spreading the gospel.

Paul uses strong language here. He pleads with them and tells them, in essence, "Get back under the yoke of Jesus!" Imagine him down on his knees begging these women to forget their differences. Envision him recruiting others to implore them as well. I expect he was also lifting numerous prayers heavenward concerning the women. This business was a serious thing.

There was someone else on their knees pleading for those he loved, and it was the Lord Jesus:

> I have revealed you to those whom you gave me out of the world. They were yours; you gave them to me and they have obeyed your word. Now they know that everything you have given me comes from you. For I gave them the words you gave me and they accepted them. They knew with certainty that I came from you, and they believed that you sent me. I pray for them. I am not praying for the world, but for those you have given me, for they are yours... My prayer is not that you take them out of the world but that you protect them from the evil one. They are not of the world, even as I am not of it . . . . My prayer is not for them alone. I pray also for those who will believe in me through their message, that all of them may be one, Father, just as you are in me and I am in you... May they be brought to complete unity to let the world know that you sent me and have loved them even as you have loved me.
>
> John 17:6-16, 20-23

First, Jesus prayed for his disciples. He described them as the ones who believed Jesus was sent from God, who accepted the message Jesus had brought, and who obeyed the message. Essentially, they had come under the yoke of Jesus. Jesus prayed that God would protect them from the world, because the evil one is rampant in the world and would try to entice them to come out from under Jesus' yoke. Jesus then prayed for all those who would come to believe in him in the future. His prayer was for unity. In other words, Jesus prayed that all of them [us] would come under his yoke as well, "to let the world know that you sent me and have loved them even as you have loved me."

The primary consideration for Jesus was that the world would know of God's love, and this was why Paul wanted the two women to forget their differences. Before, their objective had been to live the gospel of Jesus Christ and his love. He wanted them to get back to it.

## Living Your Joy Out Loud

Imagine yourself among the believers during this event with Ananias and his wife Sapphira from the book of Acts:

> Now a man named Ananias, together with his wife Sapphira, also sold a piece of property. With his wife's full knowledge he kept back part of the money for himself, but brought the rest and put it at the apostles' feet. Then Peter said, "Ananias, how is it that Satan has so filled your heart that you have lied to the Holy Spirit and have kept for yourself some of the money you received for the land? Didn't it belong to you before it was sold? And after it was sold, wasn't the money at your disposal? What made you think of doing such a thing? You have not lied just to human beings but to God." When Ananias heard this, he fell down and died. And great fear seized all who heard what had happened. Then some young men came forward, wrapped up his body, and carried him out and buried him. About three hours later his wife came in, not knowing what had happened. Peter asked her, "Tell me, is this the price you and Ananias got for the land?" "Yes," she said, "that is the price." Peter said to her, "How could you conspire to test the Spirit of the Lord? Listen! The feet of the men who buried your husband are at the door, and they will carry you out also." At that moment she fell down at his feet and died. Then the young men came in and, finding her dead, carried her out and buried her beside her husband. Great fear seized the whole church and all who heard about these events.
>
> Acts 5:1-11

Everyone in the church at Jerusalem was under the yoke of Jesus, going in his direction, loving each other and living by his power, with the result that there was unity to the glory of God the Father and Christ Jesus, his Son. Then Satan attacked. He filled the hearts of Ananias and Sapphira, who lied not only to the apostles but to the Holy Spirit of God.

Jesus knew this would occur. Before he died he prayed specifically that the Father would protect the believers from the Evil One. From personal experience, Jesus was aware of Satan's tactics. Just when God's glory seems to be unstoppable, the Devil pounces.

In Jesus' case, just after he had been baptized and was full of the Holy Spirit, Satan went out with him into the wilderness. He thought Jesus would weaken over time and tempted him in the area of three appetites: physical (food), emotional (pride), and mental (power). As he does with all temptation, Satan tried separating the other appetites from the spiritual. Warren

Wiersbe wrote, "Whenever we label different spheres of our lives 'physical,' 'material,' 'financial,' or 'spiritual,' we are bound to leave God out of areas where He rightfully belongs. Christ must be first in *everything* or He is first in nothing (Matt. 6:33)."[22]

The early church seemed unstoppable. They were united in purpose and joy. So Satan attacked a weak link. Ananias and Sapphira didn't understand that the glory in the church's midst was for God alone. They wanted some of that glory, and Satan tempted them, just as he had tempted Jesus in the wilderness. Jesus refused to take the glory from God, but Ananias and Sapphira did not. They schemed to test the Spirit of the Lord. In their pride they chose to get out from under the yoke of Jesus and make a name for themselves.

All who know Jesus as Lord and Savior are yokefellows to everyone else who knows him. As one of my pastors used to say, "Fellowship does not merely mean food and fun. It means we are all fellows in the same ship." And that ship sails a rocky sea while we live in this world.

The Enemy likes nothing better than convincing people to jump ship, and he does it by tempting us to think we are somehow due some personal provision or glory or power. May we remember that we are yokefellows (soul mates) with Christ, who, even when he was hanging on the cross, would not call down personal provision, use his own personal power, or claim for himself the glory belonging to his Father. We are also yokefellows (soul mates) with our brothers and sisters in Christ, and as such we must depend on the strength of God so all the world will know "that you sent me and have loved them even as you have loved me" (John 17:23).

Are we under the yoke of Jesus? Think about your marriage. Are you having trouble with letting your husband lead your home? Do you refuse to submit to him, for whatever reasons? Do you habitually "have a headache"? Are you a control freak? Have you given your children reason to discredit their father? Can you honestly say that next to the Lord your husband is the most important person to you, or has he fallen way down in the ranks? These are classic symptoms of putting aside the yoke of Jesus. When we put that aside, the negative effects become obvious in our households. How could our marriages and our lives be different if we got back under the yoke of Jesus and lived our joy out loud?

## Joy in Communion with Christ

Take a few minutes and go to YouTube.com, and search "Take my Life and Let it Be—Christ for the Nations worship." Sing from your heart and make this song your prayer.

"Take My Life and Let It Be"

Take my life and let it be
Consecrated, Lord, to Thee.
Take my moments and my days,
Let them flow in endless praise.
Take my hands and let them move
At the impulse of Thy love.
Take my feet and let them be
Swift and beautiful for Thee.
Take my voice and let me sing,
Always, only for my King.
Take my lips and let them be
Filled with messages from Thee.
Take my silver and my gold,
Not a mite would I withhold.
Take my intellect and use
Every pow'r as Thou shalt choose.
Take my will and make it Thine,
It shall be no longer mine.
Take my heart, it is Thine own,
It shall be Thy royal throne.
Take my love, my Lord, I pour
At Thy feet its treasure store.
Take myself and I will be
Ever, only, all for Thee.

If you've gotten out from under the yoke of Jesus, use this time to pray and repent and get back under. Remember Jesus' words: "My yoke is easy, and my burden is light."

# CHEERLEADER

OUR OLDEST DAUGHTER, Grace, and her husband, Jonathan, lived in New York City from 2004 to 2011. My husband and I tried to visit at least once a year, and every time we went, Grace took us around to museums and cafes, to her office and the places where she volunteered, to parks and to the neighborhood churches she attended. In practically every place, people regaled us with what a wonderful, loving daughter we have. I mean lots of people—café servers, fellow workers, homeless senior adults, church officials, and many others. She had a positive impact on all kinds of people in all walks of life. But I'm getting ahead of myself.

When Grace was a newborn, she cried a lot. When she was only nine days old, she was hospitalized with neonatal sepsis, the fancy name for "This newborn has an infection, and we don't really know what it is, but we think this is why she is crying so much." For ten days, they poked and prodded her little body. Every time she would finally fall asleep, they would come in to take her blood or mess with her IV or take her temperature. She would end up crying her heart out, and then they would tell me to try calming her by breastfeeding her. So I tried, but I was scared and sad and exhausted. Somehow my milk didn't pacify her! Finally, we got to go home, but neither Grace nor I got much sleep over the next few weeks.

One night in early May, I slept all night. When I woke up, my eyes shot open! Grace! I ran into her room to look in the crib. Was she dead? No, that little bundle was sleeping soundly. Whew, was that a frightening experience! Of course, David and I laughed about it, and as badly as it scared us, we were ready to try a few more nights like that one. Unfortunately, Grace wasn't. Later that month we moved from South Carolina to Alabama, and it wasn't until we were firmly settled in our new home that Grace slept all night again.

Not only were the nights miserable, but she was unhappy during the days as well. The evening hours from five to eight were horrendous. We tried every lullaby, patting technique, and dance step known to man to make her stop crying, but usually to no avail. Many of you know exactly what I'm talking about.

Along about early July, when Grace was three-and-a-half months old, she began looking at us in a different way. Before, we had been the fumbling enemy (I credit it to nervousness on our part), but suddenly, we were friends, confidants even. She began cooing at us and smacking her lips in satisfaction. She would giggle when we played "Peek-a-boo" or kissed her darling feet. She nursed gratefully, burped dutifully, and napped peacefully. In short, she got happy. And for the most part, she has had a cheerful way about her ever since.

One of my favorite memories of Grace's happy disposition revolves around her love of cheerleading. She joined a rec league cheerleading squad when she was in the sixth grade, and no one ever loved it more. I think it fed her inborn hunger for the theatrical. She loved her fellow "cast" members, loved the "stage," loved the "costumes," loved the "choreography," and loved her "lines." Everywhere she went, she jumped and pumped her arms and made cheers out of simple sentences. Everyone in our family can remember Grace's favorite cheer (each * is a clap):

I * en-<u>joy</u>ed it * * so <u>ve</u>-ry <u>much</u> ! * <u>Let's</u> have some <u>more</u> * * <u>green</u> <u>beans</u>!

Or some part of whatever we had had for dinner that night. Such as

<u>Let's</u> have some <u>more</u> * * ma-ca-<u>ro</u>-ni!
<u>Let's</u> have some <u>more</u> * * <u>Ham</u>-burger <u>Help</u>-er!

If you invited David, Grace, Shelley, Hillary, Heather, and me over for dinner tonight and asked us to do the cheer, we could do it in unison, with identical inflections and maybe even synchronized movements. We learned well because, I'm telling you, Grace cheered after practically every meal. And it was a delight!

She continued cheering through the tenth grade, and then something very difficult happened. The philosophy of our high school's cheerleading program began to change with the times, moving from basic yet excellent cheering to cheering with a huge emphasis on tumbling. The audition bar was raised to include several kinds of tumbling tricks, and although we encouraged Grace and paid for tumbling classes, it was a challenge too big for her. Before the day of tryouts for the following year, the cheerleading sponsor warned her that she just didn't have the skills it was going to take to make the team. So Grace conceded it was pointless to try out.

My happy, roll-with-the-punches sixteen-year-old daughter came home from that practice and sobbed in my arms. I still get choked up thinking about it. For a while, her spirits seemed to flag. She had to make some new friends, because all of her friends were busy cheering. I was uncertain about some of the people she began hanging around, and a few of them were not the best influence on a hurting teenager. But many of them started coming to our house now and then, and I began noticing something: They liked being around Grace, because she was full of love and joy. She truly cared for them and "cheered" for them.

## The Joyful Truth

Philippians is sometimes called the epistle of joy. Though Paul wrote from a prison cell, persecuted for his preaching of the gospel, and though he was dependent on his friends for food, clothes, and every other miscellaneous need, this letter to the Christians of Philippi is a testimony of the apostle's joy and encouragement.

> Therefore, my brothers and sisters, you whom I love and long for, my joy and crown, stand firm in the Lord in this way, dear friends! I plead with Euodia and I plead with Syntyche to be of the same mind in the Lord. Yes, and I ask you, my true companion, help these women since they have contended at my side in the cause of the gospel, along with Clement and the rest of my co-workers, whose names are in the book of life. Rejoice in the Lord always. I will say it again: Rejoice! Let your gentleness be evident to all. The Lord is near.
>
> Philippians 4:1-5

The word "rejoice" is the Greek word *chairo*, which means "to be delighted; to be cheerful; to be calmly well-off; or to be well." Notice that the connotation is not a continuous giddiness of spirit but rather a calm assurance that in the Lord we will always fare well. This theme of not being afraid because God is on our side is found elsewhere in Scripture. For example: "The word of the Lord came to Abram in a vision: 'Do not be afraid, Abram. I am your shield, your very great reward'" (Gen. 15:1); "'I am the God of your father Abraham. Do not be afraid, for I am with you; I will bless you and will increase the number of your descendants for the sake of my servant Abraham" (Gen. 26:24); "Do not be afraid of them; the Lord your God himself will fight for you" (Deut. 3:22); and, "The Lord himself goes before you and will be with you; he will never leave you nor forsake you. Do not be afraid; do not be discouraged" (Deut. 31:8).

Philippians 4:5 reads, "Rejoice! Let your gentleness be evident to all. The Lord is near." The word translated "near" is the Greek term *eggus*, which can mean near in a literal way, or near in a figurative way. The Lord is at hand; he is near in space and time. The word *eggus* can even mean "ready."

What is the Lord ready for? In the context of this chapter, it seems he is ready to help us stand firm. He is ready to fill us with joy. Paul was saying, "You are my joy, and I want you to be a joy to one another. Have joy! Let joy be your witness—because Jesus is among us in spirit and he is coming back soon in his new bodily form to take us to heaven with him!"

We've got this thing called joy that the presence of Christ has given us, that cannot be taken away from us, and that sets us apart from those who depend on circumstances to make them happy. So let's be joyful. Let's live our joy out loud! Always.

## Digesting the Joy

In a message entitled "Joy and Godliness," John MacArthur writes that, "A good definition of joy is this: it's the flag that flies on the castle of the heart when the King is in residence there." He goes on to say that, "Joy is a gift from God that is mixed with trials. In fact, joy is most clearly evident in the midst of trials."[23]

My mama used to say, "One of the good things about wearing a girdle is that it feels so good when you take if off!" And what about those first days of spring when the birds are singing at 5:00 AM and the buttercups are raising their heads towards the sun? Aren't they marvelous? And the first few nights a baby sleeps all night long? Nothing can compare to that luxury of seven or eight straight hours of rest!

Unfortunately, most of us gradually forget the glorious freedom of the un-girdled hips, the enchantment of spring's appearance after a long, hard winter, or the thankfulness we feel for a good night's sleep. Most of the time we live life in our old, humdrum ways and take our joys for granted.

One of my favorite stories in the New Testament comes to mind:

Now Peter and John were going up together to the temple complex at the hour of prayer at three in the afternoon. And a man who was lame from birth was carried there and placed every day at the temple gate called Beautiful, so he could beg from those entering the temple complex. When he saw Peter and John about to enter the temple complex, he asked for help. Peter, along with John, looked at him intently and said, "Look at us." So he turned to them, expecting to get something from them. But Peter said, "I don't have silver or gold, but what I have, I give you: In the name of Jesus Christ the Nazarene, get up and walk!" Then, taking him by the right hand he raised him up, and at once his feet and ankles became strong. So he jumped up, stood, and started to walk, and he entered the temple complex with them—walking, leaping, and praising God.

Acts 3:1-8, HCSB

Now, that man was a cheerleader! Surprisingly, undeservedly, God had given him new life. He had begged for something tangible, something small, but he had received the intangible, wholehearted mercy of God. The girdle of his lame legs had been thrown off. The long, dark winter of his life was over! He could finally have a "good night's rest" from the constant oppression of poverty and dependency. Not only did he walk into the temple, he leaped with unadulterated joy and worship.

The next verse, verse 9, tells us that all the people saw him walking and praising God. I wonder if he had already quit leaping. Had he decided the temple was no place for dancing and praising? Had he suddenly started feeling self-conscious or insecure? We know he hadn't forgotten so quickly the wonder and freedom of God's mercy, for he was continuing to praise God. Maybe he had settled into real joy, that quiet assurance and overwhelming gratefulness that God had noticed him and had acted on his behalf.

My daughter, Grace, was not a cheerleader only when she was wildly yelling and leaping about, but also when she was just hanging out with friends or working in a soup kitchen. We have been given freedom through the shed blood of Jesus Christ our Lord. At times that knowledge makes us smile, sing, and shout "Hallelujah." But we are no less cheerleaders when we are quietly seeking to serve God through tough or humdrum times.

## Living Your Joy Out Loud

**This "cheer" of David's gives us** a better understanding of the joy the Lord brings when he comes to reside in us:

That day David first appointed Asaph and his associates to give praise to the Lord in this manner: Give praise to the Lord, proclaim his name; make known among the nations what he has done. Sing to him, sing praise to him; tell of all his wonderful acts. Glory in his holy name; let the hearts of those who seek the Lord rejoice. Look to the Lord and his strength; seek his face always. Remember the wonders he has done, his miracles, and the judgments he pronounced, you his servants, the descendants of Israel, his chosen ones, the children of Jacob. He is the Lord our God; his judgments are in all the earth. He remembers his covenant forever, the promise he made, for a thousand generations, the covenant he made with Abraham, the oath he swore to Isaac.... Sing to the Lord, all the earth; proclaim his salvation day after day. Declare his glory among the nations, his marvelous deeds among all peoples. For great is the

Lord and most worthy of praise; he is to be feared above all gods. For all the gods of the nations are idols, but the Lord made the heavens. Splendor and majesty are before him; strength and joy are in his dwelling place. Ascribe to the Lord, all you families of nations, ascribe to the Lord glory and strength. Ascribe to the Lord the glory due his name; bring an offering and come before him. Worship the Lord in the splendor of his holiness. Tremble before him, all the earth! The world is firmly established; it cannot be moved. Let the heavens rejoice, let the earth be glad; let them say among the nations, "The Lord reigns!" Let the sea resound, and all that is in it; let the fields be jubilant, and everything in them! Let the trees of the forest sing, let them sing for joy before the Lord, for he comes to judge the earth. Give thanks to the Lord, for he is good; his love endures forever.

1 Chronicles 16:7-16, 23-34

Why should we rejoice and give thanks to the Lord? Because of all his wonderful acts. Because of his strength, the wonders he has done, his miracles, and the judgments he pronounced. Because of the promises he has made to his people. Because he made the heavens and is above all other gods. Because he reigns over the heavens and the earth. And because his love endures forever.

The Hebrew prophet Habakkuk also has a "cheer":

Though the fig tree does not bud and there are no grapes on the vines, though the olive crop fails and the fields produce no food, though there are no sheep in the pen and no cattle in the stalls, yet I will rejoice in the Lord, I will be joyful in God my Savior. The Sovereign Lord is my strength; he makes my feet like the feet of a deer, he enables me to tread on the heights.

Habakkuk 3:17-19

Whether the Lord's face is shining on us at the moment, or whether we are walking through a midnight hour, there is light within even when the light outside has dimmed. Following the models of David and Habakkuk, let's remember that we are cheerleaders, game day or not. "Yet he has not left himself without testimony: He has shown kindness by giving you rain from heaven and crops in their seasons; he provides you with plenty of food and fills your hearts with joy" (Acts 14:17).

A couple of winters ago, there was snow in every state but Hawaii. Snow after snow after snow in much of the mid-section of the country. I watched it snow for two days while sitting in my dad's apartment in Richmond, Virginia. It might have been nice, if Dad had been at home with me. But he was in the hospital, and I couldn't get there to be with him because my car was under two inches of snow, on top of which was a layer of ice, and then ten more inches of snow on top of that.

On the third day, I begged help from some young men who had a broom and a shovel. Once I was out on the roads, I began reflecting that you never know how really dirty the streets are until it snows and the dirt from the streets is kicked up by tires onto the mounds of snow at the edges of the roadways. Suddenly, the lovely, pristine expanses become eyesores of grimy snow clods and slush.

We want the gorgeous fields of fluffy white to last forever, and we want the ugly, dirty clumps on the shoulder of the roads to melt and disappear quickly. But what happens is the opposite. Even after the fields have returned to their winter green, the icy gray blobs on the roadsides persist for days and days like eighth-graders loitering behind the school gym.

God spoke to my soul that day by revealing the sin of my life never looks as horrid as when it is thrown onto my pure, beautiful Savior. How splendidly merciful, compassionate, and lenient he has been with my sordid soul. And on top of that, he instantaneously melts and flings the ugly stains as far as the east is from the west.

If I have loitering wayside clump reminders of my sin, Satan has put them there—not my Savior. Instead of grief, Jesus gives me hope and fills me with joy and peace. As Paul has written, "May the God of hope fill you with all joy and peace as you trust in him, so that you may overflow with hope by the power of the Holy Spirit" (Rom. 15:13).

Instead of leftovers, he gives an exquisite feast. Could there be a grander table, a more delectable menu than the love of our Father in sending his only Son to absorb our sin and die on a cross to absolve us? Once we've partaken of the meal, how can we not rejoice? How can we not say, "I * enjoyed it * * so very much!"

## Joy in Communion with Christ

I encourage you to go to hymnal.net, search, and sing "Rejoice, the Lord is King."

### "REJOICE, THE LORD IS KING"
(Charles Wesley, 1744)

Rejoice, the Lord is King! Your Lord and King adore;
Mortals give thanks and sing, and triumph evermore;
Lift up your heart, lift up your voice; Rejoice, again I say, rejoice!

Jesus, the Savior, reigns, the God of truth and love;
When He had purged our stains He took His seat above;
Lift up your heart, lift up your voice; Rejoice, again I say, rejoice!

His kingdom cannot fail, He rules o'er earth and Heav'n,
The keys of death and hell are to our Jesus giv'n;
Lift up your heart, lift up your voice; Rejoice, again I say, rejoice!

He sits at God's right hand till all His foes submit,
And bow to His command, and fall beneath His feet:
Lift up your heart, lift up your voice; Rejoice, again I say, rejoice!

He all His foes shall quell, shall all our sins destroy,
And every bosom swell with pure seraphic joy;
Lift up your heart, lift up your voice, Rejoice, again I say, rejoice!

Rejoice in glorious hope! Jesus the Judge shall come,
And take His servants up to their eternal home.
We soon shall hear the archangel's voice; the trump of God shall sound, rejoice!

Spend some time in prayer, rejoicing at the banquet table the Lord your King has prepared for you.

# PRESENTER

A COUPLE OF years ago my husband and I had the great delight of attending our oldest daughter's commencement from graduate school. After the ceremony, while Grace, Jonathan, David, and I were having a late dinner, we discussed the occasion in detail. Jonathan remarked, "The keynote speaker had some good things to say, but he is definitely not a speaker."

This comment reminded me of something my mother used to say to me. "It's not just what you say, Joy. It's how you say it." Weren't Jonathan and my mother right? Some people present things in such a way that you want to listen, you want to respond, and you want to agree. Others are just boring or offensive. I love Ward Elliot Hour's observation that "People are like holidays. Do others see you as Christmas or more like Tax Day?"

Paul evidently thinks the Philippians need to sharpen up their presentation skills. He has been trying to emphasize the value of standing firm and rejoicing in the Lord. Now he explains that one of their problems may be how they present their requests to God.

## The Joyful Truth

Do not be anxious about anything, but in every situation, by prayer and petition, with thanksgiving, present your requests to God. And the peace of God, which transcends all understanding, will guard your hearts and your minds in Christ Jesus.

Philippians 4:6-7

The word used for "present" in Greek is *gnorizo*, which means "to make known, tell, reveal, declare, or give to understand." It is the same word that is italicized in the following Scriptures:

When the angels had left them and gone into heaven, the shepherds said to one another, "Let's go to Bethlehem and see this thing that has happened, which the Lord has *told* us about."

Luke 2:15

I no longer call you servants, because a servant does not know his master's business. Instead, I have called you friends, for everything that I learned from my Father I have *made known* to you.

John 15:15

And he *made known* to us the mystery of his will according to his good pleasure, which he purposed in Christ.

Ephesians 1:9

If I am to go on living in the body, this will mean fruitful labor for me. Yet what shall I choose? I do *not know*!

Philippians 1:22

To them God has chosen to *make known* among the Gentiles the glorious riches of this mystery, which is Christ in you, the hope of glory.

Colossians 1:27

For we did not follow cleverly devised stories when we *told* you about the coming of our Lord Jesus Christ in power, but we were eyewitnesses of his majesty.

2 Peter 1:16

Notice that most of the verses are about God making himself known to us. What an incredible thing that the Creator of the universe wants to reveal himself to us and has actually done so through Jesus Christ. And here's something even more incredible. He wants the same kind of revelation from us. He wants us to "let it all hang out"—to completely reveal ourselves to him.

God wants conversation, not a text message or quick tweet. He wants to know in detail what the :) or the :( means. Someone may say, "But if God already knows everything, why do I need to tell him?" Because relationships are best nurtured by communication. You know what it feels like when your husband or your friend or your child is silent towards you. Maybe they are brooding, or they might have a quiet personality, or they might just be feeling ill. But you still want them to talk to you. You want to be able to help or pray or rejoice; more than that, you need the interaction.

Picture the following scene:

> People were bringing little children to Jesus for him to place his hands on them, but the disciples rebuked them. When Jesus saw this, he was indignant. He said to them, "Let the little children come to me, and do not hinder them, for the kingdom of God belongs to such as these. Truly I tell you, anyone who will not receive the kingdom of God like a little child will never enter it." And he took the children in his arms, placed his hands on them and blessed them.
>
> Mark 10:13-16

Everyone agrees that Jesus was teaching his disciples a lesson here. But consider another aspect of the story.

Jesus took the children in his arms. Jesus is not Santa Claus, but think about how children react to sitting in Santa's lap. Don't you imagine the children of that day did some of the same things? Some probably started crying the moment their parents put them in Jesus' lap. No doubt some were completely awed by the aura of Jesus' presence and sat there in stunned silence. Others may have talked Jesus' ears off. They introduced themselves, told him stories and asked him questions, perhaps even inappropriate ones (with their parents' faces turning scarlet in the background).

I can hear a seven or eight-year-old boy, whose parents might have been curious bystanders that day, asking, "Who are you?" When Jesus answers, "I'm Jesus," I can hear the boy replying, "*I've* never heard of you."

I can imagine that Jesus loved it when the children talked to him. It must have been refreshing to hear the viewpoints of young, untainted hearts. He must have laughed and maybe even cried. Jesus longed for all his followers to be as open and trusting as little children. After all, he said, "Truly I tell you, anyone who will not receive the kingdom of God like a little child will never enter it."

## Digesting the Joy

The Lord wants to hear from us. He wants to gather us in his arms where we can present ourselves to him. The fact is, a well-spoken word is like a caress. Our words show interest or disinterest, love or distaste, trust or distrust, gratefulness or disagreeableness. Do our presentation skills need sharpening? Remember:

Do not be anxious about anything, but in every situation, by prayer and petition, with thanksgiving, present your requests to God. And the peace of God, which transcends all understanding, will guard your hearts and your minds in Christ Jesus.

Philippians 4:6-7

There is a very explicit *how-to* in this presentation business. First and most important is the implied faith. Though we are often warned not to use the words *always* and *never*, Paul is saying, "Never worry. Always present your requests to God." So the first rule for being this type of presenter is to place complete faith in the One who is always listening in every situation.

The second thing is Paul's use of two different words for the presentation itself: *prayer* and *petition*. The New International Version of the Bible says, "By prayer and petition . . . present your requests to God." Some Bible translations, such as the King James Version, New American Standard, and the American Standard Version, say *prayer* and *supplication*, while the Contemporary English Version says *prayers* and *requests*. Could it be that Paul was saying that *praying* and *asking* are two different things? Is it like supplication (asking, requesting) is a package we give to God wrapped in prayer and tied up with faith?

If we look at the origin of *proseuche*, which is the Greek word for "prayer," we find it contains the prefix *pros*, meaning "to" or "for," and the root word *euche*, meaning "vow" or "oath." It is almost as if Paul is reminding us that we have a covenant with God and that every time we go to him in prayer, we need to remember that covenant. This idea was certainly behind one of David's psalms:

I love you, Lord, my strength. The Lord is my rock, my fortress and my deliverer; my God is my rock, in whom I take refuge, my shield and the horn of my salvation, my stronghold. . . . To the faithful you show yourself faithful, to the blameless you show yourself blameless, to the pure you show yourself pure, but to the devious you show yourself shrewd. You save the humble but bring low those whose eyes are haughty. You, Lord, keep my lamp burning; my God turns my darkness into light. With your help I can advance against a troop; with my God I can scale a wall. As for God, his way is perfect: The Lord's word is flawless; he shields all who take refuge in him. For who is God besides the Lord? And who is the Rock except our God?

Psalm 18:1-2, 25-31

David had great faith that God was his strength, rock, fortress, deliverer, salvation, and stronghold. And he had great faith in his covenant with God that if he remained faithful and humble God would keep his lamp burning: "To the faithful you show yourself faithful, to the blameless you show yourself blameless, to the pure you show yourself pure, . . . You, Lord, keep my lamp burning; my God turns my darkness into light." David was so thankful for God's delivering him from the hands of his enemies that he burst into this song of appreciation.

Like any father, God wants his children to be grateful for their many blessings. He wants them to be aware of his actions on their behalf and to express appropriate appreciation. But in the fourth chapter of Philippians, Paul asked the believers to go one step further. In effect he says, "Go ahead and thank God in advance, because he's got your best interests at heart."

A great example is my friend Melinda. She was enjoying a beach vacation with her family when her husband began feeling unwell and experienced pain in his left arm. Though he suffers from Parkinson's disease, he usually has a ball with the grandchildren at the beach. This time, uncharacteristically, he just sat around. Eventually, they decided to go to the emergency room. His EKG looked fine, so they figured the pain was part of his Parkinson's, and they came home. John did not begin feeling better, however, so they called his doctor, who ordered a heart catheterization.

During the procedure, the cardiologist found two blocked arteries, one ninety percent blocked and the other eighty-two percent blocked. When I spoke to Melinda later, she told me, "We are so thankful for the pain he was having. Otherwise, he might not be here."

I asked Melinda if they had expressed thankfulness to God for the pain John felt when they were at the beach praying John would feel better. She laughed and told me she's not sure she was thankful then, but she sure is now.

Effective presentation (prayer, asking, requesting) means thanking God for whatever is happening, even before he answers our prayers. And be assured, he always answers. Sometimes he says, "I'd love to do that for you." At other times he says, "You're not ready for that yet." And sometimes the answer is, "No, child, trust me. That wouldn't be in your best interest." It certainly wasn't in John's best interest for God to merely have relieved his pain when he was at the beach. Had that happened, Melinda and John would have never gone in for the heart catheterization. Of course, we can see that now.

Though we should welcome God's wisdom in choosing his responses to our requests, chances are we are not always that spiritually mature. Yet the only way to grow is to practice, and so Paul inserted the phrase *with thanksgiving* into the bundle when he said, "By prayer and petition, with thanksgiving, present your requests to God."

## Living Your Joy Out Loud

Let me say once more, some people present things in such a way that you want to listen, you want to respond, and you want to agree. Others are just boring or offensive. We are effective presenters, if by prayer and petition, with thanksgiving, we present our requests to God. And when we do, Philippians 4:7 tells us God responds in a positive manner: "And the peace of God, which transcends all understanding, will guard your hearts and your minds in Christ Jesus." Our omniscient God weighs the sincerity of our presentations, and if our prayers rise from pure hearts, untainted by manipulation or deceit, he grants peace. This peace that transcends has three amazing characteristics:

## It Transcends all Understanding

*Transcend* means "to pass beyond the limits of; to be greater than, in intensity and power; to exist above and independent of the material." God's peace, available through prayer, is truly indescribable. It's just there.

## It Guards our Hearts

Proverbs 4:23 says, "Guard your heart above all else, for it determines the course of your life" (NLT). God's peace, available through prayer, does this guarding for us. If we are tapped into divine power through prayer, we don't have to worry about being tossed around by our emotions, making foolish decisions, or falling into sin. God's peace will guard our hearts.

## It Guards our Minds

The Christians of Paul's time had the same problems we have. They were bombarded on every side by old and new philosophies, ungodly influences, and peer pressure. Paul urged them to guard their thoughts from these stimuli and reminded them of the power available. He wrote,

> For though we live in the world, we do not wage war as the world does. The weapons we fight with are not the weapons of the world. On the contrary, they have divine power to demolish strongholds. We demolish arguments and every pretension that sets itself up against the knowledge of God, and we take captive every thought to make it obedient to Christ.
>
> 2 Corinthians 10:3-5

When we present our prayers and supplications with thanksgiving, God endows us with peace that guards our minds. Every thought is kept captive to Christ.

## Joy in Communion with Christ

What do you need to "make known" to God today? How can you wrap it in thanksgiving? To help you, go to YouTube.com and search "What a Friend We Have in Jesus," Chonda Pierce/

full version. This video is 9.5 minutes, but well worth your time. If you don't have time right now, just sing this old hymn, paying close attention to the words.

### "What A Friend We Have in Jesus"
#### (Joseph Scriven, 1855)

What a friend we have in Jesus,
all our sins and griefs to bear!
What a privilege to carry
everything to God in prayer!
O what peace we often forfeit,
O what needless pain we bear,
all because we do not carry
everything to God in prayer.

Have we trials and temptations?
Is there trouble anywhere?
We should never be discouraged;
take it to the Lord in prayer.
Can we find a friend so faithful
who will all our sorrows share?
Jesus knows our every weakness;
take it to the Lord in prayer.

Are we weak and heavy laden,
cumbered with a load of care?
Precious Savior, still our refuge;
take it to the Lord in prayer.
Do thy friends despise, forsake thee?
Take it to the Lord in prayer!
In his arms he'll take and shield thee;
thou wilt find a solace there.

When you pray, do so believing, trusting, leaning, thanking, receiving peace.

# THINKER

MY HUSBAND, DAVID, is one of the smartest people I know. He understands all kinds of medical, financial, car, and sports stuff that my mind can't grasp. He was president of the slide rule club in high school (slide rules were the precursors of calculators). He was accepted to optometry school after only two years of college, and then graduated first in his class. I think you get my drift. He's brainy.

But my husband is unlike some smart people in that he actually uses his brain. In fact, you can tell when he is thinking hard. No, he doesn't sit down naked on a rock and put his chin on his fist. His eyes change. His eyebrows lower, and his eyes just stare up to the right. I try not to disturb him when he has that look on his face. I know eventually he will come out of the trance and tell me about it. Or not.

Right after the apostle Paul instructed the Philippians on prayer and promised that God would give a peace that would guard their minds, he continued his teaching with a lesson about what kind of thoughts are "smart" thoughts.

## The Joyful Truth

Finally, brothers and sisters, whatever is true, whatever is noble, whatever is right, whatever is pure, whatever is lovely, whatever is admirable—if anything is excellent or praiseworthy—think about such things.

Philippians 4:8

The Greek word for "think" is *logizomai*, which means "to credit, count, reckon, regard, think, or consider." We usually use *credit* as a noun, as in "I bought it on credit," or as an adjective, as in "What is your credit score?" As a verb it means "to acknowledge as sound; to believe it to be trustworthy." Evidently, credit cards were originally given only to those people who could be trusted to pay the money they owed. Imagine that!

In this context, Paul was saying that true, noble, right, pure, lovely, admirable things were trustworthy things to consider. Why? Because they are the opposite of quarrelsome and worrisome things, the two issues Paul previously addressed. And in fact, thinking these kinds of thoughts will produce true, noble, right, pure, lovely, admirable actions.

## Digesting the Joy

Since thoughts directly affect actions, thinking about the things Paul mentions in Philippians 4:8 is easier if we look at Christ's actions and trace those actions back to his thoughts. Then we can strive to make our thoughts like his. Though this is a difficult spiritual exercise, God will be faithful to bring us new understanding of the thoughts and actions of Jesus, and help us to work them out in our lives through the power of the Holy Spirit.

Paul told us to think true thoughts, noble thoughts, and right thoughts. What does this mean?

### TRUE THOUGHTS

True means genuine or trustworthy. We are bombarded daily with the world's idea of truth, and very often we are bombarded with the insistence that there is *no* absolute truth. It is a sad fact that genuine, trustworthy people are few and far between. We have to turn to Jesus to show us what it means to have true thoughts and even what it means to be true.

What do you suppose the Lord was thinking when the apostle Matthew recorded these moments?

Immediately Jesus made the disciples get into the boat and go on ahead of him to the other side, while he dismissed the crowd. After he had dismissed them, he went up on a mountainside by himself to pray. Later that night, he was there alone, and the boat was already a considerable distance from land, buffeted by the waves because the wind was against it. Shortly before dawn Jesus went out to them, walking on the lake. When the disciples saw him walking on the lake, they were terrified. "It's a ghost," they said, and cried out in fear. But Jesus immediately said to them: "Take courage! It is I. Don't be afraid." "Lord, if it's you," Peter replied, "tell me to come to you on the water." "Come," he said. Then Peter got down out of the boat, walked on the water and came toward Jesus. But when he saw the wind, he was afraid and, beginning to sink, cried out, "Lord, save me!" Immediately Jesus reached out his hand and caught him. "You of little faith," he said, "why did you doubt?"

Matthew 14:22-31

Jesus' actions in this instance suggest that his thoughts were controlled by power rather than pretention; mind rather than matter; faith rather than feelings. The truth was, he was walking on water through divine power and Peter could have done the same. But Peter's motive might have been a little pompous. On top of that, he suddenly started thinking about the fact that under his feet was wavy water, not solid ground. His final downfall (no pun intended) was that his faith faltered.

I recently had the privilege of hearing a preacher named David Ring. David was born with cerebral palsy and endured relentless teasing and discouraging remarks for many years. In addition, both of his parents died before he turned fifteen. He felt he had nothing to live for and no hope for eternity. Then he met Jesus Christ, and though the teasing and disheartening comments continued, he realized his purpose in life.

When David felt the call to preach, he went forward to tell his pastor, but the pastor told him to go sit down. David's speech is a little difficult to understand, and the pastor could not imagine God calling someone handicapped in that way to preach the Word. That pastor and many others of us would have been ones who said, "Get back in the boat, Peter. It's impossible to walk on water." But God continued pursuing David, and David continued saying yes—until someone finally believed him and helped him along on the journey.

David Ring has been preaching for over thirty years now, and he shares many truths from God's Word. There are two true thoughts he has spoken aloud to himself over and over. They are "I am blessed," and "God can and wants to use each person in ministry." These true thoughts are powerful, because they put the focus not on our weaknesses, but on where it belongs—the power of God.

## Noble Thoughts

Noble means of a magnanimous or generous nature. This definition suggests that noble thoughts are the kind of thoughts we should have when giving people the benefit of the doubt. A perfect example of this is found in Jesus' encounter with Zacchaeus:

Jesus entered Jericho and was passing through. A man was there by the name of Zacchaeus; he was a chief tax collector and was wealthy. He wanted to see who Jesus was, but because he was short he could not see over the crowd. So he ran ahead and climbed a sycamore-fig tree to see him, since Jesus was coming that way. When Jesus reached the spot, he looked up and said to him, "Zacchaeus, come down immediately. I must stay at your house today." So he came down at once and welcomed him gladly. All the people saw this and began to mutter, "He has gone to be the guest of a sinner." But Zacchaeus stood up and said to the Lord, "Look, Lord! Here and now I give half of my possessions to the poor, and if I have cheated anybody out of anything, I will pay back four times the amount." Jesus said to him, "Today salvation has come to this house, because this man, too, is a son of Abraham. For the Son of Man came to seek and to save the lost."

Luke 19:1-10

It wasn't that Jesus didn't know Zacchaeus had cheated his fellow citizens. It wasn't that Jesus was a pushover when dealing with rich tax collectors who worked at the behest of Rome. It wasn't even that he was trying to teach the crowd a lesson. What was it? Jesus had noble thoughts towards Zacchaeus. He came to Jericho to notice Zacchaeus, to speak to Zacchaeus, and to have lunch with Zacchaeus. Jesus' thoughts focused on compassion rather than condemnation. His generosity contrasted with the greed of Zacchaeus, so much so that Zacchaeus committed then and there to make amends. Likewise, our generous thoughts towards someone can translate into patient acts of love and redemption.

## RIGHT THOUGHTS

Right means righteous, upright, or without fault. This word is usually used in the context of God's thoughts towards situations. Let me give an example.

When I taught seventh grade, it was not uncommon for a student to declare something like, "I have the right to . . . ." Imagine the students' incredulity when I chimed in with, "It's not about rights. It's about doing what is right." What a novel idea, applying righteous thoughts to a situation and acting on those righteous thoughts instead of reacting out of our selfish motives. Jesus' actions showed his zeal for righteousness. He cleansed the temple twice during his three-year earthly ministry. This is the account of the second time:

When they arrived back in Jerusalem, Jesus entered the Temple and began to drive out the people buying and selling animals for sacrifices. He knocked over the tables of the money changers and the chairs of those selling doves, and he stopped everyone from using the Temple as a marketplace. He said to them, "The Scriptures declare, 'My Temple will be called a house of prayer for all nations,' but you have turned it into a den of thieves." When the leading priests and teachers of religious law heard what Jesus had done, they began planning how to kill him. But they were afraid of him because the people were so amazed at his teaching.

Mark 11:15-18, NLT

Warren Wiersbe states, "No doubt this 'religious market' began as a convenience for the Jews who came long distances to worship in the temple, but in due time the 'convenience' became a business, not a ministry."[24] Wiersbe also writes, "Suppose a foreign Jew carried his own sacrifice with him and then discovered that it was rejected, because of some blemish? The money rates were always changing, so the men who exchanged foreign currency were doing the visitors a favor, even though the merchants were making a generous profit. It was easy for them to rationalize the whole enterprise."[25]

Jesus made a right judgment concerning the situation. Why did he show righteous anger in this instance and yet have noble thoughts towards Zacchaeus, when in both cases the men were cheating others? I think it was because the men in the temple tried to pretend they were doing something helpful and kind, when their actual motive was greed. On the other hand, Zacchaeus never tried to pretend he was anything but shifty.

## Living Your Joy Out Loud

"Finally, brothers and sisters, whatever is true, whatever is noble, whatever is right, whatever is pure, whatever is lovely, whatever is admirable—if anything is excellent or praiseworthy—think about such things" (Phil. 4:8). We have discussed things that are true, noble, and right. But Paul also mentioned things that are pure, lovely, and admirable. The following passages reveal Jesus' thoughts on these themes:

### PURE (CHASTE OR UNBIASED)

Jesus cleanses a demon-possessed man (a Gentile):

They went across the lake to the region of the Gerasenes. When Jesus got out of the boat, a man with an impure spirit came from the tombs to meet him. This man lived in the tombs, and no one could bind him anymore, not even with a chain. For he had often been chained hand and foot, but he tore the chains apart and broke the irons on his feet. No one was strong enough to subdue him. Night and day among the tombs and in the hills he would cry out and cut himself with stones. When he saw Jesus from a distance, he ran and fell on his knees in front of him. He shouted at the top of his voice, "What do you want with me, Jesus, Son of the Most High God? In God's name don't torture me!" For Jesus had said to him, "Come out of this man, you impure spirit!" Then Jesus asked him, "What is your name?" "My name is

Legion," he replied, "for we are many. And he begged Jesus again and again not to send them out of the area. A large herd of pigs was feeding on the nearby hillside. The demons begged Jesus, "Send us among the pigs; allow us to go into them." He gave them permission, and the impure spirits came out and went into the pigs. The herd, about two thousand in number, rushed down the steep bank into the lake and were drowned. Those tending the pigs ran off and reported this in the town and countryside, and the people went out to see what had happened. When they came to Jesus, they saw the man who had been possessed by the legion of demons, sitting there, dressed and in his right mind; and they were afraid. Those who had seen it told the people what had happened to the demon-possessed man—and told about the pigs as well. Then the people began to plead with Jesus to leave their region. As Jesus was getting into the boat, the man who had been demon-possessed begged to go with him. Jesus did not let him, but said, "Go home to your own people and tell them how much the Lord has done for you, and how he has had mercy on you."

Mark 5:1-19

## LOVELY (FULL OF LOVE)

Jesus washes his disciples' feet:

When he had finished washing their feet, he put on his clothes and returned to his place. "Do you understand what I have done for you?" he asked them. "You call me 'Teacher' and 'Lord,' and rightly so, for that is what I am. Now that I, your Lord and Teacher, have washed your feet, you also should wash one another's feet. I have set you an example that you should do as I have done for you. Very truly I tell you, no servant is greater than his master, nor is a messenger greater than the one who sent him. Now that you know these things, you will be blessed if you do them.

John 13:12-17

## ADMIRABLE (DESERVING OF HONOR OR HIGH PRAISE)

Jesus heals on the Sabbath:

On a Sabbath Jesus was teaching in one of the synagogues, and a woman was there who had been crippled by a spirit for eighteen years. She was bent over and could not straighten up at all. When Jesus saw her, he called her forward and said to her, "Woman, you are set free from your infirmity." Then he put his hands on her, and immediately she straightened up and praised God. Indignant because Jesus had healed on the Sabbath, the synagogue leader said to the people, "There are six days for work. So come and be healed on those days, not on the

Sabbath." The Lord answered him, "You hypocrites! Doesn't each of you on the Sabbath untie your ox or donkey from the stall and lead it out to give it water? Then should not this woman, a daughter of Abraham, whom Satan has kept bound for eighteen long years, be set free on the Sabbath day from what bound her?" When he said this, all his opponents were humiliated, but the people were delighted with all the wonderful things he was doing.

Luke 13:10-17

We can all learn what it means to have pure, lovely, and admirable thoughts, and then transfer those thoughts into our daily actions. If we do, we will be living our joy out loud!

## Joy in Communion with Christ

Go to youtube.com and search for May the Mind of Christ my Savior by Jake Armerding. Listen prayerfully.

When you pray each day, give God your thought-life.

# PRACTICER

I CAN PLAY the piano. Wait. Stop applauding. You see, I *can* play the piano, but I mainly play for my own enjoyment and relaxation. Sometimes I play for my husband to sing (at home), and once in a great while I play for a small group of elderly people to sing a hymn, but the thought of playing in front of a congregation or an audience gives me a case of cold sweats. Even now my hands are shaking just writing about it. If you need some, I can give you great excuses:

- Reaching octaves is difficult, on account of my hands being small.
- My pinkies are a little double-jointed.
- I didn't get really good training in music theory until it was too late.
- God didn't call me to be a church or concert pianist.

But the truth is that the reason I don't want to play in front of people is that I don't want to practice that much. Practicing the songs is not that boring necessarily, but practicing the finger exercises to become more proficient is excruciatingly monotonous and time-consuming.

My mama had great hopes for me. She was an amazing pianist and organist, and when I could barely get on the piano bench, she began teaching me to play. I'll never forget the day I learned Middle C. I felt so accomplished! I mean, who knew a piano keyboard had a middle C? And then I learned there are seven more Cs on the piano because, for some reason, a piano does not have the whole alphabet, just A through G. Of course, then I wondered why, if it was the most important note, they decided to call it middle C and not middle A, which would have made much more sense.

I found out that on written music there are two sets of five lines called staffs, and I learned that you could figure out what note each line represented by memorizing a cute little saying. It would be years later when I learned this is called a mnemonic device. For the top staff, the saying was Every Good Boy Does Fine, and on the bottom staff the phrase was Good Boys Do Fine Always. I wondered why, if the piano keys were all about boys, I had to learn to play. Well, that didn't go over well with Mama, so I rebelliously but secretly changed the little sayings to "Every Girl Bakes Devil's Food" and "Girls Bake Devil's Food Always." So there!

Needless to say, Mama didn't last long as my piano teacher. My second teacher was Mrs. Redlips (all names have been changed to protect the innocent). She had been teaching my sister and brother for a while, because Mama had long ago thrown up her hands with them, too. Mrs. Redlips was very sweet, and her handwriting was beautiful. To this day, I love looking at my old piano books and seeing January 17 or October 5 or something else of her immaculate cursive written at the top of a piece of music.

Unfortunately, red lipstick, sweetness, and beautiful handwriting did not motivate me to practice, so the semiannual recitals Mrs. Redlips put on at the Cary Music Studio scared me practically to death.

When I was twelve, after my sister and brother had gone to college, my parents and I moved to Hong Kong for a year. I can't remember clearly, but I think Mama tried to teach me that year. When we returned, I didn't go back to Mrs. Redlips. She had filled my spot while I was gone, most likely with a huge smile on her face. My new teacher was Mrs. Harper. She was a harper. She harped on practice, practice, practice. As a result, I could barely stand her, though her daughter was a good friend of mine.

My mama's last-ditch effort to heave me out of the mass of mediocre pianists was Mrs. Maynight. I don't remember too much about Mrs. Maynight except where her house was and that she and Mama tried matchmaking between her son and me. He and I double dated with a friend of his one time, and of course, I fell for the friend. I'm quite sure this development was a disappointment to both mothers, but soon thereafter, I had some major health issues that prevented any extracurricular activities, so both the piano lessons and the boys were discontinued for some time.

My final piano teacher was Mrs. Nicelady. I had decided to major in music at college, and even though my concentration was in voice, piano was a much-to-my-dismay required course. Mrs. Nicelady had probably taught hundreds like me who were there just to satisfy the credit requirements. Nevertheless, she was patient, kind, and encouraging, and I made it through without failing, though not without my mind going completely blank during a jury (the piano equivalent of a final exam).

The moral of this story? Some things just take practice. We aren't going to get better with new catchphrases or new teachers if we don't get new attitudes and work ethics.

## The Joyful Truth

Paul admonishes us on the topic of practice with these words, "Whatever you have learned or received or heard from me, or seen in me—put it into practice. And the God of peace will be with you" (Phil. 4:9).

The Greek word used for "practice" is *prasso,* which means "to do, act, or commit." Doing and committing is what is needed in the church. If we are not actually *doing* something *for* the Kingdom, what is the use of doing so many things *about* the Kingdom? James said, "Do not merely listen to the word, and so deceive yourselves. Do what it says" (1:22).

Maybe we need to quit joining so many Bible studies, quit going to so many Bible conferences, and quit reading so many books about the Kingdom, if we are not willing to do something with the knowledge, inspiration, and revelation God has already provided. I don't see much written in the gospels about Jesus sitting around soaking up the sun of the Father's blessings. He worshiped, yes. He prayed, for sure. He fellowshipped with friends, certainly. But most of his life was spent in doing ministry and committing his life to people.

## Digesting the Joy

Putting into practice what we have learned is a common theme in the Bible. Through the inspiration and instigation of the Holy Spirit, different writers in different times speaking to different people address this issue over and over. It must matter to God! The following passages will serve as examples:

Your decrees are the theme of my song wherever I lodge. In the night, Lord, I remember your name, that I may keep your law. This has been my practice: I obey your precepts. You are my portion, Lord; I have promised to obey your words. I have sought your face with all my heart; be gracious to me according to your promise.

Psalm 119:54-58

As for you, son of man, your people are talking together about you by the walls and at the doors of the houses, saying to each other, "Come and hear the message that has come from the Lord."

My people come to you, as they usually do, and sit before you to hear your words, but they do not put them into practice. Their mouths speak of love, but their hearts are greedy for unjust gain. Indeed, to them you are nothing more than one who sings love songs with a beautiful voice and plays an instrument well, for they hear your words but do not put them into practice.

Ezekiel 33:30-32

Do not think that I have come to abolish the Law or the Prophets; I have not come to abolish them but to fulfill them. For truly I tell you, until heaven and earth disappear, not the smallest letter, not the least stroke of a pen, will by any means disappear from the Law until everything is accomplished. Therefore anyone who sets aside one of the least of these commands and teaches others accordingly will be called least in the kingdom of heaven, but whoever practices and teaches these commands will be called great in the kingdom of heaven.

Matthew 5:17-19

Therefore everyone who hears these words of mine and puts them into practice is like a wise man who built his house on the rock. The rain came down, the streams rose, and the winds blew and beat against that house; yet it did not fall, because it had its foundation on the rock. But everyone who hears these words of mine and does not put them into practice is like a foolish man who built his house on sand. The rain came down, the streams rose, and the winds blew and beat against that house, and it fell with a great crash."

Matthew 7:24-27

Now Jesus' mother and brothers came to see him, but they were not able to get near him because of the crowd. Someone told him, "Your mother and brothers are standing outside, wanting to see you." He replied, "My mother and brothers are those who hear God's word and put it into practice."

Luke 8:19-21

## Living Your Joy Out Loud

Our daughter, Shelley, was the one who swam competitively. I remember her first coach, Brad. He demonstrated the swimming strokes while standing or lying on the pool deck so the children could see what his arms and legs were doing. Then he would ask them to jump in the pool and move their limbs the way he had moved his.

If a child wasn't getting it, he would make them get out of the pool and try it on the pool deck, as he had done. He would correct the movements and then send them back into the water. Once the swimmers had the moves right, he would assign them many, many laps to put into practice what they had learned. This ingrained the strokes so the swimmers would never again be slowed down by having to think about them. Then they could concentrate on going as fast as possible.

The kids complained about all the work, but they loved it. The accomplishment they felt invigorated them and gave them such pleasure. When they won a race or perhaps the whole swim meet, their delight was tangible.

What about us? Is our joy obvious? Are we putting into practice what we've learned? If so, our joy should be complete. According to John, "If you keep my commands, you will remain in my love, just as I have kept my Father's commands and remain in his love. I have told you this so that my joy may be in you and that your joy may be complete" (John 15:10-11). "Complete" means "rendered perfect," so if we keep practicing what Jesus preached, we will have perfect joy.

## Joy in Communion with Christ

You will be blessed by the rendition of this song on YouTub.com. Search "Trust and Obey A Hymn a Week."

"TRUST AND OBEY"
(John H. Sammis, 1887)

When we walk with the Lord
In the light of His Word
What a glory He sheds on our way!
Let us do His good will;
He abides with us still,
And with all who will trust and obey.

Refrain:
Trust and obey,
For there's no other way
To be happy in Jesus,
But to trust and obey.

Not a burden we bear,
Not a sorrow we share,
But our toil He doth richly repay;
Not a grief or a loss,

Not a frown or a cross,
But is blest if we trust and obey.

Refrain:

But we never can prove
The delights of His love
Until all on the altar we lay;
For the favor He shows
And the joy He bestows
Are for them who will trust and obey.

Refrain

Take some time to pray and allow the Holy Spirit to impress on you the areas in which you can be a better doer of the Word and not merely a hearer.

# GIVER

HOW OLD ARE you? Are you young enough that your parents are still your parents? Or are you getting to the age that your parents are becoming your children? Do you know what I mean? It's the irony of life. When you are small, they take care of you. They feed you, change your diapers, and read to you. They control your finances and chauffeur you to appointments. They laugh even when your jokes aren't funny. They do it all out of love, and it brings them joy.

Then you go through twenty to thirty years when you are equals, sort of. You are all adults, supporting yourselves, taking care of yourselves, independent of each other except emotionally. But then a shift begins. Your parents start getting older, worn-out by wear, even senile. And you, the children, have to take care of them. You may have to feed them, change their diapers, and read to them. You control their finances and chauffeur them to appointments. You laugh even when their jokes aren't funny. You do it all out of love, and it brings you joy.

The apostle Paul and the converts at Philippi were not biologically related, but spiritually he was their father. He had nurtured them when they were young converts and continued to teach and encourage them. But now he senses that their roles are changing. The tables are turning, and they are taking care of him and supporting him. Paul is thankful for their devotion, though he knows God will sustain him no matter what.

## The Joyful Truth

Long before the Lottie Moon Christmas Offering for International Missions (an offering collected every year by Southern Baptists for the support of their missionaries all over the world), Paul penned these words to the Philippians:

I rejoiced greatly in the Lord that at last you renewed your concern for me. Indeed, you were concerned, but you had no opportunity to show it. I am not saying this because I am in need, for I have learned to be content whatever the circumstances. I know what it is to be in need, and I know what it is to have plenty. I have learned the secret of being content in any and every situation, whether well fed or hungry, whether living in plenty or in want. I can do all this through him who gives me strength. Yet it was good of you to share in my troubles. Moreover, as you Philippians know, in the early days of your acquaintance with the gospel, when I set out from Macedonia, not one church shared with me in the matter of giving and receiving, except you only; for even when I was in Thessalonica, you sent me aid more than once when I was in need. Not that I desire your gifts; what I desire is that more be credited to your account. I have received full payment and have more than enough. I am amply supplied, now that I have received from Epaphroditus the gifts you sent. They are a fragrant offering, an acceptable sacrifice, pleasing to God. And my God will meet all your needs according to the riches of his glory in Christ Jesus.

Philippians 4:10-19

Paul had no backing from any particular group. No collection plate was passed, and no pledge cards were signed. There were no Web site donations. Yet Paul believed a preacher should be supported financially. He said, "If we have sown spiritual seed among you, is it too much if we reap a material harvest from you? . . . In the same way, the Lord has commanded that those who preach the gospel should receive their living from the gospel" (1 Cor. 9:11, 14).

Paul hadn't taken pay while he was able to provide for himself. In his earlier travels, he had worked for a living as a tent maker, even while preaching the gospel at every opportunity. Now, however, he was imprisoned and could not work.

Timothy, his son in the faith, was there in Rome with him, doing his best to support them both. But Timothy was obviously not making "the big bucks." And Paul learned to be content whether eating steak or peanut butter, whether having a handsome new tunic or making do with his old, dirty, threadbare one. "I know what it is to be in need," Paul said, "and I know what it is to have plenty. I have learned the secret of being content in any and every situation, whether well fed or hungry, whether living in plenty or in want."

Now Epaphroditus has come bringing a gift of money from the Philippian church. Paul is touched, because he realizes they haven't forgotten him. He knows they understand it is time for them to be "parents" to him.

## Digesting the Joy

The Greek word for "concern" is *phroneo*, and it means "to think, to direct one's mind to a thing, or to be of the same mind." We have already looked at the theme of peacemaking and the Greek word for "like-minded," which is *sympsychos*. Then we explored the word *synzygos*, which is being a yokefellow of Jesus. Isn't it wonderful how God teaches us the same concept over and over, but in slightly different ways so that hopefully everyone will get it? The idea behind *phroneo* is that Christians have a connection that is brought about by being of the same mind--the mind of Christ.

Twins have been said to have a special connection that other siblings don't have. The excerpt below, from an article called "Twin Telepathy," describes this phenomenon.

One of the magical mysteries associated with multiples is that they share a special connection beyond that of ordinary siblings. While the twin bond is a special aspect of their unique relationship, sometimes it is endowed with extraordinary supernatural qualities.

There is plenty of anecdotal data to support the idea. Nearly every set of twins can relate a story. Sometimes, one twin experiences a physical sensation of something that is happening to their twin (such as labor pains or a heart attack.) Other times they will find that they perform similar actions when they're apart, such as buying the same item, ordering the same meal in a restaurant, or picking up the phone to make a call at the exact same moment. They may appear to know the other's thoughts, by speaking simultaneously or finishing each other's sentences.

For example, a friend of mine who is an identical twin shared several stories about the uncanny connection she has with her sister, especially considering that they have lived on different continents for much of their adult life. Most recently, during an online video chat, she and her sister discovered that they had purchased the exact same pair of pants, in the same color, from the same store, on the same day. Her sister lives in Belgium, while she lives in the United States. As a child, she remembers feeling physical pain when her sister was spanked for faking a report card grade. She also experienced a cramping sensation at the very moment her sister went into labor, while her sister dreamt she was holding a baby at the exact moment that my friend gave birth to her daughter.[26]

The writer of this article calls the twin phenomenon a "magical mystery of multiples." She even labels it "supernatural." But the mystery of the connection between Christians is neither magical nor supernatural in the mystical way the author applies to twins. It is, however, *spiritual*—that is, through the Holy Spirit. Because of the presence of the Holy Spirit, we can feel the pains of our brothers and sisters in Christ and desire to help them. After all, "There is one body and one Spirit, just as you were called to one hope when you were called; one Lord, one faith, one baptism; one God and Father of all, who is over all and through all and in all" (Eph. 4:4-6).

The Greek word Paul used for "concern" in Philippians 4:10 entails far more than our American English connotation of concern. It implies sympathy, compassion, and action. Paul tells the Philippians "it was good of you to share in my troubles." The word translated "troubles" is *thlipsis*, which we met in an earlier chapter. We are going to have oppression, tribulation, affliction—*thlipsis*—and we need our fellow sisters to show concern for us in these troubles.

## Living Your Joy Out Loud

Reread the following verses:

I rejoiced greatly in the Lord that at last you renewed your concern for me. Indeed, you were concerned, but you had no opportunity to show it. I am not saying this because I am in need, for I have learned to be content whatever the circumstances. I know what it is to be in need, and I know what it is to have plenty. I have learned the secret of being content in any and every situation, whether well fed or hungry, whether living in plenty or in want. I can do all this through him who gives me strength. Yet it was good of you to share in my troubles. Moreover, as you Philippians know, in the early days of your acquaintance with the gospel, when I set out from Macedonia, not one church shared with me in the matter of giving and receiving, except you only; for even when I was in Thessalonica, you sent me aid more than once when I was in need. Not that I desire your gifts; what I desire is that more be credited to your account. I have received full payment and have more than enough. I am amply supplied, now that I have received from Epaphroditus the gifts you sent. They are a fragrant offering, an acceptable sacrifice, pleasing to God. And my God will meet all your needs according to the riches of his glory in Christ Jesus.

Philippians 4:10-18

What is Paul's frame of mind? There are many clues in these verses as to how to live joy out loud. Notice especially Paul's attitude of gratitude. He is thanking the Philippians for their active concern in his ministry. But he starts this section of his letter by telling them he praises the Lord for them. He knows the source of their generosity is not their innate, ordinary human nature. The source is the Spirit who lives in them, so Paul places his praise where praise is due.

Evidently, the church at Philippi had helped Paul before, for he says, "I rejoiced greatly in the Lord that at last you renewed your concern for me." He has thanked them before, but he thanks them again.

There is a joke about the wife who is unsure of her husband's love. He says, "Of course I love you!" And she replies, "Well, you never tell me you love me." He states, "I told you on our wedding day twenty-eight years ago. If I change my mind, I'll let you know!" The apostle Paul was no different from anyone else. People long to know they are appreciated and loved. They need to hear it over and over. And joy is the sort of thing that increases exponentially; when we live our joy out loud our joy increases as we give other people joy.

It is unfortunate but true that many Christians do not know how to accept help from others. They cannot develop an attitude of gratitude because they are unwilling to admit they need help in the first place. Are we like that? If so, we need to realize this is a fault and not something of which to be proud. In fact, it is prideful, and pride stands in the way of our accepting help. God wants to help us, but before that happens we must humble ourselves and seek forgiveness: "If my people, who are called by my name, will humble themselves and pray and seek my face and turn from their wicked ways, then I will hear from heaven, and I will forgive their sin and will heal their land" (2 Chron. 7:14).

Gratitude, centered in humility, is the soil for contentment to grow. Every now and then I meet a person who says, "I'm too blessed to be stressed." That's what Paul is saying in these verses from Philippians and in Second Corinthians:

> For no matter how many promises God has made, they are "Yes" in Christ. And so through him the "Amen" is spoken by us to the glory of God. Now it is God who makes both us and you stand firm in Christ. He anointed us, set his seal of ownership on us, and put his Spirit in our hearts as a deposit, guaranteeing what is to come.
>
> 2 Corinthians 1:20-22

When we acquire something that has a guarantee, it is a win-win situation. That's why Paul says, in essence, "I'm content with plenty, and I'm content with little, because this place is not my home. I'm just passing through."

He has already spelled out that God is the true source of their generosity. Now he proclaims that Christ is the sure source of his strength in this world we have to live in. Jesus picks Paul up and carries him in any situation--good or bad, happy or sad, bountiful or scarce. Thousands claim Philippians 4:13 as their favorite Bible verse. "I can do all this through him who gives me strength" is on many a tee-shirt, mug, plaque, and bookmark. But do we really believe Christ will strengthen us in every circumstance? If the answer is yes, we will be living our joy out loud!

In verses fourteen through eighteen, Paul gushes over the incomparable love the Philippians have shown him. He describes the gift Epaphroditus has brought from them as a fragrant offering, an acceptable sacrifice, and pleasing to God. When we are at a place in our lives where we have to accept concern or help from someone, we should thank God for it. In addition, we should live our gratitude by saying, "I'm too blessed to be stressed."

## Joy in Communion with Christ

Take a few minutes and go to YouTube.com, and search "Praise to the Lord, the Almighty—Christy Nockels Passion." The pictures on the video are a little distracting, and I encourage you to pay attention instead to the words you are singing.

### "PRAISE TO THE LORD, THE ALMIGHTY"
(Joachim Neander, 1680)

Praise to the Lord, the Almighty, the King of creation!
O my soul, praise Him, for He is thy health and salvation!
All ye who hear, now to His temple draw near;
Praise Him in glad adoration.

Praise to the Lord, who over all things so wondrously reigneth,
Shelters thee under His wings, yea, so gently sustaineth!
Hast thou not seen how thy desires ever have been
Granted in what He ordaineth?

Praise to the Lord, who doth prosper thy work and defend thee;
Surely His goodness and mercy here daily attend thee.
Ponder anew what the Almighty can do,
If with His love He befriend thee.

Praise to the Lord, O let all that is in me adore Him!
All that hath life and breath, come now with praises before Him.
Let the Amen sound from His people again,
Gladly for aye we adore Him.

In your prayer time, meditate on all God has done for you through other people. Thank him and ask him to reveal circumstances where you can be a monetary blessing, a spiritual blessing, or a physical blessing (running errands, helping someone move, and so on) to someone.

# SOLUTION

PUZZLES ARE FUN. Word puzzles, number puzzles, jigsaw puzzles. I like to be able to figure them out. To me the process is invigorating. The more challenging, the better.

My daddy had a book of two hundred *New York Times* Sunday crossword puzzles. He had only finished the first ninety-one of them before he died, so I am attempting to do the rest. So far, I haven't totally completed very many of the ones I've started. They are difficult and sometimes even grueling, but it is sheer satisfaction figuring them out and checking them off! I keep going back to the ones I haven't finished, because sometimes I'll have an "Aha!" moment the second or third or fourth time around. Something will finally click, and then I'll be able to get another word, and then another. That's the thrill—finally solving something I didn't think I could.

Life is a puzzle, full of bewildering situations and people I don't get because they are so different from me and my little world. Why don't I get as excited about life puzzles as I do about Sudoku or Cryptoquote, or the *New York Times* Sunday crossword? Maybe because the stakes are so much higher. If I don't figure out the Cryptoquote today, then, . . . so what? But if I don't doggedly tackle the puzzles of poverty and wealth, being generous and yet saving for retirement, sticking my neck out there for others yet protecting my soul, loving the sinner while not condoning the sin, then what kind of Christian witness do I have?

Unfortunately, the equality, wholeness, peace, unconditional love and belonging people yearn for cannot be found in this world. Timothy Keller puts it so well in his thought-provoking book, *The Prodigal God*:

In the beginning of the book of Genesis we learn . . . that we were created to live in the garden of God. That was the world we were built for, a place in which there was no parting from love, no decay or disease. It was all these things because it was life before the face of God, in his presence . . . That was our original home, the true country we were made for . . . God was the "father" of that home, and we chafed under his authority. We wanted to live without God's interference, and so we turned away, and became alienated from him, and lost our home . . . we have been living in a world that no longer fits our deepest longings. Though we long for bodies that "run and are not weary," we have become subject to disease, aging, and death. Though we need love that lasts, all our relationships are subject to the inevitable entropy [decline and degeneration] of time, and they crumble in our hands. Even people who stay true to us die and leave us, or we die and leave them. Though we long to make a difference in our world through our work, we experience endless frustration. We never fully realize our hopes and dreams. We may work hard to re-create the home that we have lost, but, says the Bible, it only exists in the presence of the heavenly father from which we have fled."[27]

The humanistic worldview preaches that these puzzles can be solved by humans being more tolerant, more giving, and less hypocritical, but that is not the truth. The truth is that only when we have finally reached the presence of God will all we long for be fully attainable.

## The Joyful Truth

We can't create a utopia on earth, but in the last few verses of Philippians, Paul gives a hint of three things Christians are able to do about life's difficult puzzles: "To our God and Father be glory for ever and ever. Amen. Greet all God's people in Christ Jesus. The brothers and sisters who are with me send greetings. All God's people here send you greetings, especially those who belong to Caesar's household. The grace of the Lord Jesus Christ be with your spirit. Amen (Phil.4:20-23).

## Digesting the Truth

### Greet all God's People

Most of us think we know how to fellowship, especially with those who are like us. In the South, where I live, we call each other "Sweetie" and "Honey." We've got "Bless your heart" down pat. We invented the question "How in the world are you?" and we have mastered the "I'm listening" head nod. And of course, the three-back-pat hug is a trademark. The only question is whether or not our greetings are genuine or automatic "cookie cutter" words and actions. Luke shared an example of the early church's fellowship that can be our model.

Every day they continued to meet together in the temple courts. They broke bread in their homes and ate together with glad and sincere hearts, praising God and enjoying the favor of all the people. And the Lord added to their number daily those who were being saved.

Acts 2:46-47

Romans 12:9-10 also gives a clear description of uplifting Christian behavior: "Love must be sincere. Hate what is evil; cling to what is good. Be devoted to one another in love. Honor one another above yourselves."

The key to genuinely greeting fellow Christians is sincere hearts full of sincere love. Take a look at the following synonyms for "sincere:" aboveboard, actual, artless, bona fide, candid, earnest, faithful, forthright, frank, guileless, like it is, natural, no fooling, no-nonsense, on the level, on the up and up, plain, real, straightforward, sure enough, true, true-blue, trustworthy, unaffected, undesigning, unfeigned, unpretentious, up-front, and wholehearted. We want to honor others above ourselves, and we can do this only if we have pure motives and personal, Christ-like love.

## THE GRACE OF THE LORD JESUS CHRIST

Before we tackle the second solution to life's great dilemmas, the grace of the Lord Jesus Christ, let's make sure we understand what biblical grace is. According to *blueletterbible.org*, grace is "the merciful kindness by which God, exerting his holy influence upon souls, turns them to Christ, keeps, strengthens, increases them in Christian faith, knowledge, affection, and kindles them to the exercise of the Christian virtues."

I have often heard that "grace" is getting what you don't deserve and "mercy" is *not* getting what you *do* deserve. In our natural states, we are totally undeserving of God's merciful kindness and holy influence. Yet he loves us so much that he can't help himself from showing us grace. That is the whole reason behind the Father sending Jesus.

The most important truth about grace in our lives is that we can't truly give it until we have really received it through the cross of Jesus. Keller says, "He came and experienced the exile that we deserved. He was expelled from the presence of the Father, he was thrust into the darkness, the uttermost despair of spiritual alienation--in our place. He took upon himself the full curse of human rebellion, cosmic homelessness, so that we could be welcomed into our true home."[28]

In order to bestow true grace on someone else, we have to recall our own deep need for the grace of Christ. Then and only then will we be able to confront every issue with humility, to stand firm with gentleness, to analyze without condemnation, and to be thoroughly wise and yet meek. In other words, to be to others what Jesus is to us. One of my favorite passages is Ephesians 5:1-2, which says, "Follow God's example, therefore, as dearly loved children and walk in the way of love, just as Christ loved us and gave himself up for us as a fragrant offering and sacrifice to God."

Another passage that so clearly illustrates the way a woman can grant grace to all is found in 1 Peter:

> Wives, in the same way submit yourselves to your own husbands so that, if any of them do not believe the word, they may be won over without words by the behavior of their wives, when they see the purity and reverence of your lives. Your beauty should not come from outward adornment, such as elaborate hairstyles and the wearing of gold jewelry or fine clothes. Rather, it should be that of your inner self, the unfading beauty of a gentle and quiet spirit, which is of great worth in God's sight. For this is the way the holy women of the past who put their hope in God used to adorn themselves. They submitted themselves to their own husbands.
>
> 1 Peter 3:1-5

Living with purity and reverence can turn others to Christ; it "keeps, strengthens, increases them in Christian faith, knowledge, affection, and kindles them to the exercise of the Christian virtues."

We see how living this way would work and could work. The only problem is living it and actually making it work. Sylvia Gunter, Bible teacher and author, writes, "I want to live by grace, but unless God does a work of grace in me, I can't. I try to speak grace words, words of life, and only God is sufficient for that in me. I fully take all His grace, but my life presents at best only snapshots of His grace."[29]

My daughter, Heather, started a blog the week her son, Bryant, was born. Her husband encouraged her to do it so we grandparents could keep up with what our little man is accomplishing. To tell the truth, I never thought Heather would. Oh, she started and that was great and all, but I never thought she would continue. Bryant is two-years-old now, and she has written a post about once a week. The news has been fun to read, but what I've really enjoyed is all the pictures. She must keep a camera in front of that boy's face at least half of his waking hours!

That's the challenge, and that's where we will find the joy—in leaning on Jesus to make our snapshots of grace like Heather's snapshots of Bryant's life, almost continuous.

I get lazy and forgetful and apathetic. I get frustrated with this world. I get tired of people who oppress Christian values. But the only way to make my life count is to submit my laziness, forgetfulness, apathy, frustration, and weariness to the grace of Jesus.

Paul reported that Jesus said to him, "My grace is sufficient for you, for my power is made perfect in weakness." Then Paul wrote, "Therefore I will boast all the more gladly about my weaknesses, so that Christ's power may rest on me. That is why, for Christ's sake, I delight in weaknesses, in insults, in hardships, in persecutions, in difficulties. For when I am weak, then I am strong" (2 Cor. 12:9-10).

## To our God and Father be Glory

If we were capable of granting grace to everyone all on our own, then the third piece of solving life's difficult puzzles would be missing. Just as Paul expressed in the verses above, it's our weakness that brings out God's glory. And God is jealous of his glory. Anyone who tries usurping God's glory will find themselves in a wilderness. Many passages in the Bible will bear this out. You probably remember the account of Ananias and Sapphira. Here is another example:

Now the Lord was gracious to Sarah as he had said, and the Lord did for Sarah what he had promised. Sarah became pregnant and bore a son to Abraham in his old age, at the very time God had promised him. Abraham gave the name Isaac to the son Sarah bore him. When his son Isaac was eight days old, Abraham circumcised him, as God commanded him. Abraham was a hundred years old when his son Isaac was born to him. Sarah said, "God has brought me laughter, and everyone who hears about this will laugh with me." And she added, "Who would have said to Abraham that Sarah would nurse children? Yet I have borne him a son in his old age." The child grew and was weaned, and on the day Isaac was weaned Abraham held a great feast. But Sarah saw that the son whom Hagar the Egyptian had borne to Abraham was mocking, and she said to Abraham, "Get rid of that slave woman and her son, for that woman's son will never share in the inheritance with my son Isaac." The matter distressed Abraham greatly because it concerned his son. But God said to him, "Do not be so distressed about the boy and your slave woman. Listen to whatever Sarah tells you, because it is through Isaac that your offspring will be reckoned. I will make the son of the slave into a nation also, because he is your offspring." Early the next morning Abraham took some food and a skin of water and gave them to Hagar. He set them on her shoulders and then sent her off with the boy. She went on her way and wandered in the Desert of Beersheba. When the water in the skin was gone, she put the boy under one of the bushes. Then she went off and sat down about a bowshot away, for she thought, "I cannot watch the boy die." And as she sat there, she began to sob. God heard the boy crying, and the angel of God called to Hagar from heaven and said to her, "What is the matter, Hagar? Do not be afraid; God has heard the boy crying as he lies there. Lift the boy up and take him by the hand, for I will make him into a great nation." Then God opened her eyes and she saw a well of water. So she went and filled the skin with water and gave the boy a drink. God was with the boy as he grew up. He lived in the desert and became an archer.

Genesis 21:1-20

## Living Your Joy Out Loud

Jen Hatmaker blogs on *http://jenhatmaker.com/blog* and wrote concerning the idea of solving life's difficult problems and the joy we can find in letting Jesus' grace rule our lives and giving the glory to God:

I'm so over the fear mongering and hate propaganda. I'm over the political posturing and power plays. I'm over the finger pointing and name-calling. The storms are raging overhead, and let me tell you something: I'm going to the basement…

Here is what we hate down in the basement:

- We hate injustice.
- We hate our own sin and pride and arrogance, and we grieve at how it has wounded, sliced, slashed, and humiliated.
- We hate that 25,000 people will die today of hunger and we're arguing gay marriage again.
- We hate how the Gospel has been turned into a bludgeoning tool.
- We hate pointless arguments that widen the gap and devalue real human people.
- We hate abuse and violence and crowded orphanages and trafficked sixth-graders.

And it's not all hate, lest you imagine the Basement Dwellers are a sorry lot indeed. We love some things down in the basement, too:

- We love people. Because Jesus does. All of them.
- We love grace, because it rescued all of us sinners.
- We love healing and redemption, and we get to be a part of that every day, if we are brave enough to say yes.
- We love that Jesus uses broken people, because that is our zip code and He chooses us anyway. Mercy is our only sane option.
- We love the Body of Christ, when she isn't being a bully or a tyrant or trying to take over the Oval Office and the Red Carpet. I swear, she can be beautiful.

- We love Jesus, who was always in hot water with the religious folks for eating with sinners and offering scandalous grace not just to the leper but to the tax collector.
- We love *love*, and we believe in its power…

We have a whole thing going on underground. Gay friends and family, you are welcome down here. Marginalized women, come on down. Isolated and confused by organized religion, afraid your questions aren't welcomed? Join us. Activists and bleeding hearts, you are our heartbeat. Plain, old, ordinary sinners saved by grace, you belong here. Misfits, ragamuffins, and rebels, bring the party. Reformed legalists, you are my people. Pastors contending for God's glory and people, help lead us. Dissenters, dreamers, visionaries, we need you. Come on down to the basement.[30]

Living your joy out loud is really all about experiencing the glorious, miraculous grace of God, and then passing it on. So let's greet the saints, grant grace to all, and give God the glory.

## Joy in Communion with Christ

Regardless of our sins, God's amazing grace offers us forgiveness and redemption. I encourage you to prayerfully sing this famous hymn written by English poet John Newton in 1779:

### "Amazing Grace"

Amazing grace! How sweet the sound that saved a wretch like me!
I once was lost, but now am found; was blind, but now I see.
'Twas grace that taught my heart to fear, and grace my fears relieved;
How precious did that grace appear the hour I first believed!
Through many dangers, toils, and snares I have already come;
'Tis grace hath brought me safe thus far, and grace will lead me home.
The Lord has promised good to me; His Word my hope secures;
He will my Shield and Portion be as long as life endures.
When we've been there ten thousand years, bright shining as the sun,
We've no less days to sing God's praise than when we first begun!

# ENDNOTES

1   http://en.wikipedia.org/wiki/Richard_of_Chichester.

2   Randy Scruggs and John Thompson, Copyright 1982 Whole Armor Music and Full Armor Music

3   http://www.azlyrics.com/lyrics/castingcrowns/inme.html.

4   http://www.biblestudytools.com/commentaries/matthew-henry-complete/philippians/1.html.

5   © 1939 Eugene M. Bartlett, renewed 1967 Mrs. Eugene M. Bartlett, by permission of Albert E. Brumley & Sons, Inc.

6   *Strong's Exhaustive Concordance.*

7   www.searchgodsword.org.

8   Vicki Yohe, Copyright 2003

9   "Made in the USA: Spoiled Brats" WorldNet daily.com, November 20,2006.

10  Graham Kendrick, Copyright 1994 Make Way Music

11  Bill and Gloria Gaither, Copyright 1970.

12  http://www.brainyquote.com/quotes/quotes/m/marktwain100358.html

13  http://www.fivelovelanguages.com/learn.html.

14  Kurt Kaiser, Copyright 1969 by Lexicon Music, Inc.

15  Ira B. Wilson (1909), Copyright 1924. Renewed 1952 World Music, LLC, Wordspring Music, LLC.

16  Copyright unknown.

17  *Family Word Finder* (New York: The Reader's Digest Association, Inc., 1975).

18  Author unknown.

19  englishmonarchs.co.uk/crown_jewels.htm.

[20]    Copyright unknown.

[21]    Lincoln Brewster, 2005, Copyright unknown.

[22]    Warren W. Wiersbe, *The Wiersbe Bible Commentary* (Colorado Springs: David C. Cook, 2007).

[23]    www.biblebb.com/files.

[24]    Wiersbe, 234.

[25]    Ibid, 122.

[26]    http://multiples.about.com, Twin Telepathy, Pamela Prindle Fierro.

[27]    Timothy Keller, *The Prodigal God* (New York: Riverhead Books, 2008), 107-08.

[28]    Ibid, 114.

[29]    Sylvia Gunter, *The Father's Business*, "What is God Saying to Me? Part 2," July 18, 2012.

[30]    http://jenhatmaker.com/blog/2012/07/27/in-the-basement.

Printed in the United States
By Bookmasters